**Over 350 easy-to-follow recipes
you'll want to use every day**

Created for Procter & Gamble
by Prose & Concepts, Inc., New York
in association with
Culinary Arts & Services, Chicago
Helen Geist, Director.

Color Photographs: Dick Jones

Crisco Cooking will help keep your family well fed and happy for many years... and its easy-to-follow recipes will make you happy, too. A visual feast of 132 color photos will tempt you at every turn of the page.

Here are over 350 delicious recipes, carefully chosen and tested in the Crisco kitchens for great taste and family appeal. The recipes are a tasty blend of old-fashioned goodness and new-fashioned ideas... from quick and simple dishes for everyday use to more lavish entrees for entertaining with style. Each recipe is written in a series of numbered steps, which makes it easier to read and follow. The well defined procedures will be appreciated by experienced cooks as well as beginners in the kitchen.

With this one-volume menu planner in your hands, you'll be able to put flavor, variety, and imagination into every meal. The well-organized chapters and an expanded index of recipes will help you put together tasty meals quicker than ever.

Crisco Cooking is a cookbook you'll want to use every day... and your family will want you to use it every day, too! Many of the recipes are sure to become favorites at your house, just as Crisco has become the favorite shortening in America. Flaky pie crusts are "easy as pie" with Crisco... along with non-greasy fried foods, moist cakes, creamy frostings, chewy cookies, and a lot more.

Crisco Shortening... a great ingredient for all your baking and frying needs!

Table of Contents

A good dinner deserves a good start... a delicious appetizer! Here are recipes of all kinds, from simple to fancy, light to hearty.

Served alone, these tasty morsels are great party pickups or between-meal snacks. Soups are versatile as well. They can be used as appetizers, accompany appetizers, or even serve as light meals.

Cornmeal Sticks

2 cups cold water
3/4 teaspoon salt
1 1/2 cups yellow cornmeal
6 ounces sharp Cheddar cheese, finely shredded (1 1/2 cups)
Crisco shortening for deep frying

1. Combine water, salt, and cornmeal in a heavy saucepan; mix until smooth. Cook over medium heat, stirring constantly, until mixture is very stiff, thick, and pulls away from sides of pan. (This takes 6 to 9 minutes.)
2. Remove from heat. Add cheese; stir until melted.
3. Pat mixture evenly into ungreased 13x9x2-inch utility dish. Let stand uncovered 30 minutes at room temperature. Do not chill dough.
4. Cut into 3 lengthwise sections and 18 crosswise strips.
5. Heat Crisco to 365° in a deep saucepan or deep fryer.

6. Add sticks to hot Crisco, one at a time, frying 3 sticks at a time for 3 minutes or until golden brown. (If sticks run together, cut apart after frying.) Drain on paper towels. Serve warm.

4 1/2 dozen sticks

Cheese Wafers

1/2 cup Crisco shortening
1/2 pound sharp Cheddar cheese, finely shredded (2 cups)
1 1/4 cups sifted all-purpose flour
3/4 teaspoon paprika
1/4 teaspoon dry mustard
1/4 teaspoon seasoned salt
1/8 teaspoon ground red pepper

1. Put Crisco into a mixer bowl and add cheese gradually, beating at medium speed until mixture is fairly smooth.
2. Blend flour, paprika, dry mustard, seasoned salt, and red pepper. Add to cheese mixture; mix at low speed until a dough forms.
3. Shape dough into 2 rolls, each 8 inches long; wrap in waxed paper. Chill at least 2 hours or until firm.
4. Preheat oven to 400°.
5. Cut chilled dough into 1/4-inch slices and place about 1 inch apart on ungreased cookie sheets.
6. Bake at 400° for 6 to 9 minutes or until lightly browned. Serve hot or at room temperature. Garnish each with an olive slice, if desired.

64 wafers

Cheesy Corn Dogs

1 recipe Cornmeal Sticks dough (on this page)
56 cocktail wieners (about four 5 1/2-ounce packages)
Crisco shortening for deep frying

Spicy Catsup Sauce:
1 cup catsup
1/2 cup finely chopped sweet pickle
2 tablespoons brown sugar
2 teaspoons prepared mustard
2 teaspoons Worcestershire sauce

1. Have dough ready.
2. Drain wieners on paper towels.
3. Wrap 1 level measuring tablespoonful of dough around each wiener.
4. Heat Crisco to 365° in a deep saucepan or deep fryer.
5. Add corn dogs to hot Crisco, one at a time. Fry 3 to 4 corn dogs at a time for 3 minutes or until golden brown. Drain on paper towels.
6. For Spicy Catsup Sauce, stir ingredients together to make about 1 1/2 cups sauce. Serve with corn dogs.

56 corn dogs

Note: Fully cooked ham, cut in 1/2-inch slices, then in sticks 2 inches long and 1/2 inch wide, may be substituted for cocktail wieners.

Bottom Tray: Cornmeal Sticks.
Middle Tray: Cheese Wafers.
Top Tray: Cheesy Corn Dogs.

Beef 'n' Kraut Appetizers

Meat Filling:
1/2 pound ground beef
1/4 cup chopped onion
1/2 teaspoon salt
1/8 teaspoon leaf marjoram
Dash pepper
1/3 cup fine dry bread crumbs
1/4 cup drained sauerkraut

Pastry:
3 cups Homemade Crisco Pie
  Crust Mix, page 154
1/2 cup drained sauerkraut,
  finely snipped
1/4 cup sauerkraut liquid

1. For Meat Filling, cook ground beef and onion in a skillet until meat is cooked and onion is tender. Drain off excess fat; stir in remaining ingredients.
2. For Pastry, combine Crisco mix and sauerkraut in a bowl. Add sauerkraut liquid, a tablespoon at a time, mixing with a fork until dry ingredients are moistened. Shape into a ball.
3. Preheat oven to 400°.
4. Roll dough to 1/8-inch thickness on a lightly floured surface. Cut with a floured 2 3/4-inch round cutter. Place on ungreased cookie sheets.
5. Spoon 1 teaspoon Meat Filling onto each round. Moisten half the edge of each round with water. Fold pastry in half and press edges together with fork to seal. Prick top of each pastry with fork.
6. Bake at 400° for 15 to 18 minutes or until lightly browned.

About 4 dozen appetizers

Beef-Filled Macaroni Shells

1 package (12 ounces) large
  or jumbo macaroni shells
1 1/2 pounds ground beef
1/3 cup finely chopped onion
3/4 cup catsup
1 tablespoon prepared mustard
3/4 teaspoon chili powder
3/4 teaspoon garlic salt
Crisco shortening for deep
  frying
Sweet pickle slices

1. Cook macaroni shells as directed on package, using maximum cooking time. Drain; rinse with cold water. Arrange on paper towels to dry.
2. While macaroni is cooking, cook ground beef and onion in a large skillet until beef is browned and onion is tender. Drain off excess fat. Stir in catsup, mustard, chili powder, and garlic salt. Heat.
3. Heat Crisco to 365° in a deep saucepan or deep fryer.
4. Fry several shells at a time for about 2 minutes or until golden; turn once during frying. Drain on paper towels.
5. As shells are fried, spoon about 1 tablespoon warm filling into each fried shell. Garnish with a sweet pickle slice. Serve warm.

3 to 5 dozen appetizers
(depending on size of shells used)

To do ahead: Fill shells as directed above; cool. Cover and refrigerate. When ready to serve, preheat oven to 400°. Arrange shells on baking sheet. Heat at 400° for 5 minutes.

Tempting Snacks

½ cup Crisco shortening
2 cups shredded sharp
 Cheddar cheese
1 cup all-purpose flour
1 envelope (1½ ounces) onion
 soup mix
Paprika (optional)

1. Mix Crisco, cheese, flour, and soup mix in a bowl until well blended.
2. Shape into a 12-inch-long roll, wrap in waxed paper, and chill.
3. Preheat oven to 375°.
4. Cut chilled dough into ¼-inch slices. Arrange slices on ungreased cookie sheets.
5. Bake at 375° for 15 minutes or until browned. Cool on racks. Sprinkle with paprika, if desired.

4 dozen appetizers

Cheese Bran Balls

⅔ cup all-purpose flour
½ teaspoon salt
⅛ teaspoon ground red pepper
⅓ cup Crisco shortening
2 cups shredded Cheddar
 cheese (at room temperature)
1½ cups whole bran cereal

1. Preheat oven to 350°.
2. Blend flour, salt, and red pepper in a mixer bowl. Add Crisco and cheese; beat until light and fluffy. Mix in cereal.
3. Shape into balls, flatten slightly, and place on ungreased cookie sheets.
4. Bake at 350° for about 12 minutes.

3 dozen appetizers

Pizza Snacks

2¼ cups Homemade Crisco
 Pie Crust Mix, page 154
½ cup finely chopped walnuts
 or pecans
¼ cup cold water
½ cup catsup
1 teaspoon prepared mustard
1 teaspoon prepared
 horseradish
1 teaspoon dried parsley flakes
¼ teaspoon oregano
⅛ teaspoon dill weed
½ cup finely chopped cooked
 ham
½ cup shredded mozzarella
 cheese
Paprika

1. Preheat oven to 425°.
2. Combine Crisco mix and walnuts in a bowl. Add cold water, 1 tablespoon at a time, mixing until dry ingredients are moistened and dough can be gathered into a ball.
3. Roll pastry to ¼-inch thickness on a lightly floured surface.
4. Cut into fourteen to sixteen 3-inch rounds. Place on un-greased cookie sheets and prick with a fork.
5. Bake at 425° for 15 minutes or until lightly browned.
6. Combine catsup, mustard, horseradish, parsley flakes, oregano, and dill weed.
7. Spread about 1 rounded measuring teaspoon of the catsup mixture over each baked pastry round, then sprinkle about ½ tablespoon chopped ham and ½ table-spoon shredded cheese on each. Sprinkle with paprika.
8. Broil 3 to 4 inches from heat for 1 to 2 minutes or until cheese is melted. Serve hot.

14 to 16 (3-inch) pizzas

Caraway and Cheese Nibblers

2 cups sifted all-purpose flour
1 teaspoon salt
1 teaspoon caraway seed
½ teaspoon chili powder
¾ cup Crisco shortening
1 cup shredded Monterey
 Jack cheese
3 to 4 tablespoons cold water

1. Preheat oven to 425°.
2. Combine flour, salt, caraway seed, and chili powder in a bowl. Cut in Crisco with a pastry blender or 2 knives until mixture resembles coarse crumbs. Stir in cheese with a fork. Add water, 1 tablespoon at a time, tossing lightly with fork. Gently form dough into a ball.
3. Roll dough into a 12-inch square on a lightly floured surface. Cut into 1-inch squares. Place on ungreased cookie sheets.
4. Bake at 425° for 10 minutes or until golden brown. Remove from cookie sheets and cool. Store in a covered container.

12 dozen nibblers

Note: If desired, cut dough into 1½-inch squares (about 5 dozen). Bake at 425° for 12 minutes.

Appetizers

Ham Chunks in Beer Batter

*½ cup Homemade Crisco
    Quick Bread Mix, page 116*
½ cup beer or apple cider
2 eggs, separated
*2 ham steaks (about ¾ pound
    each)*
*Crisco shortening for deep
    frying*
All-purpose flour for coating
Mustard Sauce (optional)

1. Combine Crisco mix, beer, and egg yolks in a bowl; beat until smooth. Let stand for 15 minutes.
2. Beat egg whites to stiff, not dry, peaks. Fold egg whites gently into batter until combined.
3. Cut ham steaks into 2½x½-inch pieces.
4. Heat Crisco to 365° in a deep saucepan or deep fryer.
5. Coat ham pieces with flour, shaking off excess. Dip pieces in batter, letting excess drip back in bowl.
6. Fry in hot Crisco for 1 minute or until golden. Remove with slotted spoon and drain on paper towels.
7. Serve hot with Mustard Sauce, if desired.

About 8 dozen appetizers

Mustard Sauce: Blend ½ cup mayonnaise, 1 tablespoon prepared mustard, and ½ teaspoon prepared horseradish.

Deep-Fried Pretzels

1 cup all-purpose flour
¼ teaspoon salt
*1 tablespoon Crisco
    shortening*
6 tablespoons cold water
*Crisco shortening for deep
    frying*
Coarse salt

1. Combine flour and salt in a bowl. Cut in Crisco with a pastry blender or 2 knives. Add water, 1 tablespoon at a time, mixing until dry ingredients are moistened and dough can be gathered into a ball. Knead gently a few times.
2. Pinch off pieces of dough and shape into 1-inch balls.
3. Roll each ball between hands to form a 10-inch rope. Form each rope into a pretzel shape. Set on waxed paper.
4. Heat Crisco to 365° in a deep saucepan or deep fryer.
5. Fry 3 pretzels at a time in hot Crisco for 3 minutes or until golden brown.
6. Drain on paper towels; sprinkle with coarse salt.

18 soft pretzels

Baked Cheese Balls

3 cups Homemade Crisco
  Quick Bread Mix, page 116
1 package (10 ounces) sharp
  Cheddar cheese, shredded
1 pound spicy bulk pork
  sausage
¼ cup finely chopped onion

1. Preheat oven to 350°.
2. Combine ingredients in a
bowl. Mix thoroughly, using
hands if necessary; shape into
1-inch balls.
3. Arrange balls on ungreased
cookie sheets.
4. Bake at 350° for 25 minutes
or until lightly browned.

7½ dozen appetizers

Fried Cheese

4 ounces Cheddar or
  mozzarella cheese
2 eggs, beaten
⅓ cup fine dry bread crumbs
Crisco shortening for deep
  frying

1. Cut cheese into ½-inch
cubes. Dip in beaten eggs,
then coat with crumbs.
Repeat dipping and coating.
2. Chill coated cheese cubes
for at least 30 minutes before
frying.
3. Heat Crisco to 365° in a
deep saucepan or deep fryer.
4. Fry 6 coated cheese cubes
at a time for 30 seconds or
until golden brown.
5. Drain on paper towels.
Serve hot.

About 4 dozen appetizers

Sweet Potato Chips

1 large sweet potato
Crisco shortening for deep
  frying
Salt (plain, onion, garlic, or
  seasoned)

1. Pare potato with vegetable
peeler, then pull vegetable
peeler down length of potato
making long, thin strips.
2. Heat a 1½-inch layer of
Crisco to 365° in a deep heavy
saucepan.

3. Add about 1 cup of potato
strips to hot Crisco. Fry for 1
minute or until light golden
brown.
4. Remove strips from Crisco
with a slotted spoon and drain
on paper towels.
5. Sprinkle with desired salt
before serving.

4 servings

Appetizers

Fried Chicken Wings with Sweet-Sour Sauce

2 pounds chicken wings
  (about 10)
2 tablespoons dry mustard
1 tablespoon water
1 cup all-purpose flour
1 teaspoon salt
1/2 teaspoon pepper
1/4 cup Crisco shortening

Sweet-Sour Sauce:
1 cup apricot preserves
2 tablespoons brown sugar
1 teaspoon dry mustard
1/2 teaspoon ground ginger
1/4 cup cider vinegar

1. Disjoint chicken wings; discard tips.
2. Mix dry mustard and water; spread over chicken pieces.
3. Combine flour, salt, and pepper; coat chicken pieces.
4. Melt Crisco in a large skillet.
5. Fry chicken wings until golden brown (about 25 minutes), turning as needed.
6. For Sweet-Sour Sauce, combine all ingredients in a small saucepan. Heat just until sugar is melted. Makes about 1 1/4 cups sauce.
7. Serve as dipping sauce for chicken pieces.

About 20 pieces

Deviled Ham Canapés

1 can (4 1/2 ounces) deviled ham
1/4 cup dairy sour cream
1/2 teaspoon dill weed
1/4 cup finely chopped
  cucumber pickle
1 1/2 tablespoons Crisco
  shortening, melted
1 1/2 teaspoons lemon juice
1/4 teaspoon onion salt
36 toast rounds (1 3/4 inch)
Sliced pimiento-stuffed green
  olives

1. Mix deviled ham, sour cream, dill weed, and pickle. Chill thoroughly.
2. Combine melted Crisco, lemon juice, and onion salt. Brush toast rounds with Crisco mixture, then spread with ham mixture.
3. Garnish each with an olive slice.

3 dozen appetizers

Pastry Triangles

2 1/4 cups Homemade Crisco
  Pie Crust Mix, page 154
1/4 cup yellow cornmeal
1 teaspoon onion powder
Dash ground red pepper
5 tablespoons cold water
Grated Parmesan cheese
Sesame, poppy, or caraway
  seed

1. Preheat oven to 425°.
2. Combine Crisco mix, cornmeal, onion powder, and red pepper in a bowl.
3. Add water, 1 tablespoon at a time, mixing until dry ingredients are moistened and dough can be gathered into a ball.

4. Roll pastry to 1/8-inch thickness on a lightly floured surface.
5. Using a sharp knife, cut pastry into 2-inch-high triangles.
6. Place triangles on ungreased cookie sheets; prick with fork.
7. Brush triangles with cold water; sprinkle with cheese or seeds as desired.
8. Bake at 425° for 8 to 10 minutes or until lightly browned.

8 to 10 dozen appetizers

Swiss Cheese Thumbprints

1/2 cup Crisco shortening
2 cups finely shredded Swiss
  cheese
1 1/2 cups all-purpose flour
1/2 teaspoon salt
3 tablespoons water
Liver sausage spread
Sweet gherkins, sliced
Pimiento-stuffed green olives,
  sliced

1. Preheat oven to 425°.
2. Put Crisco into a mixer bowl. Add Swiss cheese gradually, beating at medium speed until fairly smooth. Combine flour and salt; add to cheese mixture alternately with water.
3. Shape rounded teaspoonfuls of dough to form 1-inch balls. Place on ungreased cookie sheets.
4. Make an indentation in center of each ball; fill with 1/2 teaspoon liver sausage spread. Top with a pickle or olive slice as desired.
5. Bake at 425° for 12 to 15 minutes. Serve warm.

3 1/2 dozen appetizers

Hot Mushroom Appetizers

1 pound large fresh mushrooms
1/4 cup Crisco shortening
1/2 pound chicken livers
1/2 teaspoon fresh onion juice
1 cup crushed wheat wafers
1/2 teaspoon salt
1/8 teaspoon tarragon leaves, crushed
1 chicken bouillon cube
1/2 cup boiling water
Sieved hard-cooked egg yolk

1. Preheat oven to 375°.
2. Clean mushrooms. Remove stems and reserve caps. Chop stems.
3. Melt Crisco in a large skillet. Add chopped mushroom stems, chicken livers, and onion juice to hot Crisco. Cook over medium heat, stirring occasionally, for 10 minutes. Remove livers and chop them.
4. Put chopped livers into skillet. Add crushed wafers, salt, tarragon, and bouillon cube dissolved in boiling water; mix well.
5. Fill mushroom caps with chicken liver mixture. Arrange in a shallow baking pan.
6. Bake at 375° for 20 minutes until hot.
7. Garnish with sieved egg yolk. Serve hot.

About 2 dozen appetizers

Sausage Pinwheels

4 cups Homemade Crisco Quick Bread Mix, page 116
1 cup milk
1 pound regular or spicy bulk pork sausage
Grated Parmesan cheese

1. Put Crisco mix into a bowl, make a well in center, and pour in milk. Mix lightly with a spoon to a soft dough.

2. Turn dough out onto a floured surface and knead for 1 minute. Divide dough in half. Roll one half into a 12-inch square. Spread with one half of sausage. Roll up as for a jelly roll. Wrap in waxed paper. Repeat with remaining dough and sausage.
3. Chill rolls several hours.
4. Preheat oven to 350°.
5. Cut rolls into 1/3-inch slices. Arrange on ungreased cookie sheets. Sprinkle with cheese.
6. Bake at 350° for 25 minutes until lightly browned.

6 dozen appetizers

Artichoke Puffs

16 to 20 slices small party rye
   bread
2 tablespoons Crisco
   shortening, melted
1 can (14 ounces) artichoke
   hearts, drained
2 egg whites
1/8 teaspoon salt
1/4 cup grated Parmesan
   cheese
2 tablespoons shredded sharp
   Cheddar cheese
Dash ground red pepper
Paprika

1. Preheat oven to 400°.
2. Brush bread slices with
melted Crisco and place on an
ungreased cookie sheet.

3. Cut artichoke hearts in half;
drain on paper towels.
4. Place an artichoke piece
cut-side-down on each bread
slice.
5. Beat egg whites and salt
until stiff, not dry, peaks
form. Fold in cheeses and red
pepper.
6. Spoon about 1 measuring
teaspoonful of egg white
mixture over each artichoke
piece; sprinkle with paprika.
7. Bake at 400° for 10 to 12
minutes or until golden brown.
Serve hot.
8. Garnish tray with celery
leaves and carrot curls, if
desired.

16 to 20 puffs

Pastry-Wrapped Patties

Patties:
1 pound ground beef
3/4 cup fine dry bread crumbs
1/4 cup chicken broth
1/2 teaspoon poultry seasoning
1/4 teaspoon seasoned salt
2 tablespoons Crisco
   shortening

Pastry:
3 cups Homemade Crisco Pie
   Crust Mix, page 154
1 1/2 teaspoons paprika
4 to 5 tablespoons cold water

1. For Patties, combine beef,
bread crumbs, chicken broth,
poultry seasoning, and
seasoned salt until well mixed.
Shape into patties using 1
tablespoonful for each.
2. Melt Crisco in a skillet, add
patties, and fry slowly until
done. Drain on paper towels.
Chill for 30 minutes.
3. Preheat oven to 400°.
4. For Pastry, put Crisco mix
and paprika into a bowl.
Sprinkle with water, 1 tablespoon at a time, and toss
lightly with a fork until just
moist enough to hold together.
Gather dough into a ball.
Pinch off small pieces of
dough and wrap around
sausage patties. Put patties
on ungreased cookie sheets.
5. Bake at 400° for 20 to 25
minutes.

4 dozen appetizers

Note: If desired, prepare patties as
directed above; do not bake. Wrap
and freeze. Preheat oven to 425°.
Place frozen patties on ungreased
cookie sheets. Bake at 425° for 25
minutes or until lightly browned.

Chicken Salad Puffs

1/2 cup Crisco shortening
1 cup boiling water
1/2 teaspoon salt
1 cup all-purpose flour
4 eggs

Chicken Salad Filling:
1 cup finely chopped cooked
* chicken*
1 cup finely chopped celery
2 tablespoons finely chopped
* pickle*
2 tablespoons finely chopped
* pimiento*
2 tablespoons mayonnaise

1. Preheat oven to 450°.
2. Put Crisco, water, and salt into a saucepan and bring to a rolling boil.

3. Add flour all at one time. Beat vigorously with a wooden spoon until mixture leaves sides of pan and forms a smooth ball. Remove from heat.
4. Add eggs, one at a time, beating until mixture is thick and smooth.
5. Drop dough by teaspoonfuls 1½ inches apart onto greased cookie sheets.
6. Bake at 450° for 10 minutes. Reduce heat to 350° and continue baking for 10 minutes. Cool.
7. For Chicken Salad Filling, combine all ingredients.
8. Cut off tops of puffs and pull out any soft moist dough. Spoon Chicken Salad Filling into puffs. Replace tops.

About 3 dozen appetizers

Teriyaki

1/3 cup soy sauce
1/4 cup honey
1 teaspoon ground ginger
1 teaspoon grated onion
1 clove garlic, minced
1 pound beef sirloin tip, cut in
* 2x1/2x1/8-inch strips*
1/2 cup water
1/8 teaspoon red food coloring
1 tablespoon cornstarch
1/4 cup Crisco shortening

1. Blend soy sauce, honey, ginger, onion, and garlic in a bowl. Add meat and stir well; marinate in refrigerator for about 1 hour.
2. Blend water and food coloring with cornstarch in a saucepan. Put strainer over saucepan. Pour marinated meat into strainer so that meat is well drained and extra marinade drains into saucepan. Set meat aside. Bring mixture to boiling; stir and cook for 2 minutes.
3. Melt Crisco in a large skillet over medium-high heat. Add meat to hot Crisco and brown quickly on all sides. Using slotted pancake turner, transfer meat from skillet to pan of sauce. Toss lightly to coat meat with sauce.
4. Serve on a hot platter; use frilled cocktail picks for servers.

About 8 servings

Note: If desired, serve with rice as a main dish (about 4 servings).

Appetizers

Olive Bites

½ cup all-purpose flour
¼ teaspoon salt
⅛ teaspoon dry mustard
1 cup finely shredded Colby cheese
¼ cup Crisco shortening, melted
1 tablespoon milk
2 drops Tabasco
18 pitted ripe olives or pimiento-stuffed green olives, drained and dried on paper towels

1. Preheat oven to 400°.
2. Combine flour, salt, and mustard in a bowl. Stir in cheese. Combine melted Crisco, milk, and Tabasco; add to bowl and stir until dry ingredients are moistened and a dough is formed.
3. Shape rounded teaspoonfuls of dough into balls. Wrap each ball around an olive. Place on an ungreased cookie sheet.
4. Bake at 400° for 10 to 12 minutes or until lightly browned. Serve hot.

18 appetizers

Deviled Ham Pastries

Filling:
1 can (4½ ounces) deviled ham
¼ cup catsup
¼ cup finely chopped celery
¼ cup finely chopped green pepper
½ teaspoon chili powder
⅛ teaspoon garlic powder

Pastry:
4 cups Homemade Crisco Pie Crust Mix, page 154
1 cup shredded Cheddar cheese
5 tablespoons cold water

1. For Filling, combine all ingredients. Cover and chill.
2. For Pastry, combine Crisco mix and cheese in a bowl. Add water, 1 tablespoon at a time, mixing with a fork until dry ingredients are moistened. Shape into a ball.
3. Preheat oven to 400°.
4. Roll dough to ⅛-inch thickness on a lightly floured surface. Cut with a floured 2¾-inch round cutter. Place on ungreased cookie sheets.
5. Spoon a scant measuring teaspoon of Filling onto each round. Moisten half the edge of each round with water. Fold pastry in half and press edges together with a fork to seal. Prick top of each pastry with fork.
6. Bake at 400° for 12 to 15 minutes or until lightly browned.

About 60 pastries

Ham Pockets

Pastry:
1 cup Crisco shortening
1 package (8 ounces) cream cheese (at room temperature)
2 cups all-purpose flour
½ teaspoon salt

Filling:
1½ cups finely chopped cooked ham
6 tablespoons sweet pickle relish, drained
2 teaspoons prepared mustard

1. For Pastry, cream Crisco and cream cheese together in a bowl. Add flour and salt; stir until smooth. Divide dough in half; wrap and chill.
2. For Filling, combine ingredients.
3. Preheat oven to 400°.
4. Roll each half of dough to ⅛-inch thickness on a lightly floured surface. Cut with a floured 3-inch round cutter. Place on an ungreased cookie sheet.
5. Spoon 1 teaspoon Filling onto each round. Moisten half the edge of each round with water. Fold pastry in half and press edges together with fork to seal. Prick top of each pastry with fork.
6. Bake at 400° for 12 to 15 minutes or until lightly browned.

About 40 appetizers

Swiss Cheese Appetizer Tarts

2 cups Homemade Crisco Pie
Crust Mix, page 154
3 to 4 tablespoons cold water

Filling:
2 eggs, slightly beaten
1/2 cup dairy sour cream
3/4 teaspoon prepared mustard
1/4 teaspoon salt
1/8 teaspoon ground nutmeg
Few grains ground red pepper
3/4 cup shredded Swiss cheese
3 tablespoons finely chopped
onion
Ground nutmeg (optional)

1. Preheat oven to 400°.
2. Put Crisco mix into a
medium bowl. Add water, 1
tablespoon at a time, mixing
just until dry ingredients are
moistened. Shape into a ball.
3. Roll dough to 1/8-inch
thickness on a lightly floured
surface. Cut with a floured
2 3/4-inch round cutter. Fit
carefully into 1 3/4-inch muffin
cups so dough is not stretched.
Press edges against rims.
4. For Filling, blend eggs, sour
cream, mustard, salt, 1/8 teaspoon nutmeg, and red pepper.
Stir in cheese and onion.
Spoon a scant 1 tablespoon
filling into each tart shell.
Sprinkle with nutmeg, if
desired.
5. Bake at 400° for 15 to 20
minutes or until filling is
golden brown. Serve piping
hot.

2 1/2 dozen appetizers

Crispy Cheese Morsels

1 cup Crisco shortening
1/2 pound sharp Cheddar
cheese, finely shredded
(2 cups)
2 cups sifted all-purpose flour
1/2 teaspoon salt
1/4 teaspoon pepper
2 cups crisp rice cereal
Pecan halves (optional)

1. Preheat oven to 350°.
2. Put Crisco into a mixer
bowl. Add cheese gradually,
beating at medium speed until
mixture is fairly smooth.
Blend flour, salt, and pepper.
Gradually add to cheese
mixture, mixing at low speed.
Stir in cereal with spoon.
Shape into balls, using 1 tablespoon for each ball.
3. Arrange balls on ungreased
cookie sheets. Lightly press
with a fork to make a criss-
cross pattern. Dip fork in
flour as needed to prevent
sticking. Press a pecan half
onto top of each, if desired.
4. Bake at 350° for 10 minutes
or until lightly browned
around edges. Cool for 10 to
12 minutes on cookie sheet,
then remove to a rack to cool.

3 to 3 1/2 dozen appetizers

Shrimp Teasers

1 medium onion, grated
1 medium raw potato, pared
and grated
1 1/2 pounds raw shrimp,
shelled, deveined, and finely
chopped
1/2 cup all-purpose flour
1 egg, slightly beaten
1/2 teaspoon salt
1/4 teaspoon pepper
1/4 teaspoon curry powder
(optional)
Crisco shortening for deep
frying

1. Combine onion, potato,
and shrimp in a large bowl.
2. Stir in flour, egg, salt,
pepper, and, if desired, curry
powder.
3. Heat Crisco to 365° in a
deep saucepan or deep fryer.
4. Drop batter by rounded
measuring teaspoonfuls into
hot Crisco. Fry 6 at a time for
3 minutes or until golden
brown.
5. Drain on paper towels.
6. Serve hot with *cocktail*
sauce.

About 6 dozen appetizers

Note: Because potatoes may darken
on standing, prepare batter just
before use.

Additional Appetizers

For other appetizer suggestions see
Sauerkraut Balls, page 35, and
Deep-Fried Strawberries, page 94.

Soups

Mushroom Soup

1/4 cup Crisco shortening
3 tablespoons chopped onion
1 small clove garlic, minced
1/2 cup all-purpose flour
1/2 teaspoon salt
1/8 teaspoon pepper
Dash ground red pepper
3 cups chicken broth
1 pound fresh mushrooms,
   cleaned and sliced lengthwise
2 cups milk

1. Melt Crisco in a saucepan.
Stir in onion and garlic; cook
until onion is crisp-tender.
Mix in a blend of flour, salt,
and peppers. Stir in chicken
broth gradually. Continuing
to stir, bring to boiling and
cook for 1 minute. Stir in
sliced mushrooms. Cook
covered over low heat for 30
minutes, stirring occasionally.
2. Stir in milk and cook uncovered over low heat for 5 to
10 minutes.

About 1 1/2 quarts soup

Asparagus Cream Soup

2 tablespoons Crisco
   shortening
1/4 cup chopped onion
2 packages (10 ounces each)
   frozen cut asparagus
1 cup chicken broth
4 egg yolks, slightly beaten
2 1/2 cups milk
1 teaspoon salt
1/4 teaspoon pepper
4 drops Tabasco

1. Melt Crisco in a saucepan,
add onion, and cook until
onion is tender.
2. Add frozen asparagus and
chicken broth to the saucepan; cook uncovered for 10
minutes over high heat.
3. Transfer mixture to a
blender and puree. (Or force
mixture through a fine wire
sieve.) Add beaten egg yolks.
4. Return mixture to saucepan
and stir in milk, salt, pepper,
and Tabasco. Reheat before
serving; do not boil.

1 1/2 quarts soup

Clam Chowder

3 tablespoons Crisco
   shortening
2 large yellow onions, peeled
   and thinly sliced
6 medium potatoes (about 2
   pounds), pared and thinly
   sliced
1 1/2 cups water
2 cans (10 ounces each)
   shelled whole baby clams or
   3 cans (6 1/2 ounces each)
   minced clams
1 quart milk
1 teaspoon salt
1/4 teaspoon ground white
   pepper

1. Melt Crisco in a large heavy
saucepan. Sauté onions and
potatoes for about 5 minutes
until golden brown. Add
water, heat to boiling, reduce
heat, and simmer covered 10
to 15 minutes or until potatoes
are tender. Stir in clams and
their liquid. Heat for 2 to 3
minutes. Remove from heat.
Add milk, salt, and pepper.
2. Cool mixture uncovered for
30 minutes, then set uncovered
in the refrigerator. About 20
minutes before serving, heat
chowder very slowly just until
steam rises from top (about
20 minutes); do not boil.

3 quarts (about 12 servings)

Beef Vegetable Soup

1/4 cup Crisco shortening
1 pound beef stew meat, cut in
   1/2-inch cubes
1 cup finely chopped onion
2 cloves garlic, minced
2 cans (20 ounces each) white
   kidney beans or 2 cans
   (15 1/2 ounces each) Great
   Northern beans, drained
   and rinsed
1 can (28 ounces) tomatoes
   (undrained)
1 1/2 quarts water
3 beef bouillon cubes
2 vegetable bouillon cubes*
2 carrots, pared and diced
2 stalks celery, sliced
4 1/2 teaspoons lemon juice
1 teaspoon salt
1/4 teaspoon Tabasco
1/2 teaspoon dried leaf basil
1/2 teaspoon dried leaf oregano
1 bay leaf
Lemon strips for garnish
   (optional)

1. Melt Crisco in a large
Dutch oven and lightly brown
beef cubes. Stir in onion and
garlic.
2. Add beans, tomatoes with
liquid, water, bouillon cubes,
carrots, celery, lemon juice,
salt, Tabasco, and herbs. Cut
tomatoes into pieces with a
spoon; mix well. Heat to
boiling, reduce heat, and simmer covered for 1 hour. If
desired, garnish with lemon
strips.

12 to 14 cups soup

* Beef bouillon cubes can be
substituted if necessary.

Easy Chicken Vegetable Soup

2 tablespoons Crisco
  shortening
$^1/_2$ cup chopped onion
1 can (10$^3/_4$ ounces) condensed
  cream of chicken soup
1 can (10$^3/_4$ ounces) condensed
  chicken vegetable soup
1 soup can milk
1 soup can water
1 can (7 ounces) whole kernel
  golden corn (undrained)

1. Melt Crisco in a large saucepan. Add onion and cook until tender.
2. Add soups, milk, water, and corn and liquid to saucepan; mix thoroughly. Heat thoroughly (5 to 10 minutes), stirring frequently.
3. Serve hot.

6 servings

Chicken Bisque

$^1/_3$ cup Crisco shortening
$^1/_2$ cup finely chopped celery
$^1/_4$ cup finely chopped onion
$^1/_4$ cup all-purpose flour
$^1/_2$ teaspoon seasoned salt
$^1/_4$ teaspoon pepper
3 cups chicken broth
1 cup minced cooked chicken
1 cup half-and-half or light
  cream

1. Melt Crisco in a heavy saucepan. Add celery and onion and cook until onion is tender. Stir in flour, seasoned salt, and pepper. Add chicken broth gradually while stirring. Bring to boiling; cook and stir for 1 to 2 minutes.
2. Stir in chicken and half-and-half; heat thoroughly.

About 5 cups soup

Onion Soup

$^1/_4$ cup Crisco shortening
6 cups sliced onions
2 quarts water
5 beef bouillon cubes
3 vegetable bouillon cubes*
$^1/_2$ teaspoon Tabasco
1 tablespoon butter or
  margarine, softened
6 slices French bread
2 tablespoons grated
  Parmesan cheese

1. Melt Crisco in a Dutch oven. Add onions and cook until tender but not brown, stirring occasionally.
2. Add water, bouillon cubes, and $^1/_4$ teaspoon Tabasco. Bring to boiling, reduce heat, and simmer covered for 30 minutes.
3. When ready to serve, blend butter and remaining $^1/_4$ teaspoon Tabasco.
4. Toast bread slices on one side under broiler. Spread untoasted side with Tabasco butter and sprinkle with Parmesan cheese. Place under broiler for 1 minute until cheese is bubbly.
5. Pour soup into a tureen and float bread slices on top.

3 quarts soup

* Beef bouillon cubes can be substituted if necessary.

Southern Ham and Shrimp Soup

1/4 cup Crisco shortening
1 cup chopped onion
1/2 cup chopped green pepper
*1 tablespoon dried parsley
  flakes*
1 1/2 quarts water
3 chicken bouillon cubes
*1/2 pound raw shrimp in the
  shell*
*1 package (10 ounces) frozen
  cut okra*
2 cups cubed cooked ham
1/2 teaspoon salt
2 cups cooked rice (optional)

1. Melt Crisco in a large saucepan over medium heat. Sauté onion and green pepper for 5 minutes.
2. Stir in parsley, water, and bouillon cubes. Bring to boiling over medium heat (about 10 minutes).
3. Add shrimp; cook uncovered for 2 to 3 minutes or until tender and opaque. Remove shrimp from soup with a slotted spoon and cool slightly.
4. Add frozen okra to soup and cook uncovered for 10 minutes; stir once. Add ham and heat thoroughly.
5. Remove shells from shrimp and devein. Stir shrimp and salt into hot soup; remove from heat.
6. Ladle over rice in soup bowls, if desired.

About 2 quarts soup

Plantation Soup

3 cups beef broth
3 carrots, pared and chopped
3 stalks celery, chopped
1/3 cup chopped onion
*3 tablespoons Crisco
  shortening*
3 tablespoons all-purpose flour
3 cups milk
*1/2 cup finely shredded
  Cheddar cheese*

1. Combine broth, carrots, celery, and onion in a saucepan. Bring to boiling; reduce heat and simmer covered for 30 minutes or until vegetables are very tender. Strain; reserve broth and vegetables separately.
2. Melt Crisco in a saucepan. Blend in flour and cook until mixture bubbles, stirring constantly. Add milk gradually while stirring. Bring rapidly to boiling; boil and stir for 1 to 2 minutes.
3. Combine reserved broth and white sauce. Simmer covered for about 20 minutes.
4. When ready to serve, stir cheese into hot soup and garnish with reserved cooked vegetables.

About 2 quarts soup

Beef

Sirloin with Special Sauce

2 tablespoons Crisco
  shortening
2 pounds beef sirloin steak,
  cut about 1½ inches thick
¼ teaspoon salt
1 lemon, thinly sliced
3 medium onions, thinly sliced
  (about 2 cups)
½ cup Crisco shortening
2 tablespoons prepared
  mustard
1 cup chili sauce
1 tablespoon Worcestershire
  sauce
1 teaspoon salt
½ teaspoon chili powder
1 can (6 ounces) tomato juice

1. Preheat oven to 350°.
2. Melt 2 tablespoons Crisco
in a large skillet with an ovenproof handle. Brown steak
about 3 minutes on each side
over medium-high heat.
Remove from heat. Season
with ¼ teaspoon salt.
3. Place lemon slices over
meat. Arrange onion slices
over lemon.
4. Blend Crisco and mustard;
blend in chili sauce, Worcestershire sauce, 1 teaspoon salt,
and chili powder. Spread over
onion and lemon. Pour tomato
juice into skillet around steak.
5. Bake at 350° about 20
minutes (for rare) or until
desired degree of doneness is
reached.

About 6 servings

Party-Perfect Stroganoff

2 pounds boneless beef sirloin,
  cut in thin slices
½ cup all-purpose flour
½ teaspoon salt
⅛ teaspoon pepper
⅓ cup Crisco shortening
1 can (4 ounces) mushroom
  stems and pieces
1 can (10½ ounces) condensed
  beef broth (undiluted)
1 can (10½ ounces) condensed
  onion soup (undiluted)
1 cup dairy sour cream
5 drops Tabasco

1. Coat meat strips evenly
with a mixture of flour, salt,
and pepper.
2. Melt Crisco in a large
heavy skillet over medium
heat. Add meat strips and
brown evenly on all sides.
3. Drain mushrooms, reserving
liquid. Add mushroom liquid,
beef broth, and onion soup
to meat. Cook, stirring constantly, until mixture boils.
Reduce heat, cover, and simmer for 20 minutes or until
meat is tender.
4. Stir in mushrooms; heat.
Remove skillet from heat.
5. Combine sour cream and
Tabasco, and add in small
amounts to the meat in
skillet, mixing well.
6. Return to heat; cook and
stir over low heat until hot.
Serve with *buttered noodles*.

8 servings

Why settle for the same old
humdrum meals when every
suppertime can be a new
taste adventure?

Choose a recipe with family
appeal, then complement it
with appropriate recipes
from other chapters. It's
easy to build a nutritious,
well-balanced meal around
a high protein meat dish.
Crisco makes it easy to do,
and easy to digest, too!

Deep-Fried Liver Strips

1 pound calf's liver
1 teaspoon salt
1 teaspoon dried leaf oregano
Dash pepper
¼ cup olive oil
2 tablespoons lemon juice
Crisco shortening for deep
  frying

1. Cut liver into strips, 2½x½
inch, and put into a bowl;
sprinkle with salt, oregano,
and pepper. Add olive oil and
lemon juice. Stir to coat liver.
Cover and refrigerate for 2
hours or longer.
2. Heat Crisco to 365° in a
deep saucepan or deep fryer.
3. Remove liver from marinade.
Fry several strips at a time in
hot Crisco for 20 to 30 seconds
or until brown.
4. Serve immediately garnish-
ed with lemon wedges and
parsley, if desired.

4 servings

Beef

Meat Patties with Zucchini Cheese Stuffing

2 tablespoons Crisco
   shortening
1½ cups shredded zucchini
¾ cup shredded Cheddar
   cheese
¼ cup dry bread crumbs
1¼ teaspoons salt, divided
2 pounds ground beef
½ teaspoon dill weed
¼ teaspoon pepper
1 can (8 ounces) tomato sauce

1. Preheat oven to 350°.
2. Melt Crisco in a large skillet. Add shredded zucchini and cook over medium heat for 3 minutes or until tender. Add cheese, bread crumbs, and ¼ teaspoon salt; mix well. Set aside.
3. Combine ground beef, remaining 1 teaspoon salt, dill weed, pepper, and ½ cup tomato sauce. Reserve remaining tomato sauce.
4. Press half of ground beef mixture into an 8x8x2-inch pan. Spread zucchini-cheese mixture on top. Shape other half of beef into four square patties and place on zucchini layer. Pour remaining ½ cup tomato sauce over meat.
5. Bake uncovered at 350° for 1½ hours or until thoroughly cooked. Cut into desired serving sizes, lift up with a slotted spoon, and allow the patties to drain slightly. Serve immediately.

4 to 6 servings

Tangy-Top Meat Loaf

2 tablespoons Crisco
   shortening
¾ cup finely chopped onion
¼ cup chopped green pepper
1½ pounds lean ground beef
½ pound bulk pork sausage
1 cup uncooked oats, quick or
   old fashioned
2 eggs, beaten
½ cup tomato juice
2 tablespoons prepared
   horseradish
2 teaspoons salt
1 teaspoon dry mustard

Topping:
2 tablespoons brown sugar
1 teaspoon dry mustard
¼ cup catsup

1. Preheat oven to 375°.
2. Melt Crisco in a skillet over low to medium heat; cook onion and green pepper until onion is soft (about 5 minutes).
3. Meanwhile, lightly mix beef, sausage, and oats in a large bowl. Add the cooked green pepper and onion. Combine eggs, tomato juice, horseradish, salt, and dry mustard. Add to meat mixture and mix lightly. Turn into a 9x5x3-inch loaf pan and press lightly.
4. For Topping, mix brown sugar with dry mustard and blend in catsup. Spread over meat loaf.
5. Bake at 375° about 1 hour. Remove from oven and allow meat to stand for 10 minutes. Loosen from edges, if necessary. Using 2 pancake turners, lift meat onto serving platter.

About 8 servings

Barbecued Beef Ribs

3 pounds beef chuck flat ribs
2 teaspoons salt
½ teaspoon pepper
¼ cup Crisco shortening
½ cup chopped green pepper
½ cup finely chopped onion
½ cup chopped celery
½ cup cider vinegar
¼ cup catsup
¼ cup packed brown sugar
1 tablespoon Worcestershire
   sauce
½ teaspoon dry mustard
½ teaspoon chili powder
2 lemon slices

1. Preheat oven to 350°.
2. Cut ribs into 2-rib pieces. Sprinkle both sides of ribs with salt and pepper. Place ribs meaty-side-up in a shallow roasting pan. Bake at 350° for 30 minutes, turning once; drain.
3. Melt Crisco in a heavy saucepan over medium heat. Add green pepper, onion, and celery, and cook until onion is tender, stirring occasionally. Blend in vinegar, catsup, brown sugar, Worcestershire sauce, mustard, and chili powder. Add lemon slices. Simmer for 10 minutes, stirring frequently. Remove from heat; set aside.
4. Reserve lemon slices, then spoon half of the sauce over ribs. Cover and continue baking for 30 minutes, basting once. Turn ribs meaty-side-up; baste with remaining sauce. Cover and bake, basting several times, for 1 hour longer or until meat is tender. Garnish with reserved lemon slices and a *green pepper ring*.

6 servings

Mini Meat Loaves

²/₃ cup milk
2 eggs, slightly beaten
¹/₂ cup finely chopped onion
³/₄ teaspoon salt
¹/₄ teaspoon pepper
1 cup finely crushed herb-
  seasoned stuffing mix
2 pounds ground beef
¹/₄ cup Crisco shortening
¹/₂ pound fresh mushrooms,
  cleaned and sliced
¹/₂ cup sliced onion
1 can (10³/₄ ounces) condensed
  golden mushroom soup
¹/₂ cup dairy sour cream

1. Combine milk, eggs, chopped onion, salt, and pepper in
a large bowl. Stir in stuffing
mix; let stand for 5 minutes.
Add ground beef; mix well.
2. Divide meat into 6 portions;
shape each into a loaf. Place
in a greased shallow 2-quart
baking dish. Make a depression
down center of each loaf.

3. Preheat oven to 350°.
4. Melt Crisco in a heavy
skillet over medium heat. Add
mushrooms and sliced onion;
cook for 5 minutes, stirring
frequently. Remove 1 cup
mushroom mixture and
reserve. Add soup and sour
cream to remaining mushroom
mixture in skillet; stir gently
to combine as sauce.
5. Put 1 tablespoon mushroom
sauce in depression of each
loaf. Seal meat over filling.
Reserve remaining sauce.
6. Bake at 350° for 35 minutes.
While meat loaves are baking,
heat reserved sauce and
reserved mushroom mixture.
7. Arrange meat loaves on
serving platter. Spoon reserved
sauce over each loaf. Top with
reserved mushrooms and
onions. Garnish with parsley
and carrot curls, if desired.

6 servings

Hamburger Onion Cups

1¹/₂ pounds lean ground beef
1 egg, slightly beaten
2 tablespoons dry bread crumbs
¹/₂ teaspoon salt
¹/₄ teaspoon pepper
2 small onions, peeled and
  sliced in thirds

Cheese Sauce:
2 tablespoons Crisco
  shortening
2 tablespoons all-purpose flour
1 cup milk
³/₄ cup shredded sharp
  Cheddar cheese
¹/₄ teaspoon salt
Dash white pepper

1. Preheat oven to 350°.
2. Combine ground beef, egg,
bread crumbs, salt, and
pepper. Line 6 custard cups
(6 ounces each) with ¹/₂ cup
of meat mixture; make a
depression in the center of
meat and press an onion slice
in center of each hamburger
cup. Place custard cups on a
baking sheet.
3. Bake at 350° for 25 minutes.
4. For Cheese Sauce, melt
Crisco in a saucepan. Add
flour and cook for 1 minute or
just until bubbly. Add milk
gradually, stirring constantly.
Cook and stir for 3 minutes or
until thickened. Add cheese
and stir until melted. Season
with salt and white pepper.
Remove from heat; cover and
keep warm.
5. Remove meat cups from
custard cups with slotted
spoon; drain off fat. Spoon 2
tablespoons of Cheese Sauce
over each meat cup. Serve
with remaining Cheese Sauce.

6 servings

Corned Beef Dinner

1 corned beef brisket (about 5 pounds)
2 medium onions, peeled and quartered
4 peppercorns
1 bay leaf
1/2 teaspoon rosemary, crushed
1 quart water
6 medium potatoes (about 2 pounds), pared and quartered
6 medium carrots, pared and cut in 2-inch pieces
1 cup cut celery (2-inch pieces)
1 medium head green cabbage, cut in wedges

Horseradish Sauce:
2 tablespoons Crisco shortening
2 tablespoons all-purpose flour
1/2 teaspoon salt
1/8 teaspoon pepper
1 egg yolk
1 cup milk
2 teaspoons prepared horseradish
1 tablespoon lemon juice

1. Put meat into a large Dutch oven having a tight-fitting cover. Add onion quarters, peppercorns, bay leaf, rosemary, and water. Bring to boiling and simmer covered for 3½ hours or until meat is fork tender.
2. Add vegetables, placing cabbage on top of meat. Cover and cook for 1 hour or until tender.
3. Remove vegetables and meat to a large heated platter. Serve with Horseradish Sauce.

4. For Horseradish Sauce, melt Crisco in a saucepan. Stir in flour, salt, and pepper. Mix well and cook until bubbly (about 1 minute). Remove from heat.
5. Beat egg yolk; add milk and mix well. Stir into Crisco-flour mixture. Cook, stirring constantly, for 3 minutes or until smooth and thickened. Remove from heat. Stir in horseradish and lemon juice.

12 servings

Company Hash

1 can (about 15 ounces) corned beef hash
1 tablespoon Crisco shortening, melted
1 teaspoon prepared horseradish
1 teaspoon prepared mustard
1 large tomato
1/4 teaspoon salt
Dash pepper
1/4 cup shredded sharp Cheddar cheese

1. Cut hash into 4 equal slices. Place hash slices on a broiler rack; brush tops with 1½ teaspoons melted Crisco.
2. Broil 3 inches from heat for 5 minutes or until browned. Turn and spread tops thinly with a mixture of horseradish and mustard. Broil for 3 minutes.
3. Remove from broiler. Cut tomato into 4 equal slices. Place 1 tomato slice on each hash slice. Brush tomato slices with remaining 1½ teaspoons melted Crisco. Sprinkle with salt, pepper, and cheese.
4. Broil for 1 to 2 minutes or until cheese is melted.

4 servings

Mexicali Stew

3/4 pound bologna
3 tablespoons Crisco shortening
1/2 cup sliced celery
1/2 cup chopped green pepper
1/2 cup chopped onion
1 clove garlic, minced
1 can (16 ounces) kidney beans, drained and rinsed
1 can (about 16 ounces) golden whole kernel corn, drained
3/4 cup sliced pitted ripe olives
2 cups tomato juice
1 tablespoon Worcestershire sauce
1 teaspoon chili powder
1/2 teaspoon salt
1/8 teaspoon pepper
1 cup shredded sharp Cheddar cheese

1. Cut bologna into ½-inch cubes and set aside.
2. Melt Crisco in a large heavy saucepan over medium-high heat. Add celery, green pepper, onion, and garlic. Cook, stirring frequently, until onion is tender. Mix in bologna, beans, corn, olives, tomato juice, Worcestershire sauce, chili powder, salt, and pepper.
3. Bring to boiling, stirring frequently. Reduce heat and simmer for 15 minutes, stirring occasionally. Remove from heat; add 3/4 cup cheese and stir until melted.
4. Spoon into 6 ramekins or soup bowls. Sprinkle with remaining 1/4 cup cheese.
5. Serve with *toasted corn-bread squares* or *French bread slices*.

6 servings

Country Pot Roast

$1/3$ cup all-purpose flour
2 teaspoons salt
$1/8$ teaspoon pepper
1 beef chuck pot roast (3 to 4
  pounds)
3 tablespoons Crisco
  shortening
2 cups water
1 bay leaf, crushed
8 small onions
8 small potatoes (about
  1 pound)
8 small carrots
2 medium turnips, quartered
1 clove garlic, minced
$1/4$ cup chopped green pepper
$1/2$ cup cold water
$1/4$ cup all-purpose flour

1. Combine $1/3$ cup flour, salt, and pepper; coat meat evenly.
2. Melt Crisco in a Dutch oven over medium heat. Brown meat well on all sides. Add 2 cups water and bay leaf. Cover and simmer for 2 hours; do not boil. If needed, add water during cooking.
3. Peel onions and pare potatoes, carrots, and turnips.
4. When meat has simmered for 2 hours, add vegetables to Dutch oven. Cover and simmer for 1 hour or until meat and vegetables are tender.
5. Remove meat and vegetables and arrange on a heated platter; keep warm. Strain liquid and add water, if necessary, to make $1/2$ cups liquid. Return to Dutch oven.
6. Blend $1/2$ cup cold water and $1/4$ cup flour until smooth. Slowly stir into pot roast liquid. Cook and stir until gravy thickens and comes to boiling. Cook and stir for 1 minute. Serve with meat.

8 servings

Oven Pot Roast, Italian Style

$1/2$ teaspoons salt
$1/4$ teaspoon pepper
$1/4$ cup Crisco shortening
1 beef bottom round roast or
  rolled rump roast ($4^1/2$ to 5
  pounds)
1 can (28 ounces) Italian
  tomatoes, cut in pieces
$1/2$ cup dry red wine
2 tablespoons instant minced
  onion
2 tablespoons dried parsley
  flakes
1 bay leaf
$1/4$ teaspoon garlic powder
6 medium carrots, pared and
  sliced
$1^1/2$ pounds zucchini, sliced
2 cups cherry tomatoes,
  pricked with fork
$1/2$ cup cold water
$1/4$ cup cornstarch

1. Preheat oven to 350°.
2. Rub salt and pepper over surface of meat.
3. Melt Crisco in heavy Dutch oven over medium-high heat. Add meat and brown well on all sides. Drain off fat.
4. Combine tomatoes, wine, onion, parsley, bay leaf, and garlic powder. Pour over meat. Cover tightly.
5. Cook in a 350° oven for $2^1/2$ hours. Mix in carrots; cover and cook for 20 minutes. Mix in zucchini; cover and cook for 15 minutes. Mix in cherry tomatoes; cover and cook for 5 to 10 minutes or until heated.
6. Arrange meat and vegetables on a warm serving platter; keep warm.

7. Pour pan juices into a large measuring cup. Add water, if needed, to make 4 cups liquid. Return liquid to Dutch oven. Stir in a blend of cold water and cornstarch. Cook over medium-high heat, stirring constantly, until liquid comes to boiling. Cook and stir for 5 minutes. Serve with meat.

12 to 15 servings

Corny Beef Casserole

3 tablespoons Crisco
  shortening, divided
1 pound ground beef
1 cup chopped onion
$1/2$ cup chopped green pepper
1 can (17 ounces) cream-style
  corn
1 teaspoon salt
$1/8$ teaspoon pepper
$1/2$ cup dry bread crumbs
$1/8$ teaspoon paprika

1. Preheat oven to 350°.
2. Melt 2 tablespoons Crisco in a heavy skillet and brown ground beef. Add onion and green pepper and cook until tender.
3. Drain mixture thoroughly and turn into a $1^1/2$-quart casserole. Stir in corn, salt, and pepper.
4. Melt remaining 1 tablespoon Crisco in the same skillet and lightly brown bread crumbs (about 5 minutes). Top casserole with crumbs.
5. Bake at 350° for 25 to 30 minutes or until heated. Remove from oven and sprinkle with paprika.

4 to 6 servings

Beef 'n' Cheese Tart

1 pound lean ground beef
1/4 cup chopped onion
3/4 cup prepared barbecue
sauce
Crisco pastry for a double-
crust 9-inch pie, page 154
5 slices (about 4 ounces)
American pasteurized
process cheese food
1 teaspoon milk
1/4 teaspoon poppy seed

1. Preheat oven to 425°.
2. Brown meat lightly in a skillet (about 5 minutes). Add onion and cook for 3 minutes or until tender. Drain excess fat. Add barbecue sauce and stir; set aside.

3. Prepare Crisco pastry. Roll half into a 15x6½-inch rectangle on a lightly floured surface. Place on a 15½x12-inch cookie sheet. Spread meat mixture along center of pastry leaving a 1-inch border at edges. Place cheese slices, slightly overlapping, on meat. Moisten pastry edge with water. Roll out remaining pastry on a lightly floured surface to a 15x6½-inch rectangle. Carefully place pastry over meat and cheese filling matching edges of bottom pastry. If necessary, fold bottom pastry up to meet edge of top pastry. Seal edges with fork. Brush pastry with milk and sprinkle with poppy seed.
4. Bake at 425° for 20 minutes or until lightly browned. Let stand for 5 minutes before serving.

6 servings

Zesty Beef Turnovers

1 tablespoon Crisco
shortening
3/4 pound lean ground beef
1/4 cup finely chopped green
pepper
1/4 cup finely chopped celery
1/4 cup finely chopped onion
1 tablespoon chopped
pimiento-stuffed green olives
1 tablespoon chopped seedless
raisins
1 tablespoon chopped parsley
1 teaspoon salt
1/4 teaspoon dry mustard
1/4 teaspoon dried marjoram
1/8 teaspoon dried thyme
1/8 teaspoon black pepper
Crisco pastry for a double-
crust 9-inch pie, page 154
1 egg, slightly beaten

1. Melt 1 tablespoon Crisco shortening in a skillet. Add ground beef and brown lightly (about 5 minutes). Add green pepper, celery, onion, olives, raisins, parsley, salt, dry mustard, marjoram, thyme, and black pepper. Cover and simmer for 30 minutes.
2. Preheat oven to 400°.
3. Divide pastry in half. Roll out pastry on a lightly floured surface. Using the lid from a 3-pound Crisco can as a pattern, cut 6 circles (about 5¼ inches) from each half.
4. Place a scant ¼ cup meat filling on each pastry round. Moisten edges with water. Fold in half over filling, pressing with a fork to seal. Prick tops with fork. Brush pastry with beaten egg. Place on an ungreased cookie sheet.
5. Bake at 400° for 20 minutes or until golden. Serve hot.

12 turnovers

Beef Wellington

3¹/₂ to 4 pounds beef tenderloin, rolled for roasting
Dash salt
Dash pepper
4 ounces liver sausage spread

Crisco Pastry:
3¹/₃ cups sifted all-purpose flour
1¹/₂ teaspoons salt
1¹/₄ cups Crisco shortening
6 to 7 tablespoons cold water
1 egg yolk, fork beaten
1 teaspoon water

1. Preheat oven to 425°.
2. Set beef on a rack in a shallow roasting pan. Roast at 425° for 25 minutes (rare). Remove roast from oven and cool completely.
3. Discard any fat on roast. Season with salt and pepper. Spread with liver sausage.
4. For Crisco Pastry, combine flour and salt in a bowl. Cut in Crisco with pastry blender or 2 knives until mixture is uniform (mixture should be fairly coarse). Sprinkle with water, 1 tablespoon at a time, tossing lightly with fork. When all water has been added, work dough into a firm ball.
5. On a lightly floured surface, roll out pastry large enough to wrap around the roast. Place roast on one edge of pastry and bring other edge over roast to cover completely; reserve extra pastry for decorations. Moisten edges with water and pinch together firmly. Place on a cookie sheet. Cut a few small slits on top to allow steam to escape.
6. Cut out decorative shapes from reserved pastry. Moisten underside of each with water and place on top. Combine egg yolk and water in a small bowl. Brush entire surface of pastry with mixture.
7. Bake at 425° for 30 to 35 minutes or until pastry is golden brown.
8. Garnish serving platter with crab apples and green leaves, if desired.

6 to 8 servings

Stuffed Cabbage Rolls

1 tablespoon Crisco shortening
1 small onion, peeled and chopped
1¹/₄ pounds ground beef
1¹/₂ teaspoons salt
¹/₄ teaspoon pepper
³/₄ cup cooked rice
2 cans (8 ounces each) tomato sauce
12 large cabbage leaves
¹/₄ cup packed brown sugar
2 tablespoons vinegar

1. Melt Crisco in a large skillet; add onion and sauté until tender. Remove from heat and mix in ground beef, salt, pepper, cooked rice, and 1 can tomato sauce.
2. Remove center vein from cabbage leaves. Put leaves into boiling water; return to boiling; boil for 3 to 4 minutes or until tender; drain.
3. Spoon meat mixture in center of cabbage leaves. Fold ends over meat mixture and roll up. Put rolls into skillet.
4. Mix remaining can of tomato sauce with brown sugar and vinegar; pour over rolls. Bring to boiling; simmer covered for 30 minutes, basting occasionally. Uncover and continue cooking for 30 minutes.

6 servings

Easy Beef Slices

1 egg, well beaten
2 tablespooons milk
1 teaspoon salt
1 teaspoon dry mustard
¹/₈ teaspoon pepper
¹/₃ cup fine dry bread crumbs
¹/₄ cup grated Parmesan cheese
8 slices cooked beef, cut about ¹/₈ inch thick
¹/₄ cup all-purpose flour
¹/₄ cup Crisco shortening
8 slices (6 ounces) American pasturized process cheese food
1 can (8 ounces) tomato sauce

1. Combine egg, milk, salt, mustard, and pepper in a bowl.
2. Combine bread crumbs and Parmesan cheese.
3. Dip beef slices in flour to coat on both sides. Dip in egg mixture and coat well. Dip in bread crumb mixture to coat on both sides.
4. Melt Crisco in a large skillet. Add 4 coated beef slices; brown over medium heat for 1 minute on each side. Transfer to a cookie sheet. Repeat with remaining slices.
5. Top each slice with a slice of cheese. Spoon tomato sauce over cheese.
6. Place under broiler 4 to 6 inches from heat. Broil for 2¹/₂ to 3 minutes until cheese is melted and sauce is hot.

4 servings

Prune-Filled Pork Roast

1 boneless pork loin roll (2½ pounds)
16 pitted prunes
3 tablespoons Crisco shortening
1 teaspoon salt
¼ teaspoon pepper
2 tablespoons water
3 tablespoons all-purpose flour
1½ cups milk

1. Untie roast. Arrange prunes in center. Securely tie roast with string.
2. Melt Crisco in a Dutch oven over medium heat. Brown meat well on all sides. Sprinkle with salt and pepper. Add water. Cover and cook slowly for 2 hours or until meat is tender. If necessary, add water during cooking. Remove meat and place on heated platter; keep warm.
3. Pour drippings into a measuring cup. Remove 3 tablespoons of fat and ½ cup drippings; pour into Dutch oven. Blend in flour and cook until bubbly. Remove from heat; gradually stir in milk. Cook, stirring constantly, until gravy thickens and boils. Cook and stir for 1 minute.
4. Slice pork and serve with gravy.

8 servings

Oriental Pork Casserole

2 pounds boneless pork, cut in thin strips
⅓ cup all-purpose flour
½ teaspoon salt
¼ teaspoon pepper
⅓ cup Crisco shortening, divided
1 clove garlic, minced
½ cup coarsely chopped onion
1 green pepper, cored and cut in strips
1 cup diagonally sliced celery
2 cans (8 ounces each) sliced water chestnuts, drained
½ cup uncooked long grain rice
2 tablespoons soy sauce
1 envelope (about 1¾ ounces) dry chicken noodle soup mix
2½ cups boiling water

1. Preheat oven to 350°.
2. Coat meat strips evenly with a mixture of flour, salt, and pepper.
3. Melt 2 tablespoons Crisco in a large heavy skillet over medium heat. Add one half of the meat strips and brown evenly on all sides. Transfer to a 3-quart casserole. Add 2 tablespoons Crisco to skillet and brown remaining meat. Transfer meat to casserole.
4. Melt remaining Crisco; add garlic, onion, green pepper, and celery. Cook for 3 minutes, tossing lightly to mix.
5. Add the vegetables, water chestnuts, rice, and soy sauce to casserole. Add soup mix and boiling water; mix thoroughly. Cover tightly.
6. Bake at 350° for 45 minutes.
7. Remove from oven and stir mixture with a fork before serving.

8 servings

Stuffed Spareribs

¼ cup Crisco shortening
⅓ cup chopped onion
⅓ cup chopped celery
4 cups ½-inch soft bread cubes
1 cup diced pared apple
2 cups drained sauerkraut
1 teaspoon caraway seed
2 sections pork spareribs (about 1½ pounds each)
2 teaspoons salt
¼ teaspoon pepper

1. Preheat oven to 350°.
2. Melt Crisco in a heavy skillet over medium heat. Add onion and celery and cook until onion is tender, stirring occasionally. Toss lightly with bread cubes, apple, sauerkraut, and caraway seed.
3. Sprinkle both sides of sparerib sections with salt and pepper. Place one sparerib section on rack in a shallow roasting pan. Spread stuffing over it; cover with second section. Fasten the sections together with skewers.
4. Roast at 350° for 2 hours or until meat is tender. Remove skewers. Cut spareribs into serving-size pieces and serve with stuffing.

6 servings

Sausage Lima Bean Skillet

1 package (10 ounces) frozen
  lima beans
1/4 teaspoon salt
1 tablespoon Crisco
  shortening
1/4 cup finely chopped onion
1 pound bulk pork sausage
1/4 cup water
1/4 teaspoon ground nutmeg
1/8 teaspoon dried leaf
  marjoram
2 tablespoons cold water
1 tablespoon all-purpose flour
1/2 cup sliced pitted ripe olives
1 cup dairy sour cream
Toasted cornbread or French
  bread slices

1. Cook lima beans following package directions; drain. Season with salt.
2. Melt Crisco in a large heavy skillet over medium heat. Add onion and cook until crisp-tender, stirring occasionally. Separate sausage into small pieces and add to skillet. Pour in 1/4 cup water. Bring to boiling. Cover and simmer for 15 minutes.
3. Drain off drippings. Stir in nutmeg and marjoram. Stir in a blend of 2 tablespoons cold water and the flour. Cook and stir for 1 minute.
4. Mix in lima beans and olives. Blend in sour cream, a small amount at a time. Heat thoroughly (do not boil).
5. Serve at once with slices of cornbread.

4 to 6 servings

Dill Pickle Pork Chops

3 tablespoons Crisco
  shortening
8 pork chops, cut 1/2 inch thick
1 teaspoon salt
1/4 teaspoon black pepper
4 teaspoons prepared mustard
7 or 8 baby dill pickles, thinly
  sliced
2 tablespoons dill pickle liquid
1/4 cup apple cider

1. Melt Crisco in a large skillet. Add pork chops and brown well on both sides. Sprinkle with a mixture of salt and pepper. Spread each pork chop with 1/2 teaspoon mustard.
2. Arrange one layer of pork chops in a Dutch oven and cover with half of the dill pickle slices. Repeat layering with chops and remaining pickles.
3. Add pickle liquid; cover and cook over low heat for 1 hour; add apple cider 20 minutes before end of cooking time.
4. Remove from heat and place chops on a heated serving platter. Skim fat from top of pan gravy. Place over high heat and cook for 3 to 5 minutes or until reduced to half. Serve sauce with chops.

8 servings

Pork Pie with Apple Kraut Filling

Shell:
1½ pounds ground lean pork
1½ teaspoons salt
¼ teaspoon pepper
¼ teaspoon crushed rosemary
    leaves
¼ cup catsup
2 eggs, slightly beaten
1 cup coarse dry bread crumbs

Filling:
¼ cup Crisco shortening
1 medium onion, halved and
    sliced
3 cups well-drained
    sauerkraut
3 cups coarsely chopped
    unpeeled tart cooking apples
½ cup apple cider, divided
¼ teaspoon dried leaf thyme
¼ teaspoon rubbed sage
⅛ teaspoon pepper
2 tablespoons all-purpose flour
4 ounces Swiss cheese, cut in
    strips

1. Preheat oven to 350°.
2. For Shell, combine pork, salt, ¼ teaspoon pepper, and rosemary in a bowl. Mix in catsup, eggs, and bread crumbs.
3. Turn mixture into a 10-inch pie plate and press lightly against the bottom and sides, shaping into a shell. Make a high rim that extends 1 inch higher than rim of pie plate. Set pie plate in a shallow pan to catch any spillovers.
4. Bake at 350° for 35 to 40 minutes or until browned. Remove from oven and spoon off any excess fat.
5. For Filling, melt Crisco in a large heavy saucepan over medium heat. Add onion and cook until crisp-tender, stirring occasionally. Mix in sauerkraut, chopped apples, ¼ cup apple cider, thyme, sage, and ⅛ teaspoon pepper. Simmer covered for 20 minutes or until apple is tender. Stir in a blend of remaining ¼ cup apple cider and the flour.

Cook and stir for 2 minutes or until thickened.
6. Spoon kraut mixture into hot meat shell. Arrange Swiss cheese strips in a lattice pattern over top. Return to oven for 4 to 5 minutes or until cheese is melted. Serve immediately.

6 to 8 servings

Sauerkraut Goulash

1½ pounds boneless pork
    shoulder, cut in 1½-inch
    cubes
2 tablespoons all-purpose flour
2 teaspoons paprika
2 teaspoons salt
2 tablespoons Crisco shortening
3 tablespoons finely chopped
    onion
¼ cup hot water
2½ cups drained sauerkraut
½ teaspoon caraway seed
1 cup hot water
1 cup dairy sour cream

1. Coat meat evenly with a mixture of flour, paprika, and salt.
2. Melt Crisco in a large saucepan. Add onion and cook until soft, stirring occasionally. Add meat and brown evenly on all sides. Add ¼ cup hot water. Cover and simmer for 45 minutes; stir occasionally.
3. Mix sauerkraut and caraway seed with the meat; add 1 cup hot water. Cover and simmer for 30 minutes or until meat is tender.
4. Gradually add sour cream to hot mixture blending well. Heat for 5 minutes, stirring constantly. Serve with *boiled potatoes.*

6 to 8 servings

Sauerkraut Balls

3 tablespoons Crisco
   shortening
1/2 cup finely chopped onion
1 cup finely chopped cooked
   ham
1 cup finely chopped cooked
   corned beef
1 clove garlic, minced
6 tablespoons all-purpose flour
1/2 teaspoon dry mustard
1 can (16 ounces) sauerkraut,
   drained and finely chopped
1 tablespoon snipped parsley
1/2 cup beef broth
1 1/4 cups all-purpose flour
1 cup milk
1 egg, fork beaten
1 cup fine dry bread crumbs
Crisco shortening for deep
   frying

1. Melt 3 tablespoons Crisco
in a saucepan. Add onion and
cook over low heat for 5 minutes or until tender, stirring
occasionally. Add ham, corned
beef, and garlic; heat well.
2. Mix 6 tablespoons flour
with dry mustard and stir in
until well blended. Add
sauerkraut, parsley, and beef
broth; cook and stir for 2 to 3
minutes or until mixture
forms a thick paste. Spread
mixture in a shallow pan;
cover and chill for 2 hours.
3. Shape mixture into 1-inch
balls. Beat 1 1/4 cups flour,
milk, and egg in a medium
bowl until smooth. Dip balls
into batter, then roll in bread
crumbs. Set aside.
4. Heat Crisco to 375° in a
deep saucepan or deep fryer.
5. Fry balls in hot Crisco for 2
minutes or until well browned
and cooked inside. Serve as
main dish or appetizer.

About 32 balls

Ham Roll-Ups

2 packages (10 ounces each)
   frozen asparagus spears,
   cooked following package
   directions
8 slices baked ham, cut about
   1/8 inch thick
2 tablespoons Crisco
   shortening
2 tablespoons all-purpose flour
1/4 teaspoon salt
Few grains white pepper
1/2 cup chicken broth
1/2 cup milk
2 egg yolks, slightly beaten
1/4 cup shredded sharp
   Cheddar cheese
1 tablespoon lemon juice

1. Preheat oven to 325°.
2. Place 5 or 6 asparagus
spears in the center of each
ham slice. Fold slice around
asparagus to form a roll;
secure with a toothpick. Place
roll-ups on a baking sheet.
3. Bake at 325° for 15 to 20
minutes or until ham is
thoroughly heated.
4. Meanwhile, melt Crisco in a
heavy saucepan and blend in
flour, salt, and pepper; heat
until bubbly. Stir in broth
and milk. Bring rapidly to
boiling, stirring constantly,
and cook for 1 to 2 minutes.
Stir about 3 tablespoons of
the hot mixture into egg yolks
and immediately blend into
hot mixture. Cook and stir for
3 to 5 minutes over low heat.
Remove from heat and add
cheese; stir until cheese is
melted. Blend in lemon juice.
5. Transfer roll-ups to a hot
platter; remove picks. Spoon
sauce over roll-ups. Sprinkle
with *paprika* and garnish
with *parsley*. Serve hot.

8 servings

Fruited Ham Slice

1 large center cut ham slice
   (1 1/2 inches thick)
4 medium Golden Delicious
   apples, cored and cut in
   rings
2 orange slices
3/4 cup apple cider
1/2 cup packed brown sugar

Mustard Sauce:
2 tablespoons Crisco
   shortening
2 tablespoons all-purpose flour
2 teaspoons dry mustard
1/4 teaspoon salt
1/4 teaspoon pepper
1 cup water
2 tablespoons cider vinegar
2 tablespoons prepared
   mustard

1. Preheat oven to 350°.
2. Place ham slice in a large
shallow baking dish.
3. Cut unpared apple rings in
half and place around outer
edge of ham, slightly overlapping slices.
4. Place orange slices in center
of ham slice.
5. Pour cider over ham and
fruit; sprinkle brown sugar
over all.
6. Bake covered at 350° for 45
minutes.
7. For Mustard Sauce, melt
Crisco in a heavy saucepan.
Stir in flour, dry mustard,
salt, and pepper. Gradually
add water and vinegar. Cook
and stir until boiling. Cook for
1 to 2 minutes. Remove from
heat and stir in prepared
mustard to make about 1 1/4
cups sauce. Serve with ham.

6 to 8 servings

Lamb Prune Patties

1¹/₂ pounds ground lamb
¹/₄ cup chopped onion
²/₃ cup finely snipped dried prunes
2 teaspoons dried parsley flakes
1 teaspoon salt
¹/₈ teaspoon pepper
1 cup soft bread crumbs
2 tablespoons Crisco shortening

Gravy:
1¹/₂ cups chicken broth
1 teaspoon dried parsley flakes
¹/₄ cup crushed ginger snaps
¹/₃ cup finely snipped dried prunes

1. Combine ground lamb, onion, prunes, dried parsley, salt, pepper, and bread crumbs, mixing thoroughly. Shape into 6 patties.
2. Melt Crisco in a skillet and cook patties over medium heat until done as desired. Transfer to a serving plate and keep warm.
3. For Gravy, drain off all but 1 tablespoon drippings. Stir in chicken broth and dried parsley. Cook and stir over medium heat for 1 minute. Stir in crushed ginger snaps and snipped prunes. Cook and stir until thickened (about 2 minutes). Serve over lamb patties.

6 servings

Curried Lamb

3 tablespoons Crisco shortening
³/₄ cup chopped onion
³/₄ cup chopped celery
1 teaspoon curry powder
¹/₂ teaspoon salt
1 tablespoon Worcestershire sauce
2 cups chicken broth
1¹/₂ cups cubed cooked lamb
¹/₄ cup water
2 tablespoons all-purpose flour
Cooked rice

1. Melt Crisco in a large saucepan. Add onion and celery and cook until onion is tender (about 5 minutes). Pour off drippings. Add seasonings, chicken broth, and lamb; mix well. Bring to boiling; reduce heat and cook covered for 20 minutes over low heat.
2. Mix water and flour, stir into hot lamb mixture, and cook until thickened. Serve over cooked rice.

4 servings

Lamb Kabobs

2 pounds boneless lamb, cut in 1-inch cubes
6 tablespoons lemon juice
3 tablespoons Crisco shortening, melted
1 onion, peeled and finely chopped
1 teaspoon salt
¹/₂ pound fresh medium mushroom caps, cleaned
Green pepper squares

1. Put lamb into a shallow baking dish. Mix lemon juice, melted Crisco, onion, and salt. Pour over lamb. Let marinate for at least 1 hour; stir once or twice.

2. Drain lamb and arrange alternately with mushroom caps and green pepper squares on skewers. Place on rack of broiler pan.
3. Broil 4 inches from heat for 12 to 15 minutes, turning to cook evenly.

8 servings

Mountain Lamb Chops

¹/₄ cup olive oil
2 tablespoons lemon juice
1¹/₂ teaspoons salt
³/₄ teaspoon dried oregano leaves, crushed
¹/₄ teaspoon pepper
4 lamb shoulder chops (about 2 pounds)
2 tablespoons Crisco shortening

1. Combine oil, lemon juice, salt, oregano, and pepper in a large shallow baking dish. Add lamb chops; turn to coat both sides with marinade. Cover and marinate for 3 to 4 hours in refrigerator.
2. Melt Crisco in large heavy skillet over medium heat. Remove lamb chops from marinade and put into skillet. Cook, turning once, until browned and meat is tender. For well done, cook for 10 to 13 minutes per side; for medium rare, cook for 6 to 9 minutes per side.

4 servings

Oven Lamb Stew

1/2 cup all-purpose flour
1 3/4 teaspoons salt
1/4 teaspoon crushed thyme
2 pounds boneless lean lamb
  shoulder, cut in 2-inch cubes
1/4 cup Crisco shortening
1 bay leaf
4 whole allspice
2 tablespoons chopped parsley
1 clove garlic, minced
1/4 small head cabbage,
  shredded
2 leeks, thinly sliced
1 medium onion, peeled and
  sliced
1 quart water
3 medium potatoes, pared and
  quartered

4 carrots, pared and cut in 2-
  inch pieces
1 white turnip, pared,
  quartered, and quarters
  halved
Boiling water

1. Preheat oven to 350°.
2. Combine flour, salt, and
thyme in a paper or plastic
bag. Add lamb and shake to
coat well. Reserve any excess
flour.
3. Melt Crisco in a Dutch
oven. Add lamb and cook to
brown evenly. Add bay leaf,
allspice, parsley, garlic, cabbage, leeks, and onion. Add 1
quart water and mix well.

Cover tightly and bring
rapidly to boiling.
4. Cook in 350° oven for 1½
hours or until meat is tender.
5. About 20 to 30 minutes
before end of cooking time,
put remaining vegetables into
boiling water in a saucepan,
bring to boiling, reduce heat
to simmer, and cook covered
about 20 minutes or until
vegetables are tender. Drain,
cover to keep warm, and stir
into finished stew.

6 to 8 servings

Note: If a thicker stew is desired,
blend equal parts of reserved flour
and cold water; add to boiling stew.

Veal

Veal 'n' Spaghetti Casserole

1½ pounds boneless veal
  shoulder, cut in 1-inch cubes
¾ cup chopped onion
1 teaspoon salt
½ teaspoon pepper
2 cups water
1 package (7 ounces) thin
  spaghetti, cooked
1 can (6 ounces) sliced
  mushrooms (undrained)
1 cup dairy sour cream

Topping:
3 tablespoons Crisco
  shortening
1 cup fresh bread crumbs
½ cup grated Parmesan
  cheese
½ cup snipped parsley

1. Put veal, onion, salt, pepper, and water into a Dutch oven. Bring to boiling and simmer covered until meat is tender (about 30 minutes).
2. Preheat oven to 350°.
3. Mix cooked spaghetti, undrained mushrooms, and sour cream into veal mixture. Turn into a greased 2½-quart casserole.
4. For Topping, melt Crisco in a skillet and stir in bread crumbs. Remove from heat; stir in cheese and parsley. Sprinkle over mixture in casserole.
5. Bake uncovered at 350° for 35 to 40 minutes or until mixture is bubbly and crumb topping is golden brown.

8 servings

Italian Veal Parmesan

2 pound veal cutlets, thinly
  sliced
1 teaspoon salt
⅛ teaspoon pepper
1 egg
2 teaspoons water
⅓ cup grated Parmesan
  cheese
½ cup dry bread crumbs
¼ cup Crisco shortening
1 medium onion, finely
  chopped (about ½ cup)
1 can (15 ounces) tomato
  sauce
½ teaspoon salt
½ teaspoon basil
½ teaspoon marjoram
6 slices mozzarella cheese

1. Cut veal into 12 to 16 pieces; sprinkle with 1 teaspoon salt and the pepper.
2. Lightly beat together egg and 2 teaspoons water.
3. Combine Parmesan cheese and bread crumbs.
4. Dip veal in egg mixture, then Parmesan mixture. Refrigerate for 1 hour.
5. Melt Crisco in a skillet. Brown veal on both sides. Remove to a 3-quart baking dish.
6. Preheat oven to 350°.
7. Sauté onion in same skillet. Stir in tomato sauce, ½ teaspoon salt, basil, and marjoram. Simmer for 5 minutes. Reserve ½ cup sauce. Pour remaining sauce over veal. Top with mozzarella cheese. Pour reserved sauce over cheese.
8. Bake uncovered at 350° for 20 to 25 minutes or until mixture is bubbly.

6 to 8 servings

Veal Patties

*2 tablespoons Crisco
   shortening*
*2 tablespoons finely chopped
   celery*
*2 tablespoons finely chopped
   onion*
3 tablespoons all-purpose flour
1 cup chicken broth
*2 cups finely chopped cooked
   veal*
*1¹/₂ cups saltine cracker
   crumbs, divided*
1 teaspoon summer savory
³/₄ teaspoon salt
¹/₈ teaspoon pepper
2 eggs, beaten
¹/₃ cup Crisco shortening

1. Melt 2 tablespoons Crisco
in a skillet. Add celery and
onion and cook over medium
heat for 2 minutes or until
tender. Add flour; stir.
Gradually add chicken broth,
blending until smooth. Cook
over medium heat for 1
minute or until thickened.
2. Remove skillet from heat.
Add veal, ¹/₂ cup cracker
crumbs, savory, salt, and
pepper; mix well.
3. Shape mixture into 6 patties.
Coat with eggs and remaining
cracker crumbs.
4. Melt ¹/₃ cup Crisco in a
large skillet. Add patties and
fry for 3 to 4 minutes on each
side or until golden brown.

6 servings

Veal Burger

1 pound ground veal
¹/₄ pound ground smoked ham
¹/₂ teaspoon salt
¹/₈ teaspoon pepper
2 eggs, slightly beaten
¹/₄ cup all-purpose flour
¹/₄ cup Crisco shortening
¹/₂ cup finely chopped carrot
¹/₃ cup finely chopped onion
¹/₄ cup finely chopped celery
*2 tablespoons finely chopped
   parsley*
*1¹/₂ cups broth (1¹/₂ vegetable
   or chicken bouillon cubes
   dissolved in 1¹/₂ cups boiling
   water)*

1. Mix meat, salt, and pepper
in a bowl. Add eggs and mix.
Turn onto waxed paper and
shape into a large patty. Coat
with flour; set aside.
2. Melt Crisco in a 10-inch
skillet. Add carrot, onion,
celery, and parsley; cook for 5
minutes, stirring occasionally.
Push vegetables to edge of
skillet. Add meat patty and
brown on both sides.
3. When meat is browned, add
about half the vegetable broth
to the skillet. Cover and
simmer for 25 minutes or until
meat is cooked. If necessary,
add a little more broth to
keep meat from sticking. With
a large meat turner, remove
patty from skillet and place
on a hot platter; set aside and
keep hot.
4. Add remaining broth to
skillet and mix; pour into an
electric blender and puree.
Return sauce to skillet and
heat. Pour some sauce over
veal patty and serve with
remaining sauce.

4 to 6 servings

Breaded Veal
Cutlets

*2 pounds veal cutlets (about
   ¹/₄ inch thick)*
¹/₃ cup all-purpose flour
1¹/₂ teaspoons salt
¹/₂ teaspoon paprika
¹/₄ teaspoon pepper
3 eggs, slightly beaten
*1 cup fine French bread
   crumbs*
*Crisco shortening for deep
   frying*

1. Cut veal into 6 to 8 serving-
size pieces. Coat with a mixture of flour, salt, paprika,
and pepper. Dip veal in eggs,
then lightly coat with crumbs.
Let stand for 5 to 10 minutes
to seal.
2. Heat Crisco to 365° in a
large saucepan or deep fryer.
3. Add only as many pieces of
veal at one time as will lie
uncrowded one layer deep in
the hot Crisco. Fry until
brown on each side (3 to 4
minutes); turn slices several
times during cooking (do not
pierce). Remove meat with
tongs and drain over fat for a
few seconds, then place on
paper towels. Serve with
lemon wedges.

6 to 8 servings

Pizza-Topped Meat Ring

Meat Ring:
2 pounds ground beef
1/2 pound Italian sausage, crumbled
2 eggs
1/2 cup dry bread crumbs
1 1/2 teaspoons salt
1/2 teaspoon garlic salt
1/4 teaspoon pepper

Pizza Topping:
1 can (8 ounces) tomato sauce
1/4 teaspoon marjoram
1/4 teaspoon oregano
1/4 teaspoon basil
1 cup shredded mozzarella cheese

Sautéed Vegetables:
2 tablespoons Crisco shortening
1/2 pound fresh mushrooms, cleaned and sliced
1/2 cup coarsely chopped green pepper
1/3 cup coarsely chopped onion

1. Preheat oven to 350°.
2. For Meat Ring, combine ground beef, Italian sausage, eggs, bread crumbs, salt, garlic salt, and pepper in a large bowl; mix well. Press meat mixture into an ungreased 6 1/2-cup ring mold.
3. Bake at 350° for 35 to 40 minutes or until thoroughly cooked.
4. Drain meat ring well. Using a spatula, loosen the sides of meat ring from mold; invert onto an ovenproof serving plate. Keep warm.
5. For Pizza Topping, combine tomato sauce, marjoram, oregano, and basil in a small bowl. Pour sauce mixture over meat ring. Sprinkle mozzarella cheese on top.
6. Place meat ring in oven. Bake for 5 to 10 minutes or until cheese is melted. Meanwhile, prepare vegetables.
7. For Sautéed Vegetables, melt Crisco in a medium skillet. Add mushrooms, green pepper, and onion. Cook for 3 minutes or until tender. Remove vegetables with slotted spoon and serve in center of meat ring.

8 to 10 servings

Beef and Ham Vegetable Roll-Ups

5 tablespoons Crisco shortening, divided
1/2 pound fresh mushrooms, cleaned and chopped
1/2 pound fully cooked ham, coarsely chopped
1/4 cup snipped parsley
1/2 cup soft bread crumbs
1 clove garlic, minced
1 teaspoon salt, divided
1/4 teaspoon pepper, divided
8 pieces (4x6 inches each) beef round steak, 1/2 inch thick
1/4 cup all-purpose flour
1 cup coarsely chopped onion
1 cup finely chopped carrot
1 cup chopped celery with leaves
1 teaspoon leaf thyme
4 whole cloves
1 small bay leaf
1 can (10 1/2 ounces) condensed beef broth (undiluted)

1. Melt 3 tablespoons Crisco in a large heavy skillet over medium heat. Add mushrooms and ham and cook, stirring occasionally, until mushrooms are lightly browned. Remove from heat and stir in parsley, crumbs, garlic, 3/4 teaspoon salt, and 1/8 teaspoon pepper.
2. On a wooden board, pound each piece of meat with a meat hammer. Spoon dressing lengthwise on center of each piece. Beginning with longer side, roll and tie securely with cord. Coat evenly with a mixture of flour, remaining 1/4 teaspoon salt, and remaining 1/8 teaspoon pepper.
3. Melt remaining 2 tablespoons Crisco in a large heavy skillet over medium heat. Add roll-ups and brown on all sides; remove. Add to skillet a mixture of onion, carrot, celery, thyme, cloves, and bay leaf. Place roll-ups over vegetables. Cover tightly and cook for 10 minutes.
4. Pour broth over meat, cover, and reduce heat. Simmer for 1 1/4 hours or until tender.
5. Remove meat from skillet and cut off cord. Place roll-ups on a heated serving platter.
6. Meanwhile, cook vegetable mixture uncovered for 3 minutes or until slightly thickened. Remove bay leaf and cloves. Spoon mixture over roll-ups.

8 servings

Mixed Meats

6. Remove meat loaf from oven. Invert loaf in a shallow baking pan or on ovenproof serving platter. Spoon sauce over loaf. Bake at 350° for 30 minutes. Garnish as desired.

8 to 10 servings

Three-Meat Chop Suey

1¹/₄ pounds boneless pork
1 pound boneless beef
³/₄ pound boneless veal
3 tablespoons Crisco
  shortening
1¹/₄ cups water, divided
2 cups diagonally sliced celery
1 cup coarsely chopped onion
3 tablespoons cornstarch
¹/₄ cup soy sauce
¹/₄ cup bead or dark molasses
1 can (16 ounces) bean
  sprouts, drained
1 can (14 ounces) fancy mixed
  Chinese vegetables, drained
1 can (8 ounces) sliced water
  chestnuts, drained

1. Cut meat into 1-inch cubes.
2. Melt Crisco in large heavy skillet. Cooking one layer of meat at a time, brown pieces on all sides. Return meat to skillet; cover and cook over low heat for 30 minutes.
3. Mix in 1 cup water, celery, and onion. Bring to boiling and simmer covered for 20 minutes.
4. Blend cornstarch, remaining ¹/₄ cup water, soy sauce, and molasses. Stir into meat mixture. Bring to boiling; cook and stir for 2 minutes.
5. Mix in remaining ingredients; heat. Serve on *rice*.

8 servings

Triple-Meat Loaf

1 pound ground cooked ham
³/₄ pound ground pork
³/₄ pound ground veal
2 eggs, beaten
¹/₂ teaspoon salt
¹/₂ teaspoon ground nutmeg
¹/₂ teaspoon dry mustard
¹/₈ teaspoon pepper
2 tablespoons Crisco
  shortening
¹/₂ cup finely chopped onion
¹/₂ cup finely chopped green
  pepper
3 tablespoons finely chopped
  parsley
³/₄ cup soft bread crumbs
³/₄ cup apple juice

Sauce:
²/₃ cup packed brown sugar
4 teaspoons cornstarch
1 teaspoon dry mustard
1 teaspoon ground allspice
²/₃ cup apricot nectar
3 tablespoons lemon juice
2 teaspoons vinegar

1. Preheat oven to 350°.
2. Combine ham, pork, and veal with eggs, salt, nutmeg, dry mustard, and pepper.
3. Melt Crisco in a skillet and sauté onion, green pepper, and parsley. Add to meat mixture and toss to blend. Add bread crumbs and apple juice; mix thoroughly but lightly. Turn into a 9x5x3-inch loaf pan and flatten top.
4. Bake at 350° for 1 hour.
5. For Sauce, blend brown sugar, cornstarch, dry mustard, and allspice in a saucepan. Add apricot nectar, lemon juice, and vinegar. Bring to boiling; cook and stir for 2 minutes. Reduce heat and simmer for 10 minutes.

Chicken

POULTRY

Chicken Amandine

1/4 cup all-purpose flour
1 broiler-fryer chicken (about
  3 pounds), cut up
1/4 cup Crisco shortening
1 clove garlic, minced
1/4 cup chopped onion
2 tablespoons all-purpose flour
2 tablespoons tomato paste
1 1/2 cups chicken broth
1/2 teaspoon salt
1/4 teaspoon each dried basil,
  paprika, black pepper, and
  crushed dried leaf tarragon
3/4 cup dairy sour cream
1/4 cup toasted slivered
  blanched almonds
2 tablespoons grated
  Parmesan cheese

1. Put 1/4 cup flour in paper or
plastic bag. Add chicken
pieces and shake to coat well.
2. Melt Crisco in a skillet over
medium-high heat. Add chicken
pieces and brown on all sides;
remove pieces as they brown.
3. Add garlic and onion to
skillet and sauté.
4. Reduce heat to medium; stir
in flour and tomato paste. Pour
in chicken broth and stir until
mixture boils. Return chicken
to skillet. Combine salt, basil,
paprika, pepper, and tarragon;
sprinkle over chicken. Cover
and cook over low heat for 45
to 55 minutes.
5. Remove chicken to a serving
dish. Skim off fat. Using low
heat add sour cream, stirring
constantly; do not boil. Pour
half of sauce over chicken.
Sprinkle with almonds and
cheese. Serve with remaining
sauce.

4 to 6 servings

Country Fried Chicken

1 cup all-purpose flour
2 teaspoons garlic salt
2 teaspoons MSG
1 teaspoon black pepper
1 teaspoon paprika
1/4 teaspoon poultry seasoning
1/2 cup milk
1 egg, lightly beaten
1 frying chicken (2 1/2 to 3
  pounds), cut up or use
  chicken pieces
Crisco shortening for frying

1. Combine flour, garlic salt,
MSG, pepper, paprika, and
poultry seasoning in plastic
or paper bag. Shake chicken
pieces in seasoned flour.
2. Combine milk and egg. Dip
chicken pieces in milk mixture. Shake chicken pieces a
second time in seasoned flour
to coat thoroughly and evenly.
3. To pan fry: melt Crisco in
skillet to about 1/2 to 1 inch in
depth; heat to 365°. Brown
chicken on all sides. Reduce
heat to 275° and continue
cooking until chicken is tender, about 30 to 40 minutes.
Do not cover. Turn chicken
several times during cooking.
Drain on paper towels.
4. To deep fry: heat Crisco
in deep fryer to 365°. Cook
chicken pieces for 15 to 18
minutes. Drain on paper
towels.

4 servings

For Extra Spicy Chicken: increase
poultry seasoning to 1/2 teaspoon and
black pepper to 2 teaspoons.

Poultry is very adaptable.
It can be used for a simple
low-cost casserole or great
holiday dinner with all the
trimmings. Chicken and
turkey are economical,
while a roast duckling is a
good excuse for an elegant
dinner party.

Here is a varied collection of
recipes that will inspire you
to use poultry more often.

Southern Chicken

1/4 cup Crisco shortening
4 split chicken breasts
  (2 pounds)
1 cup undiluted evaporated
  milk
2 tablespoons honey
1 teaspoon salt
1/4 teaspoon ground nutmeg
1/8 teaspoon ground allspice
1 can (16 ounces) sweet
  potatoes in syrup, drained

1. Preheat oven to 350°.
2. Melt Crisco in a large heavy
skillet over medium-high heat.
Add chicken breasts and cook
until golden brown, turning as
needed. Drain on paper towels.
3. Arrange chicken in a
greased 2-quart baking dish.
Combine evaporated milk,
honey, and seasonings; pour
over chicken.
4. Bake at 350° for 10 minutes. Remove from oven and
arrange sweet potatoes around
chicken. Spoon sauce over all.
Return to oven and bake for
30 minutes or until chicken is
tender.

4 servings

Chicken

Roast Chicken

Bread Stuffing:
4 slices bread, cut in 1/2-inch
* cubes*
1/4 cup milk
1 egg, slightly beaten
1/2 teaspoon salt
1 teaspoon dried parsley flakes
1/8 teaspoon pepper
1/8 teaspoon poultry seasoning
2 tablespoons Crisco
* shortening*
1/2 cup chopped celery
1/4 cup chopped onion

Chicken and Gravy:
1 roaster chicken (3 to 4
* pounds)*
1/2 teaspoon salt
1 tablespoon Crisco shortening
2 tablespoons water
2 tablespoons all-purpose flour
1/4 teaspoon salt
1 teaspoon instant chicken
* bouillon granules*
1 cup hot water
1 cup dairy sour cream

1. For Bread Stuffing, combine bread cubes, milk, egg, 1/2 teaspoon salt, parsley, pepper, and poultry seasoning in a bowl. Let stand for 5 minutes. Melt 2 tablespoons Crisco in a small heavy skillet over medium heat. Add celery and onion; cook until onion is tender. Add to bread mixture; stir lightly until combined.
2. Preheat oven to 400°.
3. For Chicken and Gravy, rub inside of chicken with 1/2 teaspoon salt. Fill with stuffing; sew, or skewer and lace with cord. Rub outside of chicken with 1 tablespoon Crisco.
4. Put chicken into a greased roasting pan and add 2 table-spoons water; cover.
5. Roast at 400° for 1 hour, basting every 20 minutes with pan drippings. Uncover and roast an additional 30 minutes or until chicken is golden brown and tender; baste twice with pan drippings.
6. Place chicken on a serving platter. Stir flour and remaining 1/4 teaspoon salt into pan drippings. Dissolve bouillon granules in hot water. Gradually stir into drippings. Cook, stirring constantly, until gravy comes to boiling. Cook and stir for 1 minute. Remove from heat; gradually stir in sour cream. Cook over very low heat, stirring con-stantly, just until gravy is hot. Serve with chicken.

4 to 6 servings

Crumb-Coated Fried Chicken

1/2 cup Crisco shortening
1 broiler-fryer chicken (2 1/2
* pounds), cut up*
2/3 cup finely crushed herb-
* seasoned stuffing mix*
3/4 teaspoon salt
1/4 teaspoon pepper
1/4 teaspoon paprika

1. Heat Crisco to 365° in a large electric skillet.
2. Moisten chicken pieces with water, then coat with a mixture of stuffing mix, salt, pepper, and paprika. Put chicken pieces into skillet and brown evenly on all sides.
3. Reduce heat to 260° and cook chicken uncovered for 30 minutes or until tender, turning occasionally.
4. Remove chicken pieces to serving platter; garnish with cherry-filled peaches, if desired.

4 servings

Chicken Deluxe

1 broiler-fryer chicken (2 1/2 to
* 3 pounds), cut in parts and*
* skinned*
1/2 teaspoon celery salt
3 tablespoons Crisco
* shortening*
4 small yellow onions, peeled
* and quartered*
1 can (16 ounces) artichoke
* hearts, drained and halved*
1 tablespoon chopped parsley
2 tablespoons water
1 teaspoon Italian seasoning
1/8 teaspoon garlic powder
1 large tomato (3 to 3 1/2 inches
* in diameter), cored and*
* coarsely chopped*
1/4 cup white grape juice or
* Chablis wine*
1/4 cup grated Parmesan
* cheese*

1. Preheat oven to 350°.
2. Place chicken in an 11x7x 1 1/2-inch baking pan or baking dish. Sprinkle with celery salt and set aside.
3. Melt Crisco in a skillet; add onion, artichoke hearts, parsley, water, Italian season-ing, and garlic powder. Cook, stirring occasionally, over medium heat for 5 minutes or until onion is tender. Stir in tomato and grape juice; pour over chicken. Cover pan.
4. Bake at 350° for 50 minutes or until chicken is fork-tender. Remove cover, sprinkle with cheese, and return to oven for 5 minutes or until cheese melts.

4 servings

Chicken and Cabbage Skillet

1 broiler-fryer chicken (2¹/₂ pounds), cut up
¹/₂ cup all-purpose flour
¹/₄ cup Crisco shortening
1 pound cabbage, coarsely chopped (about 8 cups)
2 tablespoons all-purpose flour
1 teaspoon caraway seed
¹/₂ teaspoon salt
1 cup cider vinegar
1 cup water
3 medium tart red apples, cored and cut in ¹/₂-inch rings
3 tablespoons brown sugar
1 teaspoon salt

1. Melt Crisco in a large heavy skillet. Coat chicken evenly with ¹/₂ cup flour. Add chicken pieces and brown evenly on all sides over medium heat; cook until done. Remove from skillet and drain on paper towels. Pour off drippings.
2. Put cabbage in skillet. Combine 2 tablespoons flour, caraway seed, and ¹/₂ teaspoon salt; sprinkle over cabbage. Stir in vinegar and water.
3. Arrange apple rings over cabbage; sprinkle with brown sugar.
4. Arrange chicken pieces over apple rings and cabbage. Sprinkle with remaining 1 teaspoon salt.

5. Cover and cook for 10 minutes over medium heat. Uncover and cook for 5 minutes or until cabbage and chicken are tender.
4 to 6 servings

Barbecued Chicken

2 broiler-fryer chickens (3 pounds each), quartered
¹/₃ cup Crisco shortening, melted
1¹/₂ teaspoons salt
¹/₄ teaspoon pepper

Barbecue Sauce:
¹/₃ cup light molasses
¹/₃ cup cider vinegar
¹/₄ cup prepared mustard
1 tablespoon Worcestershire sauce
¹/₂ teaspoon Tabasco
¹/₈ teaspoon dried leaf marjoram

1. Preheat oven to 350°.
2. Put chicken in a greased roasting pan and brush generously with Crisco; sprinkle with salt and pepper.
3. Roast at 350° for 50 minutes or until golden brown, brushing occasionally with Crisco.
4. While chicken is roasting, prepare Barbecue Sauce. Pour molasses into bowl. Gradually add vinegar, mustard, Worcestershire sauce, Tabasco, and marjoram, blending well after each addition. Mix thoroughly before using.
5. Brush browned chicken with Barbecue Sauce; continue to roast for 30 minutes or until chicken is tender, basting several times with sauce. Serve immediately.

8 servings

Chicken

Pineapple Drumsticks

1 egg, slightly beaten
¼ cup water
2 tablespoons milk
¼ cup all-purpose flour
1 tablespoon cornstarch
1 tablespoon cornmeal
⅛ teaspoon baking powder
12 broiler-fryer chicken drumsticks
Crisco shortening for deep frying
1 cup green pepper chunks
½ cup coarsely chopped onion
1 tablespoon Crisco shortening
1 can (20 ounces) pineapple chunks in pineapple juice, drained; reserve juice
⅔ cup cider vinegar
½ cup packed brown sugar
2 tablespoons soy sauce
4 teaspoons cornstarch
2 tablespoons water

1. Combine egg, water, and milk. Combine flour, 1 tablespoon cornstarch, cornmeal, and baking powder; add to first mixture and mix until smooth. Dip each drumstick into batter, letting excess batter drain for a couple of seconds.
2. Heat Crisco to 350° in a deep fryer or a large heavy saucepan. Fry drumsticks in hot Crisco for 14 to 16 minutes or until chicken is crisp, brown, and tender. Remove with slotted spoon and place on paper towels.
3. While chicken is frying prepare sauce. Melt 1 tablespoon Crisco in a saucepan. Sauté green pepper and onion for 3 to 4 minutes or until crisp-tender. Add reserved pineapple juice, vinegar, brown sugar, and soy sauce.

Mix cornstarch into water. Add to sauce until blended, stirring constantly. Add pineapple chunks. Bring to boiling, stirring occasionally. Cook for 2 minutes.
4. Spoon half of sauce over fried drumsticks. Serve with *cooked rice* and remaining sauce.

4 to 6 servings

Saucy Chicken

½ cup Crisco shortening
1 broiler-fryer chicken (about 3 pounds), cut in pieces
1 teaspoon salt
¼ teaspoon pepper
2 tablespoons all-purpose flour
1 cup chicken broth
1½ teaspoons dry mustard
¼ teaspoon paprika
2 teaspoons Worcestershire sauce
2 teaspoons catsup
Cooked rice

1. Melt Crisco in a large skillet, add chicken pieces, and brown on all sides. Remove chicken from skillet; sprinkle with salt and pepper.
2. Add flour to fat in skillet and stir until blended. Add broth gradually, stirring until smooth. Cook and stir until thickened. Blend in dry mustard, paprika, Worcestershire sauce, and catsup.
3. Return chicken to skillet. Simmer covered for 30 minutes or until chicken is tender.
4. Serve with rice.

4 servings

Sweet-Sour Chicken

3/4 cup all-purpose flour
1 teaspoon salt
2 broiler-fryer chickens (2 1/2 to
  3 pounds each), cut up
1/2 cup Crisco shortening
2 tablespoons brown sugar
1 tablespoon cornstarch
1/4 teaspoon salt
1/4 teaspoon ground ginger
1 can (20 ounces) pineapple
  chunks in pineapple juice
1/4 cup cider vinegar
1/4 cup light molasses
1/4 cup prepared mustard
1 teaspoon soy sauce
1 can (11 ounces) mandarin
  oranges, drained

1. Combine flour and 1 teaspoon salt in paper or plastic bag; add chicken pieces and shake to coat well.
2. Melt Crisco in a large heavy skillet. Add chicken pieces and brown evenly on all sides. Drain on paper towels. Arrange in a shallow 3-quart baking dish.
3. Preheat oven to 350°.
4. Combine brown sugar, cornstarch, 1/4 teaspoon salt, and ginger in a heavy saucepan. Drain pineapple, reserving juice. If necessary, add water to make 1 cup liquid. Set fruit aside. Add pineapple juice, vinegar, molasses, mustard, and soy sauce to saucepan; mix until smooth. Cook over medium-high heat, stirring constantly, until sauce comes to boiling. Cook and stir for 2 minutes. Pour 3/4 cup sauce over chicken. Cover tightly with aluminum foil.
5. Bake at 350° for 40 minutes. Stir pineapple chunks and oranges into remaining sauce. Uncover chicken; pour sauce and fruit over chicken. Bake an additional 10 minutes or until chicken is tender.

8 servings

Crispy Broiler Chicken

2 broiler-fryer chickens
  (2 pounds each)
1 tablespoon lemon juice
1/3 cup Crisco shortening,
  melted
1 1/2 teaspoons salt
1/2 teaspoon paprika
1/4 teaspoon pepper

1. Place broiler pan 11 inches from heat. Turn oven control to Broil.
2. Split chickens into halves lengthwise. Remove backbone, neck, and giblets. Crack drumstick joint and joints of wings. Tuck wings under thighs and skewer legs and wings to body.
3. Sprinkle both sides of chicken with lemon juice and brush with half of the melted Crisco. Combine salt, paprika, and pepper; sprinkle over both sides of chicken.
4. Arrange chicken pieces skin-side-down in broiler pan without rack. Broil for 50 to 60 minutes or until done, turning pieces every 10 minutes and brushing each time with Crisco. Place chicken on serving platter and pour pan juices over pieces.

4 servings

Sour Cream Chicken Quiche

Crisco pastry for a single-
  crust 9-inch pie, page 154
2 tablespoons Crisco
  shortening
2 tablespoons chopped green
  pepper
2 tablespoons chopped onion
1 cup cubed cooked chicken
1 tablespoon all-purpose flour
1/4 teaspoon salt
Dash ground nutmeg
Dash pepper
1/2 cup shredded sharp
  Cheddar cheese
1/4 cup shredded Swiss cheese
2 eggs, slightly beaten
3/4 cup milk
3/4 cup dairy sour cream

1. Line a 9-inch pie plate with pastry; set aside.
2. Preheat oven to 400°.
3. Melt Crisco in a skillet. Add green pepper and onion. Cook over medium-high heat for 3 minutes, stirring frequently. Add cubed chicken and flour; cook and stir for 2 minutes.
4. Spread chicken mixture over bottom of unbaked pie shell. Sprinkle with salt, nutmeg, and pepper. Top with Cheddar cheese and Swiss cheese. Combine eggs, milk, and sour cream; mix until smooth. Carefully pour into pie shell.
5. Bake at 400° for 20 minutes. Reduce oven temperature to 350° and bake an additional 30 to 35 minutes or until knife inserted near center comes out clean. Cool for 10 minutes before cutting.

6 to 8 servings

Chicken

Chicken Stroganoff

2 pounds boneless chicken
 breasts, skinned and cut in
 thin strips
1/2 cup all-purpose flour
1 1/2 teaspoons salt
1/8 teaspoon pepper
1/3 cup Crisco shortening
1/2 cup finely chopped onion
2 cups chicken broth
3 tablespoons Crisco
 shortening
1/2 pound fresh mushrooms,
 cleaned and sliced
3/4 cup dairy sour cream
3 tablespoons tomato paste
1 teaspoon Worcestershire
 sauce

1. Coat chicken strips evenly
with a mixture of flour, salt,
and pepper.
2. Melt 1/3 cup Crisco in a large
heavy skillet. Add chicken
strips and onion; brown evenly
on all sides. Add broth, cover,
and simmer about 20 minutes
or until meat is tender.
3. Melt 3 tablespoons Crisco
in a skillet over medium heat.
Add mushrooms and cook
until lightly browned and
tender. Add mushrooms to the
chicken. Remove skillet from
heat.
4. Combine sour cream, tomato
paste, and Worcestershire
sauce; add in small amounts
to the meat in skillet, mixing
well.
5. Return to heat. Cook and
stir over low heat until hot.
Serve with *buttered noodles.*

8 servings

Chicken Kiev

4 large whole chicken breasts,
 skinned and boned
1 teaspoon salt
1/3 cup butter or margarine
1 tablespoon minced parsley
1 teaspoon lemon juice
1 clove garlic, minced
1/3 cup all-purpose flour
1 1/2 cups dry bread crumbs
2 eggs, lightly beaten
Crisco shortening for deep
 frying

1. Cut chicken breasts in half
and sprinkle with salt.
2. Cream butter, parsley,
lemon juice, and garlic. Spread
2 teaspoons along the center
length of each chicken breast
half. Tuck in ends and long
sides around flavored butter;
skewer or tie to close.
3. Place flour and bread
crumbs in separate flat dishes;
beat eggs in a shallow bowl.
Dip each prepared chicken
breast first in flour, then eggs,
and then crumbs. Place
seam-side-down on a plate;
refrigerate for at least 2 hours
or until crumbs are set.
4. Heat a 1 1/2-inch layer of
Crisco to 365° in a deep
saucepan or deep fryer. Fry
chicken rolls in hot Crisco for
5 minutes or until done.
Remove with slotted spoon.
Serve immediately with
brown rice.

8 servings

Chicken Divan

2 packages (10 ounces each)
 frozen broccoli spears
1/4 cup Crisco shortening
1/4 cup all-purpose flour
1/2 teaspoon salt
1 cup chicken broth
1/4 cup crumbled blue cheese
1 cup whipping cream
3 large whole chicken breasts,
 cooked, skinned, boned, and
 sliced
3/4 cup grated Parmesan
 cheese, divided in half

1. Preheat oven to 375°.
2. Cook broccoli just until
tender; drain.
3. Melt Crisco in a saucepan.
Blend in flour and salt and
cook until mixture bubbles;
stir constantly. Gradually add
chicken broth; stir constantly.
Bring sauce to boiling and
cook for 2 minutes or until
thickened. Remove from heat.
Add blue cheese and stir until
melted. Using a wire whisk,
blend in cream.
4. Divide cooked broccoli
among 6 greased ramekins or
10-ounce custard cups. Using
half of the sauce, spoon 1/4 cup
sauce over each serving of
broccoli. Top each serving
with 2 or 3 slices of chicken.
5. Stir half of Parmesan cheese
into the remaining sauce.
Spoon 1/3 cup sauce over each
serving. Sprinkle each with 1
tablespoon of cheese.
6. Bake at 375° for 15 minutes
or until bubbly and lightly
browned. Place broiler rack 6
inches from heat and turn
oven control to Broil. Broil for
1 to 2 minutes. Serve hot.

6 servings

Chicken

Chicken Breasts Hawaiian

*4 large whole chicken breasts
  (about 1 pound each)*
*¼ cup butter or margarine,
  softened*
2 teaspoons chili powder
¼ cup flaked coconut
1 egg, slightly beaten
*¾ cup coarse dry bread
  crumbs*
1 teaspoon salt
¼ cup Crisco shortening

Sweet and Sour Sauce:
*2 tablespoons Crisco
  shortening*
¼ cup finely chopped onion
½ cup catsup
½ cup apricot preserves
1 tablespoon brown sugar
1 tablespoon cider vinegar
½ teaspoon curry powder
*2 tablespoons Crisco
  shortening*
4 pineapple slices
*2 cooked sweet potatoes,
  quartered*
*2 firm bananas, peeled and
  cut in half lengthwise*

1. Split chicken breasts in half lengthwise. Remove skin and bones; rinse and pat dry. Flatten chicken pieces slightly using a meat hammer.
2. Cream butter and chili powder. Blend in coconut. Divide into 8 portions.
3. Spoon one portion onto each chicken piece. Tuck in sides, roll, and skewer. Chill at least 2 hours.
4. Preheat oven to 400°.

5. Dip chicken rolls into egg, then roll in a mixture of bread crumbs and salt to coat evenly.
6. Melt ¼ cup Crisco in a large heavy skillet over medium-high heat. Add the chicken rolls and brown evenly on all sides. Transfer to a greased shallow baking dish and bake at 400° for 20 to 25 minutes or until chicken is tender. Remove skewers.
7. For Sweet and Sour Sauce, melt 2 tablespoons Crisco in a small heavy saucepan over medium heat. Add onion; cook until tender. Stir in catsup,

apricot preserves, brown sugar, vinegar, and curry powder; blend well. Heat and keep warm.
8. Melt remaining 2 table-spoons Crisco in a large heavy skillet over medium heat. Heat pineapple, sweet potatoes, and bananas. Arrange with chicken rolls on a serving platter. Garnish with toasted nuts and coconut, if desired. Serve with Sweet and Sour Sauce.

4 to 6 servings

Oriental Chicken Crepes

Crepes:
1 cup sifted all-purpose flour
4 teaspoons sugar
1/4 teaspoon salt
4 eggs, slightly beaten
1 cup milk
2 teaspoons Crisco shortening, melted

Sauce:
3 tablespoons cornstarch
3/4 cup apple juice
3 tablespoons soy sauce
1 teaspoon sugar
3 cups chicken broth

Filling:
2 tablespoons Crisco shortening
1/2 cup chopped green onion
1 cup cooked rice
1/4 cup snipped parsley
1 can (8 ounces) sliced water chestnuts, drained
2 cups cubed cooked chicken or turkey
1/2 teaspoon vinegar

1. For Crepes, combine flour, sugar, and salt. Add eggs; mix in milk and Crisco; beat until smooth.
2. Grease a 6-inch skillet or crepe pan with Crisco. Heat skillet. For each crepe, pour into skillet just enough batter to cover bottom. Tilt skillet back and forth to spread batter thinly and evenly. Cook over medium heat until lightly browned on bottom. Remove from skillet; continue to cook crepes to make a total of 16.
3. For Sauce, dissolve cornstarch in apple juice in saucepan. Stir in soy sauce, sugar, and chicken broth.

Cook over medium-high heat; stir to boiling. Cook for 1 minute; remove from heat. Reserve 1 cup sauce for filling and pour remainder into a 10-inch skillet. Set aside.
4. For Filling, melt Crisco in a large skillet. Add green onion and rice; cook and stir for 5 minutes over low heat. Remove from heat; add remaining ingredients. Stir in 1 cup sauce.
5. To assemble crepes, spoon a rounded 1/4 cup of filling along the center of one crepe. Roll edges over filling and place seam-side-down in sauce. Place 8 filled crepes in sauce and heat over low heat for 8 to 10 minutes or until heated through. Remove crepes to serving plate and repeat with remaining 8 crepes.

8 servings

Tangy Livers

1/3 cup Crisco shortening
1 pound chicken livers, rinsed, dried, and halved
2 tablespoons chopped onion
2 tablespoons catsup
2 tablespoons brown sugar
1/2 teaspoon salt
1/4 teaspoon ground ginger

1. Melt Crisco in a skillet. Sauté livers over medium heat for 10 to 15 minutes or until medium brown, turning occasionally.
2. Pour 1 tablespoon of pan drippings into a second skillet. Sauté onion until tender. Add the livers. Combine catsup, brown sugar, salt, and ginger; add to skillet. Heat and stir for 2 minutes. Serve at once.

About 4 servings

Sour Cream Chicken Livers

2 pounds chicken livers
1/4 cup all-purpose flour
1/2 cup Crisco shortening
3/4 cup finely chopped onion
2 tablespoons Crisco shortening
5 ounces fresh mushrooms, cleaned and sliced lengthwise
2 tablespoons Worcestershire sauce
2 tablespoons chili sauce
1 teaspoon salt
1/2 teaspoon thyme
1/4 teaspoon pepper
1/4 teaspoon rosemary
2 cups dairy sour cream

1. Rinse and drain chicken livers. Pat free of excess moisture with paper towels. Coat lightly with flour. Set aside.
2. Melt 1/2 cup Crisco in a large skillet. Add onion and brown lightly; stir occasionally. Add half the chicken livers. Cook, turning with a spoon, for 5 to 10 minutes or until lightly browned. Remove and keep warm. Fry remaining livers.
3. Melt 2 tablespoons Crisco in a medium skillet. Add mushrooms and cook until lightly browned (about 3 minutes). Combine Worcestershire sauce, chili sauce, salt, thyme, pepper, and rosemary. Add mushrooms and stir. Heat thoroughly.
4. Slowly add sour cream to mushroom mixture, stirring constantly until well blended. Heat thoroughly (do not boil). Mix gently with livers to coat.
5. Serve warm with *buttered toasted English muffins* or *party rye slices.*

6 to 8 servings

Turkey

Fried Turkey for Two

6 tablespoons all-purpose flour
1 teaspoon salt
1/2 teaspoon dried summer savory
1/4 teaspoon dried sage
1/4 teaspoon dried marjoram
1/4 teaspoon dried thyme
1/8 teaspoon pepper
2 turkey legs (about 1 1/4 to 1 1/2 pounds each)
Crisco shortening for frying
1 3/4 cups water

1. Combine flour, salt, summer savory, sage, marjoram, thyme, and pepper. Remove 1/4 cup seasoned flour and set aside. Coat turkey legs well with remaining flour.
2. Melt enough Crisco, about 1 1/2 cups, in a deep 10-inch skillet to measure 1/2 inch at bottom of skillet. Add coated turkey legs and cook for 15 minutes over medium heat, turning to brown well on all sides. Remove turkey from skillet.
3. Remove all but 1/4 cup fat from skillet. Return turkey legs to skillet and add 1/4 cup water. Cook covered over low heat for 1 hour to 1 hour and 10 minutes or until fork-tender, turning several times.
4. Place turkey legs on serving platter. Add reserved seasoned flour to remaining 1 1/2 cups water. Stir into hot drippings over medium-high heat. Continue to stir until boiling; cook for 2 to 3 minutes. Serve hot gravy with turkey legs.

2 servings

Turkey Croquettes

2 tablespoons Crisco shortening
2 tablespoons finely chopped onion
2 tablespoons all-purpose flour
1/2 cup chicken broth
1 egg, lightly beaten
2 cups very finely chopped or ground cooked turkey
1 tablespoon chopped parsley
1/2 teaspoon salt
1/8 teaspoon pepper
1 egg, lightly beaten
3/4 cup dry bread crumbs
Crisco shortening for deep frying
Cheese sauce or hollandaise

1. Melt Crisco in a skillet. Add onion and cook over medium heat for 2 minutes or until tender. Add flour; stir. Gradually add chicken broth, stirring until sauce is thick and smooth.
2. Remove skillet from heat and mix in egg. Add turkey, parsley, salt, and pepper; combine.
3. Spread mixture on a plate and refrigerate at least 2 hours.
4. Shape mixture into 6 balls. Roll in egg, then in bread crumbs.
5. Heat Crisco to 365° in a deep fryer or deep saucepan. Fry turkey croquettes for 5 to 6 minutes. Drain on paper towels. Serve with cheese sauce.

6 croquettes

Creamed Turkey with Avocado

1/2 cup Crisco shortening
1/2 pound fresh mushrooms, cleaned and sliced
1/4 cup finely chopped onion
1/2 cup all-purpose flour
1/2 teaspoon salt
1/4 teaspoon dried basil
1/4 teaspoon paprika
1/8 teaspoon pepper
1/8 teaspoon ground nutmeg
1 1/2 cups whipping cream
1 1/2 cups chicken broth (dissolve 2 chicken bouillon cubes in 1 1/2 cups boiling water)
3 cups cooked turkey pieces
2 medium avocados, halved, pitted, and cut in balls with melon baller

1. Melt Crisco in a skillet. Add mushrooms and onion. Cook, stirring frequently, until onion is soft and mushrooms are tender and lightly browned. With a slotted spoon remove mushrooms and set aside.
2. Blend flour, salt, basil, paprika, pepper, and nutmeg into hot Crisco. Heat until bubbly (about 1 minute). Stir in cream and chicken broth. Bring rapidly to boiling; cook and stir for 1 minute. Mix in mushrooms and turkey pieces; heat thoroughly (about 3 to 5 minutes).
3. Combine avocado with creamed turkey just before serving. Serve over *toast points*.

6 to 8 servings

Curried Turkey Pie

¼ cup Crisco shortening
1 cup chopped onion
3 apples, pared, cored, and
  sliced (about 2 cups)
4 cups cubed cooked turkey
1 cup cooked green peas
½ cup toasted slivered
  almonds
¼ cup golden raisins
½ cup flaked coconut
1 can (10½ ounces) condensed
  chicken noodle soup
1 cup milk

2 teaspoons curry powder
2 tablespoons chutney
Crisco pastry for a double-
  crust 9-inch pie, page 154
1 egg, beaten

1. Melt Crisco in a large saucepan. Add onion and apples; cook for 3 minutes or until soft and tender, stirring occasionally. Stir in turkey, peas, almonds, raisins, and coconut; stir lightly to mix. Turn into a shallow 2-quart baking dish. Set aside.
2. Preheat oven to 425°.

3. Blend soup, milk, curry, and chutney in blender or food processor until smooth. Pour over turkey mixture in baking dish.
4. Prepare Crisco pastry. Roll out pastry a little larger than baking dish, cut several slits in pastry, and fit loosely over top of baking dish. Trim pastry, seal, and flute edge. Brush pastry with beaten egg.
5. Bake at 425° about 25 minutes or until top is golden.

About 8 servings

53

Turkey with Herb Dressing

4 quarts 1/2-inch bread cubes
1/3 cup dried parsley flakes
2 teaspoons salt
2 teaspoons rosemary, crushed
2 teaspoons ground thyme
1 teaspoon ground sage
1/2 cup Crisco shortening
1 cup coarsely chopped onion
1 cup coarsely chopped celery
  with leaves
1 1/2 cups chicken broth
1 turkey (14 to 15 pounds)

1. Preheat oven to 325°.
2. Combine bread cubes and parsley in a large bowl. Blend salt, rosemary, thyme, and sage; add to bread cube mixture and toss to mix.
3. Melt Crisco in a skillet over medium heat. Mix in onion and celery; cook for 3 minutes, stirring occasionally. Toss with the bread mixture. Add chicken broth, mixing lightly until ingredients are thoroughly blended.
4. Rinse turkey with cold water; pat dry, inside and out, with paper towels. Lightly fill body and neck cavities with the stuffing. Fasten neck skin to back with a skewer. Bring wing tips onto back of bird. Push drumsticks under band of skin at tail, if present, or tie to tail with cord.
5. Place turkey breast-side-up on a rack in a shallow roasting pan. Insert meat thermometer in the thickest part of the inner thigh muscle; be sure tip does not touch bone.
6. Roast in 325° oven for 4 to 5 hours or until thermometer registers 180 to 185°; baste during roasting.

10 to 14 servings

Turkey in Orange Sauce

2 tablespoons Crisco
  shortening
1 can (6 ounces) frozen orange
  juice concentrate, thawed
1/2 cup water
1 tablespoon lemon juice
2 tablespoons brown sugar
1/2 teaspoon salt
1/2 teaspoon ground ginger
1/8 teaspoon ground thyme
1/8 teaspoon poultry seasoning
1 1/2 teaspoons cornstarch
1 tablespoon cold water
1 1/2 pounds roast turkey white
  meat, thinly sliced

1. Melt Crisco in a large heavy skillet over medium heat. Add orange juice concentrate, 1/2 cup water, and lemon juice; stir until blended. Combine brown sugar, salt, ginger, thyme, and poultry seasoning; mix with ingredients in skillet. Bring to boiling, stirring constantly. Cover and simmer for 15 minutes, stirring occasionally.
2. Blend cornstarch and 1 tablespoon cold water; stir into orange sauce. Cook, stirring constantly, until sauce comes to boiling. Cook and stir for 2 minutes.
3. Add sliced turkey and heat thoroughly.
4. Garnish with parsley, if desired.

6 servings

Quick Turkey Hash

1/4 cup Crisco shortening
1 cup sliced mushrooms
1/2 cup finely chopped onion
2 cups diced cooked turkey
2 cups diced cooked potatoes
1 tablespoon snipped parsley
1 teaspoon salt
1/8 teaspoon black pepper
2/3 cup undiluted evaporated
  milk

1. Melt Crisco in a saucepan. Add mushrooms and onion and sauté about 5 minutes.
2. Remove from heat and stir in turkey, potatoes, parsley, salt, and pepper. Gradually add evaporated milk, stirring gently. Heat mixture thoroughly (about 5 minutes).

6 servings

Hash Cakes

Quick Turkey Hash (see
  recipe above; finely chop
  mushrooms, turkey, and
  potatoes, and reduce
  evaporated milk to 1/3 cup)
1/4 cup all-purpose flour
2 tablespoons Crisco
  shortening

1. Prepare hash; cool.
2. Shape hash into 6 patties and coat well with flour.
3. Melt Crisco in a skillet. Add hash cakes and brown on both sides.

6 servings

Duckling

Fricassee of Duckling

1 ready-to-cook duckling
  (5 pounds), cut in pieces
1/2 cup all-purpose flour
1 teaspoon salt
1/4 teaspoon thyme
1/8 teaspoon pepper
1/4 cup Crisco shortening
1/4 cup finely chopped onion
Water (about 2 1/2 cups)
1 small bay leaf
1 can (8 ounces) sliced
  mushrooms, drained

1. Rinse and dry duckling pieces. Coat with a mixture of flour, salt, thyme, and pepper.
2. Melt Crisco in a large skillet, add onion, and cook over medium heat until tender (about 2 minutes). Add duckling pieces; cook over medium heat until lightly browned, turning as necessary. Pour off drippings.
3. Add enough water to skillet to almost cover duckling; add bay leaf. Bring to boiling and cook covered over low heat until tender (about 1 hour).
4. Add mushrooms to duckling and heat thoroughly. Remove bay leaf before serving.

About 6 servings

About poultry stuffings

A different-tasting stuffing will add variety and excitement to your poultry.

All the stuffing recipes in this chapter can be used for any bird. To estimate how much stuffing to use, allow one cup of stuffing per pound of poultry, ready-to-cook weight.

Remember that stuffing may be baked separately and served as a substitute for potatoes, rice, or pasta.

Glazed Duckling Gourmet

2 ducklings (about 4 1/2 pounds
  each), quartered (do not use
  wings, necks, and backs)
  and skinned
2 teaspoons salt
1/4 teaspoon ground nutmeg
1/4 cup Crisco shortening
1 clove garlic, minced
1 1/2 teaspoons rosemary,
  crushed
1 1/2 teaspoons thyme
1 1/2 cups apple cider
1/2 cup orange marmalade
2 teaspoons apple cider
  vinegar
1 teaspoon cornstarch
1/4 cup cold water
3 medium apples, cored and
  sliced (about 1 1/2 cups)

1. Remove excess fat from duckling pieces, rinse duckling and pat dry with paper towels. Rub pieces with salt and nutmeg.
2. Melt Crisco in a large skillet over medium heat; add garlic and the duckling pieces, and brown well on all sides.
3. Add rosemary, thyme, apple cider, marmalade, and vinegar to skillet. Bring to boiling; cover and simmer over low heat until duckling is tender (about 45 minutes). Remove duckling to a heated platter and keep it warm.
4. Combine cornstarch and water and stir into liquid in skillet; bring to boiling and cook for 1 to 2 minutes, stirring constantly. Add apple slices and stir gently until thoroughly heated. Serve sauce immediately with warm duckling.

6 to 8 servings

Roast Duckling with Wild Rice and Grape Stuffing

1 ready-to-cook duckling
  (4 to 5 pounds)
1/4 cup Crisco shortening
2 medium onions, peeled and
  chopped
1/2 cup chopped celery
2 cups cooked wild rice
1 cup seedless grapes
1/4 cup apple cider

1. Preheat oven to 325°.
2. Melt Crisco in a skillet over medium heat. Cook onion and celery until tender (about 5 minutes). Stir in wild rice, grapes, and cider.
3. Lightly fill body and neck cavities of duckling with the stuffing; do not pack. To close body cavities, lace with cord; fasten neck skin to back and wings to body with skewers. Place duckling breast-side-up on a rack in a shallow roasting pan.
4. Roast uncovered at 325° for 2 1/2 to 3 hours. Brush frequently with drippings. Pour off excess drippings as they accumulate.
5. Place duckling on heated platter and garnish platter with clusters of grapes and parsley, if desired.

About 6 servings

Duckling

Roast Goose with Stuffing

1 ready-to-cook goose (8 to 10 pounds)
1 tablespoon salt
¼ teaspoon black pepper
2 tablespoons Crisco shortening
1 medium onion, finely chopped
1 pound cooking apples, pared and quartered
1 pound dried prunes, soaked in warm water, drained, and pitted
1 tablespoon sugar

1. Preheat oven to 325°.
2. Rinse goose and remove any large layers of fat from the body cavity. Pat dry with paper towels. Rub body and neck cavities with a mixture of salt and pepper.
3. Melt Crisco in a skillet and sauté onion until tender. Mix onion, apples, prunes, and sugar; lightly spoon mixture into body cavities. Fasten neck skin to back with skewer.
4. Place goose breast-down on a rack in a shallow roasting pan.
5. Roast uncovered at 325° for 2½ hours, removing fat from pan several times during this period. Turn goose breast-up and roast for 45 to 60 minutes or until goose tests done. To test for doneness, move leg gently by grasping end of bone. When done, drumstick-thigh joint moves easily or twists out.
6. Transfer goose to a heated platter and garnish with *crab apples* and *parsley.*

8 servings

Walnut Stuffing

Giblets from one 8- to 10-pound ready-to-cook goose
1 small onion, sliced
1 bay leaf
1 tablespoon salt, divided
Water
8 slices dry bread, crushed to fine crumbs
2 cups walnuts, chopped
2 teaspoons poultry seasoning
¼ cup Crisco shortening, melted

1. Put giblets, onion, bay leaf, 2 teaspoons salt, and water to cover into a saucepan. Bring to boiling; reduce heat and cook covered over low heat until giblets are tender. Remove bay leaf. Drain giblets, reserving broth. Chop giblets finely. Add water to broth to measure 1 cup liquid; reserve.
2. Put bread crumbs into a bowl and add chopped giblets, walnuts, remaining 1 teaspoon salt, poultry seasoning, and melted Crisco; toss lightly to mix. Add the reserved liquid, tossing to mix.
3. Use as stuffing for goose.

2 quarts stuffing

Cornish Hens

Raisin Cherry Dressing

3 tablespoons Crisco
   shortening
2 tablespoons chopped onion
2 cup raisins
1 can (16 ounces) tart red
   cherries, drained
4 cups herb-seasoned croutons
1 cup warm chicken broth
2 eggs, beaten
1 cup milk

1. Melt Crisco in a large skillet. Add onion and cook until tender (about 3 minutes). Stir in raisins and cherries and heat for 1 minute.
2. Put croutons into a large bowl. Stir in raisin mixture. Add chicken broth and stir well. Combine eggs and milk and stir into raisin mixture.
3. Use immediately as a stuffing for 4 Rock Cornish hens or turn mixture into a 1½-quart casserole and bake at 350° for 30 minutes or until mixture is set in center.

6 to 8 servings

Almond Stuffing

4 cups soft bread crumbs
¼ cup milk
¼ teaspoon salt
Dash pepper
¼ cup Crisco shortening,
   melted
1 cup sliced almonds

1. Put bread crumbs and milk into a bowl. Add salt, pepper, and melted Crisco; mix well. Stir in almonds.
2. Use to stuff Rock Cornish hens.

2 cups stuffing

Fruit-and-Nut Stuffed Rock Cornish Hens

1½ cups herbed seasoned
   stuffing croutons
1 can (8 ounces) crushed
   pineapple in pineapple
   juice, drained; reserve 2
   tablespoons juice
⅓ cup dried apricots, cut
   in ½-inch pieces
⅓ cup chopped pecans
2 tablespoons Crisco
   shortening, melted
1 tablespoon snipped parsley
¼ teaspoon salt
4 Rock Cornish hens (1 to 1½
   pounds each), thawed if
   frozen
Salt and pepper
⅓ cup apricot preserves
2 teaspoons soy sauce
2 tablespoons Crisco
   shortening, melted

1. Preheat oven to 350°.
2. Combine croutons, pineapple, reserved pineapple juice, apricot pieces, pecans, 2 tablespoons melted Crisco, parsley, and ¼ teaspoon salt in a bowl; mix lightly.
3. Sprinkle cavities of hens lightly with salt and pepper. Fill each hen with a rounded ½ cup stuffing; sew, or skewer and lace with cord. Place hens breast-side-up on a rack in a shallow roasting pan.
4. Combine apricot preserves, soy sauce, and remaining 2 tablespoons melted Crisco. Brush hens with half of sauce.
5. Roast at 350° for 60 to 75 minutes or until hens are tender and leg joints move easily; baste occasionally with sauce. Cover ends of legs and wings with aluminum foil during last 15 minutes to prevent excessive browning.

4 servings

Baked Fish

FISH AND SHELLFISH

Baked Halibut Dinner

4 halibut steaks, fresh or
frozen (about 2 pounds)
¼ cup Crisco shortening,
melted
2 tablespoons olive oil
1 tablespoon wine vinegar
2 teaspoons lemon juice
¾ teaspoon salt
¼ teaspoon dry mustard
¼ teaspoon dried leaf
marjoram
⅛ teaspoon garlic powder
⅛ teaspoon pepper
6 small zucchini
1 package (10 ounces) frozen
green peas
1 can (8¼ ounces) tiny whole
carrots or crinkle sliced
carrots
2 tablespoons snipped parsley

1. Preheat oven to 450°.
2. Thaw frozen halibut; rinse and pat dry. Place fish in a greased baking pan or large ovenproof serving platter.
3. Combine melted Crisco, olive oil, vinegar, lemon juice, salt, mustard, marjoram, garlic powder, and pepper. Drizzle over fish.
4. Bake at 450° for 10 to 12 minutes or until fish is almost done. Keep warm.
5. Meanwhile, halve zucchini lengthwise and scoop out center portion. Cook in boiling salted water for 5 minutes or until just tender.
6. Cook peas according to directions on package. Heat carrots; drain.

7. Fill zucchini with peas and carrots. Sprinkle with parsley. Arrange in pan with fish.
8. Return pan to oven and heat at 450° for 5 minutes.
9. Garnish with *dill weed* and *lemon wedges*.

8 servings

Baked Sole Fillets

2 tablespoons Crisco
shortening
⅓ cup finely chopped onion
½ pound sliced fresh
mushrooms
¼ cup snipped parsley
½ teaspoon salt
1 teaspoon lemon juice
1 pound sole fillets, fresh or
frozen
½ cup dry white wine or
cooking sherry

1. Melt Crisco in a heavy saucepan over medium heat. Stir in onion. Cook until tender, stirring occasionally. Stir in mushrooms; cook 2 to 3 minutes longer. Remove from heat. Stir in parsley, salt, and lemon juice.
2. Preheat oven to 350°.
3. Thaw frozen fish; rinse and pat dry. Place in a greased 11x7x1½-inch pan or broiler-proof serving platter. Spoon vegetable mixture over fish. Pour wine over all.
4. Bake at 350° for 20 minutes or until fish flakes easily. Serve with *lemon and lime wedges*.

4 servings

Delicious and nutritious! That's fresh fish… delicate flavor combined with an abundance of vitamins and minerals.

Today, with quick freezing and better transportation, fresh fish is available everywhere! Why not serve your family delicious seafood meals more often?

Baked Haddock Fillets

¼ cup Crisco shortening
1 cup chopped celery
½ cup chopped onion
¼ cup snipped parsley
2 pounds haddock fillets
1 tablespoon curry powder or
dried leaf tarragon
1 teaspoon salt
¼ teaspoon pepper
6 bacon slices, cooked and
crumbled

1. Preheat oven to 350°.
2. Melt Crisco in a heavy skillet over medium heat. Add celery, onion, and parsley. Cook for 2 to 3 minutes or until celery and onion are tender, stirring occasionally. Spoon into a 2-quart baking dish.
3. Rinse haddock and pat dry. Combine curry powder, salt, and pepper; sprinkle over both sides of fish. Arrange fish on celery mixture.
4. Bake at 350° for 25 to 30 minutes or until fish flakes easily. Garnish with bacon.

6 servings

Baked Snapper with Creamy Sauce

Stuffing:
1 cup water
1 stick (1/2 cup) butter or margarine
1 bag (7 ounces) herb-seasoned cube stuffing (4 cups)
2/3 cup finely chopped celery
1/2 cup finely chopped green onion
1/4 cup snipped parsley
1 egg, slightly beaten

Red Snapper:
2 pounds red snapper fillets, fresh or frozen
1 tablespoon lemon juice
1 teaspoon salt
1 teaspoon grated lemon peel
1/4 cup Crisco shortening, melted

Creamy Sauce:
3 tablespoons Crisco shortening
3 tablespoons all-purpose flour
1/2 teaspoon salt
Dash pepper
1 1/2 cups milk
1/2 cup chili sauce
2 tablespoons lemon juice

1. For Stuffing, heat water and melt butter in hot water. Add stuffing cubes; toss lightly until liquid is absorbed. Mix in celery, green onion, parsley, and egg. Spoon into bottom of a greased 13x9x2-inch baking dish.
2. Preheat oven to 350°.
3. For Red Snapper, thaw frozen fish. Cut into 6 serving-size pieces. Rinse and pat dry. Combine lemon juice, salt, and lemon peel. Brush over cut surfaces of fish. Place fish skin-side-up on stuffing. Brush with melted Crisco.
4. Bake at 350° for 30 to 40 minutes or until fish flakes easily. Brush with melted Crisco twice during baking.
5. While fish is baking, prepare Creamy Sauce.
6. For Creamy Sauce, melt Crisco in a heavy saucepan over medium heat. Blend in flour, salt, and pepper; cook until bubbly. Remove from heat. Gradually stir in milk. Cook over medium heat, stirring constantly, until sauce boils and thickens. Cook, stirring constantly, for 1 minute.
7. Remove from heat. Stir chili sauce and lemon juice into sauce. Serve hot sauce with fish and stuffing.

6 servings

Tuna Skillet

1/4 cup Crisco shortening
2/3 cup chopped onion
1 small green pepper, slivered (about 1/2 cup)
1 can (10 3/4 ounces) condensed tomato soup
2 teaspoons soy sauce
2 to 3 tablespoons brown sugar
1 teaspoon grated lemon peel
3 tablespoons lemon juice
2 cans (6 1/2 or 7 ounces each) tuna, drained

1. Melt Crisco in a large heavy skillet over medium heat. Stir in onion and green pepper. Cook until almost tender, stirring occasionally.
2. Mix in tomato soup, soy sauce, brown sugar, lemon peel, and lemon juice. Bring to boiling; simmer for 5 minutes.
3. Mix in tuna, separating it into small pieces. Heat.
4. Serve with *hot cooked rice.* Garnish with *red pepper rings.*

4 to 6 servings

Tuna Surprise Loaf

Crisco shortening for greasing
1/4 cup Crisco shortening
1/2 cup chopped green pepper
1/4 cup chopped celery
1/4 cup chopped onion
1/4 cup chopped pimiento
3 cans (6 1/2 or 7 ounces each) chunk tuna, drained
1 1/2 cups dry bread crumbs
1 tablespoon dried parsley flakes
1/2 teaspoon salt
3 eggs
1/2 cup milk

1. Preheat oven to 375°.
2. Line bottom and sides of an 8 1/2x4 1/2x2 1/2-inch loaf pan with aluminum foil, leaving 2-inch overhang. Grease generously with Crisco.
3. Melt 1/4 cup Crisco in a small heavy skillet. Add green pepper, celery, and onion; sauté over medium heat until soft (4 to 5 minutes). Remove from heat.
4. Add pimiento to sautéed vegetables and set aside.
5. Combine tuna, crumbs, parsley, salt, eggs, and milk; mix well.
6. Spread half of mixture in prepared pan. Make a depression along the center of the loaf, leaving 1/2-inch border at edge. Fill with vegetable mixture. Cover with remaining tuna mixture.
7. Bake at 375° for 1 hour. Invert onto plate and remove foil. Invert again onto serving platter. Slice with serrated knife and serve with Creamed Peas, page 90.

6 to 8 servings

Tuna

Tuna Pie

3 tablespoons Crisco
    shortening
1/2 cup chopped green pepper
3 tablespoons all-purpose flour
1/2 teaspoon salt
Dash pepper
2 cups milk
2 cans (6 1/2 ounces each) solid-
    pack tuna, drained
1 jar (16 ounces) boiled whole
    onions, drained
1 can (17 ounces) green peas,
    drained
3 tablespoons chopped
    pimiento
Crisco pastry for a double-
    crust 9-inch pie, page 154

1. Preheat oven to 425°.
2. Melt Crisco in a medium
saucepan. Add green pepper
and cook over medium heat
until tender (about 3 minutes).
Stir in flour, salt, and pepper.
Add milk gradually, stirring
to mix well. Cook and stir
over medium heat until
thickened (about 5 minutes).
3. Add tuna, onions, peas, and
pimiento; stir to mix lightly.
4. Divide pastry in half. Roll
out and line a 9-inch pie plate.
Fill with tuna mixture. Roll
out remaining pastry and
place on top of tuna mixture.
Seal and flute edges. Cut slits
for steam to escape.
5. Bake at 425° for 30 to 35
minutes or until crust is
lightly browned.

6 servings

Codfish and Rice Supreme

2 cups flaked cooked fish
    (cod or other firm fish)
1 cup cooked rice
2 teaspoons dried parsley
    flakes
1/2 teaspoon seasoned salt
1/4 teaspoon onion salt
1/4 teaspoon lemon-pepper
    seasoning
2 eggs, beaten
1/2 cup fine saltine cracker
    crumbs
Crisco shortening for deep
    frying

1. Combine fish, rice, parsley,
seasoned salt, onion salt, and
lemon-pepper seasoning. Add
eggs and mix well.
2. Using 2 level tablespoons
of mixture, firmly press into
balls. Roll in crumbs, keeping
balls round.
3. Heat Crisco to 365° in a
deep saucepan or deep fryer.
Fry several balls at a time in
hot Crisco for 3 1/2 minutes or
until browned. Drain on paper
towels.
4. Serve with *lemon wedges*.

4 to 6 servings

Note: If fish is very moist, add 1 or 2
tablespoons cracker crumbs to fish-
rice mixture so that it can be formed
easily into balls.

Cod

Cod Florentine with Mornay Sauce

Cod Florentine:

1½ pounds cod fillets, fresh or frozen
¼ cup Crisco shortening, melted
2 tablespoons lemon juice
½ teaspoon salt
1 package (10 ounces) frozen chopped spinach

Mornay Sauce:

1 chicken bouillon cube
¾ cup boiling water
¼ cup Crisco shortening
3 tablespoons all-purpose flour
¾ cup milk
2 egg yolks, beaten
¼ cup grated Parmesan cheese

1. For Cod Florentine, thaw frozen fish. Cut into 6 serving-size pieces. Rinse and pat dry. Place fish skin-side-down on a greased broiler rack. Combine melted Crisco and lemon juice and brush fish with half of mixture. Broil 4 inches from heat for 6 minutes. Brush with remaining Crisco mixture. Broil for 4 to 6 minutes longer or until fish flakes easily. Sprinkle salt over fish. Cover with aluminum foil to keep warm if needed.
2. While fish is broiling, cook spinach according to package directions. Drain well.
3. For Mornay Sauce, dissolve bouillon cube in boiling water; set aside. Melt Crisco in a heavy saucepan over medium heat. Blend in flour; cook until bubbly. Remove from heat. Gradually stir in broth and milk. Cook over medium heat, stirring constantly, until sauce boils and thickens. Cook and stir for 1 minute.
4. Stir a small amount of hot sauce into beaten egg yolks, mixing thoroughly, then stir into hot sauce. Cook, stirring constantly, for 1 minute.
5. Remove from heat; add cheese and stir until cheese is melted.
6. Combine spinach with 1 cup Mornay Sauce; spoon onto broilerproof platter. Carefully place fish over spinach. Spoon remaining Mornay Sauce over fish. Broil for 2 to 3 minutes or just until sauce is lightly browned.
7. Garnish platter with *parsley sprigs* and *lemon wedges.*

6 servings

Cod Creole

¼ cup Crisco shortening
1 cup minced celery and leaves
¼ cup chopped onion
1 can (28 ounces) peeled whole tomatoes (undrained)
1 teaspoon salt
⅛ teaspoon pepper
1 bay leaf
4 potatoes (about 1½ pounds), pared and cut in ½-inch slices
2 pounds fresh or frozen cod (thaw first, if frozen)

1. Melt Crisco in a large skillet, add celery and onion, and cook until tender. Stir in tomatoes and juice, salt, pepper, and bay leaf. Arrange potato slices in skillet. Bring to boiling; cook covered over medium heat for 5 minutes.
2. Put cod on top. Cover and simmer for 20 to 25 minutes or until fish flakes easily; baste fish frequently. Serve with a slotted spoon.

4 to 6 servings

Codfish Balls

1 pound salt codfish
4 to 6 medium potatoes
¼ cup chopped onion
2 eggs, beaten
½ teaspoon paprika
⅛ teaspoon pepper
Crisco shortening for deep frying

Dill Sauce:

½ cup dairy sour cream
½ cup mayonnaise
1 teaspoon dried dill weed
1 teaspoon lemon juice

1. Cover fish with cold water to freshen. Let stand in cold water 4 hours, changing water 3 to 4 times (or follow directions on package). Drain fish and remove any pieces of bone. Flake and set aside.
2. Wash, pare, and cut potatoes into pieces. Combine fish, potatoes, and onion in a large saucepan. Add cold water to cover. Cover saucepan and bring to boiling. Cook until potatoes are tender.
3. For Dill Sauce, combine all ingredients. Mix well. Refrigerate.
4. Thoroughly drain and mash potatoes, fish, and onion. Add eggs, paprika, and pepper; whip until mixture is fluffy. Using 2 tablespoons of batter for each, shape into balls.
5. Heat Crisco to 365° in a deep saucepan or deep fryer. Drop only as many fish balls at one time into hot Crisco as will float uncrowded one layer deep. Fry for 2 to 5 minutes or until golden brown, turning balls as they brown. Drain on paper towels.
6. Serve with Dill Sauce.

6 servings

Deep-Dish Turbot Pie

Filling:
1 pound fresh or frozen turbot
  (or other fish)
Milk
1/3 cup Crisco shortening
1/4 cup chopped onion
1/3 cup all-purpose flour
1 teaspoon salt
1/8 teaspoon pepper
1 package (10 ounces) frozen
  mixed vegetables

Pastry:
2¼ cups Homemade Crisco
  Pie Crust Mix, page 154
1/4 cup cold water

1. For Filling, cook fish as desired; drain, reserving liquid, and flake fish. Add enough milk to reserved liquid to make 2 cups.
2. Melt Crisco in a large heavy saucepan over medium heat. Add onion; cook until tender, stirring occasionally. Blend in flour, salt, and pepper; cook until bubbly. Remove from heat. Gradually stir in liquid. Cook over medium heat, stirring constantly, until sauce boils and thickens. Cook and stir for 1 minute.
3. Stir in frozen vegetables and fish. Set aside.
4. Preheat oven to 425°.
5. For Pastry, place Crisco mix in a bowl. Add cold water, 1 tablespoon at a time, mixing with a fork until dry ingredients are moistened and dough can be gathered into a ball.
6. On a lightly floured surface, roll two-thirds of pastry to fit the bottom and sides of a round 2-quart casserole. Carefully ease pastry into casserole. Pour in filling.
7. Roll remaining pastry into a circle the diameter of the casserole. Cut slits for steam to escape. Place over filling. Seal edges and flute.
8. Bake at 425° for 35 to 40 minutes or until crust is brown.

6 servings

Lemon Turbot

1/4 cup Crisco shortening
2 medium onions, peeled and
  sliced
2 pounds fresh or frozen
  turbot or other fish fillets
1 teaspoon salt
1/4 teaspoon pepper
8 tomato slices
8 lemon slices
1 bay leaf
2 tablespoons lemon juice

1. Melt Crisco in a large skillet. Stir in sliced onions and cook over medium heat until tender.
2. Thaw turbot if frozen and pat dry. Cut turbot into 8 slices and arrange over onions in skillet. Sprinkle with salt and pepper. Place a tomato slice over each piece of turbot and top with lemon slice. Add bay leaf; drizzle lemon juice over all.
3. Simmer covered for 10 to 15 minutes or until fish flakes easily.
4. Remove fish with slotted spoon to a serving platter.

8 servings

Salmon Patties

Salmon Patties:
1 can (15½ ounces) salmon,
  drained and flaked
2 eggs, slightly beaten
3/4 cup shredded sharp
  Cheddar cheese
1/2 cup fine dry bread crumbs
1/3 cup finely chopped onion
1/4 teaspoon seasoned salt
2 tablespoons all-purpose flour
1/4 cup Crisco shortening

Cheese Broccoli Sauce:
2 tablespoons Crisco
  shortening
2 tablespoons all-purpose flour
1/2 teaspoon salt
1²/3 cups half-and-half or light
  cream
1 cup shredded sharp
  Cheddar cheese
1 tablespoon lemon juice
1/2 teaspoon Worcestershire
  sauce
1 package (10 ounces) frozen
  chopped broccoli, cooked
  and drained

1. For Salmon Patties, combine salmon, eggs, cheese, bread crumbs, onion, and seasoned salt; mix well. Divide into 6 portions. Shape into patties. Coat well with flour.
2. Melt Crisco in a large heavy skillet over medium heat. Cook patties for 5 to 10 minutes per side over low to medium heat or until golden brown on each side.
3. For Cheese Broccoli Sauce, melt Crisco in a saucepan over medium heat. Blend in 2 tablespoons flour and ½ teaspoon salt; cook until bubbly. Remove from heat. Gradually stir in half-and-half. Cook and stir until sauce boils and thickens. Cook and stir for 1 minute.

4. Reduce heat to low. Stir in remaining ingredients; heat only until cheese melts.
5. Serve immediately over salmon patties.

6 servings

Salmon Ring

2¹/₂ cups Homemade Crisco Quick Bread Mix, page 116
¹/₂ cup milk
1 can (15¹/₂ ounces) salmon, drained
1 small onion, chopped
¹/₂ green pepper, chopped
¹/₂ teaspoon salt
¹/₄ cup milk
1 tablespoon butter or margarine, melted

1. Preheat oven to 375°.
2. Put Crisco mix into a bowl, make a well in center, and pour in ¹/₂ cup milk. Mix lightly with a spoon to form a dough.
3. Turn dough onto a floured surface and roll into a 14x10-inch rectangle.
4. Combine salmon, onion, green pepper, salt, and ¹/₄ cup milk. Spread mixture over dough and roll up as for a jelly roll, beginning with 14-inch side. Place sealed-edge-down on a lightly greased cookie sheet. Join ends to form a ring; seal. With scissors, make 12 cuts two-thirds of the way through ring at 1-inch intervals. Turn each section on its side. Brush with butter.
5. Bake at 375° for 35 minutes or until golden brown. Using pancake turner, slide baked ring onto serving plate. Serve with Creamed Peas, page 90.

6 servings

Broiled Salmon Steaks

6 salmon steaks, cut 1¹/₄ inches thick
³/₄ cup sauterne or other dry white wine
1 tablespoon white wine vinegar
1¹/₂ teaspoons soy sauce
1 tablespoon finely chopped green onion
¹/₄ cup Crisco shortening

1. Rinse salmon steaks and pat dry. Arrange in a large shallow dish.
2. Blend sauterne, vinegar, soy sauce, and green onion and pour over salmon steaks.
Cover and marinate in refrigerator several hours or overnight, turning occasionally.
3. Drain marinade into saucepan. Add Crisco and heat until melted.
4. Brush rack of broiler pan with marinade. Arrange salmon steaks on rack. Brush with marinade. Broil 6 inches from heat for 12 to 15 minutes per side or until fish flakes easily. Brush fish generously with marinade several times during broiling.
5. Arrange salmon steaks on bed of *rice*; garnish with *lime slices* and *curled onion tops*.

6 servings

Fried Fish

Fried Smelts

1 pound smelts (about 30)
1/4 cup all-purpose flour
1/2 teaspoon salt
1/4 teaspoon onion salt
1/4 teaspoon pepper
1 egg
1 tablespoon water
1 cup coarse dry bread crumbs
*Crisco shortening for deep
    frying*

1. Clean smelts, leaving on the heads and tails. Rinse and pat dry.
2. Combine flour, salt, onion salt, and pepper; set aside. Beat egg and water. Coat smelts with flour mixture, then dip into egg mixture; drain well.
3. Using a small amount of crumbs at a time and adding more as needed, coat each smelt lightly with crumbs. Let stand for 15 minutes.
4. Heat Crisco to 360° in deep saucepan or deep fryer. Fry 4 smelts at a time in hot Crisco for 3 minutes or until browned. Drain on paper towels. Let temperature return to 360° before frying more smelts.
5. If desired, serve with Tartar Sauce, page 69.

4 servings

Fried Fish Fillets

*1 1/2 pounds fresh or frozen fish
    fillets (rainbow trout)*
1/2 cup yellow cornmeal
1 1/4 teaspoons salt
1/8 teaspoon pepper
1/2 cup Crisco shortening
1/2 cup sliced almonds

1. Thaw frozen fish; rinse and pat dry. Cut fillets into 6 serving-size pieces. Coat with a mixture of cornmeal, salt, and pepper.
2. Melt Crisco in a large heavy skillet over medium heat. Fry fish for 5 minutes per side or until crisp and browned.
3. Remove to heated platter. Add almonds to skillet and stir until lightly browned. Sprinkle over fish and serve with *lemon wedges.*

6 servings

Fish Sticks, Taco Style

*Crisco shortening for deep
    frying*
*1 package (9 ounces) frozen
    fish sticks*
1/4 cup taco sauce
*1/2 cup shredded Monterey
    Jack cheese*

1. Heat Crisco to 365° in deep saucepan or deep fryer. Fry frozen fish sticks in hot fat for 3 minutes or until browned. Drain on paper towels.
2. Arrange fried fish sticks on a broilerproof serving platter. Drizzle taco sauce over fish sticks; sprinkle with cheese.
3. Broil 4 inches from heat for 1 to 2 minutes or until cheese is melted.

4 servings

Fried Frog Legs

Frog Legs:
*2 pounds skinned frog legs,
    separated*
3/4 cup all-purpose flour
1 1/2 teaspoons salt
1/8 teaspoon pepper
1/3 cup Crisco shortening

Sauce:
1/2 cup mayonnaise
*2 teaspoons chopped green
    onion*
*2 teaspoons dried leaf
    tarragon*
*1 teaspoon dried parsley
    flakes*

1. For Frog Legs, wash frog legs. Soak legs in salted water (1 tablespoon per 2 quarts water) for 15 minutes; drain.
2. Coat legs evenly with a mixture of flour, salt, and pepper by shaking 2 or 3 at a time in a plastic bag containing flour mixture.
3. Melt Crisco in a large heavy skillet over medium heat. Cook frog legs for 25 minutes or until golden brown and tender when pierced with a fork; brown all sides by turning legs as necessary with two spoons or tongs. Drain legs on paper towels; set aside and keep warm.
4. For Sauce, combine mayonnaise, green onion, tarragon, and parsley. Mix until well blended. Serve with frog legs. Garnish with *lemon wedges.*

4 servings

Fried Fish

Crispy Catfish

Tartar Sauce:
1/2 cup mayonnaise
1/4 cup sweet pickle relish
2 tablespoons chopped
  pimiento-stuffed green olives
1 tablespoon finely chopped
  onion

Catfish:
2 pan-dressed catfish (1 pound
  each), fresh or frozen
1/3 cup all-purpose flour
1/3 cup yellow cornmeal
1 teaspoon salt
1/2 teaspoon paprika
1/4 teaspoon onion powder
1/8 teaspoon pepper
1 egg
1 tablespoon water
1/2 cup Crisco shortening

1. For Tartar Sauce, combine all ingredients. Mix until well blended. Refrigerate until serving time.
2. For Catfish, thaw frozen fish. Split in half lengthwise, rinse, and pat dry.
3. Combine flour, cornmeal, salt, paprika, onion powder, and pepper; set aside. Beat egg and water.
4. Dip fish into egg mixture, then coat with flour mixture.
5. Melt Crisco in a large heavy skillet over medium heat. Fry fish for 10 minutes per side or until fish is crisp and browned. Drain on paper towels.
6. Serve fish with Tartar Sauce.

4 to 6 servings

Mackerel Cakes

1 can (15 ounces) mackerel
1/2 cup finely chopped onion
1 egg, beaten
1 teaspoon lemon juice
2 tablespoons all-purpose flour
1/4 teaspoon salt
1/4 teaspoon ground nutmeg
1/4 teaspoon pepper
1/2 cup fine cheese cracker
  crumbs
1/4 cup Crisco shortening

1. Drain mackerel; flake with fork. Stir in onion, egg, lemon juice, flour, salt, nutmeg, and pepper. Mix well. Shape into eight 2 1/2-inch patties.
2. Coat patties with crumbs.
3. Melt Crisco in a large heavy skillet over medium heat. Fry cakes for 2 1/2 to 3 minutes per side or until browned.
4. Serve with *tomato wedges* and Cream Cheese Sauce, page 75.

4 servings

Newburg in Pastry Shells

Pastry Shells:
2 cups all-purpose flour
1 teaspoon salt
¾ cup Crisco shortening
¼ cup cold water

Newburg:
1 pound ocean perch fillets, cooked
½ pound frozen cooked salad shrimp
¼ cup Crisco shortening
½ pound sliced fresh mushrooms
1 teaspoon lemon juice
¼ cup all-purpose flour
¾ teaspoon salt
¼ teaspoon white pepper
2 cups half-and-half or light cream
2 egg yolks, beaten
2 tablespoons snipped parsley
2 tablespoons sherry or cooking sherry

1. Preheat oven 425°.
2. For Pastry Shells, mix flour and salt in a bowl. Cut in Crisco using a pastry blender or 2 knives until mixture resembles coarse crumbs. Sprinkle with water, 1 tablespoon at a time, mixing lightly with fork until dough can be formed into a ball.
3. Divide dough into 6 equal portions. Roll each on a lightly floured surface into a circle 1 inch larger than the lid from a 3-pound Crisco can (about 6¼ inches). Prick pastry circles with fork.
4. Set six 10-ounce custard cups upside-down on a baking sheet. Place pastry circles over cups; pinch 10 to 12 times so they fit closely.

5. Bake at 425° for 12 to 15 minutes or until golden brown. Remove from oven and set on rack. When ready to use, carefully remove Pastry Shells from custard cups.
6. For Newburg, cut cooked perch into bite-size pieces. Thaw shrimp; rinse with cold water and pat dry. Set aside, reserving a few shrimp for garnish.
7. Melt Crisco in a heavy skillet over medium heat. Add mushrooms; cook for 2 to 3 minutes, stirring occasionally. Sprinkle with lemon juice. Remove from heat; blend in flour, salt, and pepper. Add a small amount of half-and-half and stir until sauce is smooth. Gradually stir in remaining half-and-half. Cook over medium heat, stirring constantly, until sauce boils and thickens. Cook and stir for 1 minute.
8. Stir a small amount of hot sauce into beaten egg yolks, mixing thoroughly, then stir into sauce. Stir in perch, shrimp, and parsley. Bring just to boiling, stirring gently. Stir in sherry.
9. Set Pastry Shells on serving plates and immediately fill with Newburg. Garnish with reserved shrimp and parsley, if desired.

6 servings

Flounder Roll-Ups

Herb Stuffing:
¼ cup Crisco shortening
½ cup chopped carrot
¼ cup chopped celery
¼ cup chopped onion
2 cups fine soft bread crumbs
1 teaspoon salt
⅛ teaspoon each: basil, oregano, rosemary, and thyme
2 tablespoons water
1 tablespoon lemon juice
6 thin flounder fillets

Creole Sauce:
2 tablespoons Crisco shortening
½ cup chopped green pepper
2 tablespoons chopped onion
1½ cups cooked tomatoes
¼ cup sliced pimiento-stuffed green olives
½ teaspoon salt
Dash pepper

1. Preheat oven to 350°.
2. For Herb Stuffing, melt Crisco in a skillet. Sauté carrot, celery, and onion until tender (about 7 minutes). Add bread crumbs, seasonings, water, and lemon juice to sautéed vegetables; mix well.
3. Divide stuffing into 6 equal parts. Spread one part on each fillet. Roll up fillet. Place each in a greased large muffin cup.
4. Bake at 350° for 25 to 30 minutes or until tender.
5. For Creole Sauce, melt Crisco in a saucepan. Add green pepper and onion; sauté until tender. Add tomatoes and olives; heat for 2 minutes. Stir in salt and pepper. Serve over roll-ups.

6 servings

Fried Shrimp Deluxe

1 pound small fresh shrimp in
  the shell (about 50)
3/4 cup fine corn flake crumbs
2 1/2 tablespoons dry onion
  soup mix (half of one 1 3/8-
  ounce envelope)
2 tablespoons snipped parsley
2 tablespoons grated
  Parmesan cheese
1 to 2 eggs, beaten
1/3 cup Crisco shortening

1. Shell shrimp leaving on
tail; devein. Rinse and pat dry.
2. Combine crumbs, soup mix,
parsley, and cheese.
3. Dip shrimp into egg; drain
well. Using a small amount of
crumbs at a time and adding
more as needed, coat each
shrimp lightly with crumbs.
4. Melt Crisco in a large
heavy skillet over medium
heat. Fry shrimp in a single
layer for 3 minutes per side or
until browned. Drain on paper
towels.

4 servings

How much shrimp to buy

One pound of fresh or frozen shrimp,
cooked and peeled, will yield 1/2
pound. When a recipe calls for one
pound of raw shrimp, fresh or frozen,
you may substitute one-half pound
of cooked and peeled (or canned)
shrimp.

Shrimp Jambalaya

3 tablespoons Crisco
  shortening
1/2 cup chopped onion
1/3 cup chopped green onion
1/2 cup chopped green pepper
1/2 cup chopped celery
1/4 pound diced cooked ham
1/4 teaspoon garlic powder
2 cups chicken broth
3 large tomatoes, coarsely
  chopped
1/4 cup snipped parsley
1/2 teaspoon salt
1/8 teaspoon pepper
1/4 teaspoon dried leaf thyme
1/8 teaspoon chili powder or
  ground red pepper
1 bay leaf
1 cup uncooked rice
3 cans (4 1/2 ounces each)
  shrimp, rinsed under
  running cold water
1/4 cup chopped green pepper

1. Melt Crisco in a large
heavy skillet over medium
heat. Stir in onion, green
onion, 1/2 cup chopped green
pepper, celery, ham, and garlic
powder. Cook for 5 minutes or
until onion is tender, stirring
occasionally.
2. Stir in chicken broth, tomatoes, parsley, salt, pepper,
thyme, chili powder, and bay
leaf; cover and bring to
boiling.
3. Add rice gradually, stirring
with a fork. Cover and simmer
for 20 minutes or until rice is
tender.
4. Mix in shrimp and remaining 1/4 cup green pepper.
Simmer uncovered for 5 minutes longer. Remove bay leaf
before serving.

6 to 8 servings

French-Fried Shrimp

1 pound small fresh shrimp in
  the shell (about 50)
1/2 teaspoon salt
1/4 teaspoon onion salt
1/4 teaspoon pepper
1/8 teaspoon garlic powder
1/4 cup all-purpose flour
1 egg
2 tablespoons water
1 cup coarse dry bread crumbs
Crisco shortening for deep
  frying

1. Shell shrimp leaving on
tails; devein. Rinse and pat
dry.
2. Combine salt, onion salt,
pepper, and garlic powder.
Blend 3/4 teaspoon of the
combined seasonings with
flour; set aside.
3. Beat egg, water, and remaining combined seasonings.
4. Coat shrimp with flour
mixture, then dip into egg
mixture; drain well.
5. Using a small amount of
crumbs at a time and adding
more as needed, coat each
shrimp lightly with crumbs.
6. Heat Crisco to 350° in a
deep saucepan or deep fryer.
Fry 6 shrimp at a time in hot
Crisco for 3 minutes or until
well browned. Drain on paper
towels. Let temperature
return to 350° before frying
more shrimp.
7. Serve with *lemon wedges,
seafood cocktail sauce, or*
Tartar Sauce, page 69.

4 servings

Crab Meat Imperial

¹/₄ cup Crisco shortening
¹/₂ cup chopped green pepper
2 cans (6¹/₂ ounces each) crab meat, drained thoroughly
2 tablespoons pimiento strips
¹/₂ cup Crisco shortening
¹/₂ cup all-purpose flour
4 cups milk
¹/₄ cup mayonnaise
1 teaspoon salt
¹/₂ teaspoon dry mustard
Dash chili powder or ground red pepper
Dash Worcestershire sauce
2 tablespoons fine dry bread crumbs

1. Preheat oven to 375°.
2. Melt ¹/₄ cup Crisco in a large heavy skillet over medium heat. Stir in green pepper. Cook until tender, stirring occasionally. Stir in crab meat and pimiento.
3. Melt ¹/₂ cup Crisco in a heavy saucepan over medium heat. Blend in flour; cook until bubbly. Remove from heat. Gradually stir in milk. Cook over medium heat, stirring constantly, until sauce boils and thickens. Cook and stir for 1 to 2 minutes.
4. Combine mayonnaise, salt, mustard, chili powder, and Worcestershire sauce. Stir into hot sauce. Stir in crab meat mixture.

5. Spoon into 6 shell ramekins or 10-ounce custard cups. Top each serving with 1 teaspoon crumbs. Place on a baking sheet.
6. Bake at 375° for 15 to 20 minutes or until sauce is lightly browned and bubbly. Sprinkle lightly with paprika, if desired.

6 servings

Crab Meat Superb

2 tablespoons Crisco shortening
2 tablespoons chopped green pepper
3 tablespoons all-purpose flour
³/₄ teaspoon salt
¹/₄ teaspoon dry mustard
Few grains pepper
³/₄ cup tomato juice
¹/₂ cup milk
1 cup shredded Cheddar cheese
1 can (6¹/₂ ounces) white crab meat, drained (about 1 cup)
Toast slices

1. Melt Crisco in a saucepan, add green pepper, and cook for 5 minutes over low heat. Blend in flour and seasonings. Add tomato juice gradually while stirring. Cook and stir until thickened. Add milk gradually while stirring. Add cheese. Cook over low heat, stirring constantly, until cheese is melted. Stir in crab meat and heat thoroughly.
2. Serve on toast.

4 to 6 servings

Crab-Filled Crepes

Crab Filling:

2 tablespoons Crisco
   shortening
1/2 cup chopped fresh
   mushrooms
2 tablespoons finely chopped
   onion
2 tablespoons all-purpose flour
1/2 teaspoon salt
1/8 teaspoon white pepper
3/4 cup milk
1/4 teaspoon Worcestershire
   sauce
3 drops Tabasco
3 tablespoons sherry or
   cooking sherry
2 packages (6 ounces each)
   snow crab meat, thawed and
   drained
1/2 teaspoon snipped parsley

Crepes:

1/2 cup sifted all-purpose flour
2 teaspoons sugar
1/4 teaspoon salt
2 eggs
1/2 cup milk
1 teaspoon Crisco shortening,
   melted

Cream Cheese Sauce:

12 ounces cream cheese
1/2 teaspoon seasoned salt
1/4 teaspoon garlic powder
1 cup milk

1. For Crab Filling, melt Crisco in a large heavy saucepan over medium heat. Add mushrooms and onion; cook until onion is transparent. Blend in flour, salt, and pepper. Cook until bubbly. Remove from heat. Gradually stir in milk. Stir in Worcestershire sauce and Tabasco. Cook over medium heat, stirring constantly, until sauce boils and thickens. Cook, stirring constantly, for 1 minute. Remove from heat.

2. Stir in sherry, crab meat, and parsley. Cool; refrigerate.
3. For Crepes, sift flour, sugar, and salt together. Beat eggs slightly in a bowl and mix in milk and melted Crisco. Add the flour mixture and beat until smooth.
4. Preheat oven to 375°.
5. Lightly grease a 6-inch skillet with Crisco. Heat the skillet. For each crepe, pour into skillet just enough batter to cover bottom, about 2 tablespoons of batter. Immediately tilt skillet back and forth to spread batter thinly and evenly. Cook over medium heat until lightly browned on bottom. Loosen edges with spatula and transfer to a large plate.
6. When ready to complete crepes, spoon about 3 tablespoons of the chilled filling onto center of each crepe; roll up. Put each filled crepe seam-side-down in a lightly greased large shallow baking dish; cover with aluminum foil.
7. Bake at 375° for 20 minutes or until hot.
8. While crepes are baking, prepare Cream Cheese Sauce.
9. For Cream Cheese Sauce, heat cream cheese in a heavy saucepan over low heat, stirring occasionally until softened. Blend in seasoned salt and garlic powder. Gradually stir in milk. Cook, stirring constantly, until sauce is hot. Add additional milk if needed until sauce is of desired consistency. Remove from heat.
10. Serve hot sauce with crab-filled crepes.

4 servings

Crab Soufflé

3 tablespoons Crisco
   shortening
3 tablespoons all–purpose
   flour
3/4 teaspoon salt
1 1/2 cups milk
4 eggs, separated
2 cans (6 1/2 ounces each) white
   crab meat, drained (about 2
   cups)
1/2 cup dry bread crumbs
1/2 teaspoon onion powder
1/4 teaspoon paprika
Sliced blanched almonds
   (optional)

1. Preheat oven to 350°.
2. Melt Crisco in a saucepan. Add flour and salt; blend well. Heat until bubbly. Add milk gradually, stirring constantly. Bring to boiling; cook and stir for 1 to 2 minutes.
3. Beat egg yolks thoroughly in a bowl. Add sauce gradually, mixing to blend. Add crab meat, bread crumbs, onion powder, and paprika; mix well.
4. Beat egg whites to stiff, not dry, peaks. Fold into crab mixture. Turn into an ungreased 1 1/2-quart soufflé dish.
5. Bake at 350° for 45 to 50 minutes or until golden brown and a knife inserted near center comes out clean. Serve at once. Garnish with almonds, if desired.

6 servings

Clam Casserole

1 can (10 ounces) shelled whole
  baby clams, or 2 cans (6½
  ounces each) minced clams,
  drained; reserve liquid
Milk
3 eggs, beaten
1 can (8¾ ounces) cream-style
  corn
½ cup saltine cracker crumbs
2 tablespoons chopped pimiento
1 tablespoon minced onion
1 tablespoon Crisco
  shortening, melted
¾ teaspoon salt
Dash ground red pepper

1. Preheat oven to 375°.
2. Combine reserved clam
liquid and enough milk to
make 1 cup liquid. Pour into a
large bowl and stir in beaten
eggs. Add clams and remaining
ingredients; stir until well
blended. Pour into a greased
1½-quart casserole.
3. Bake at 375° for 45 minutes
or until firm.

6 servings

Clam Fritters

1 can (6½ ounces) minced
  clams
¾ cup all-purpose flour
1 teaspoon baking powder
½ teaspoon salt
¼ teaspoon paprika
Dash pepper
2 tablespoons finely chopped
  onion
1 egg
Crisco shortening for deep
  frying

1. Drain clams, reserving ¼
cup juice.
2. Combine flour, baking powder, salt, paprika, and pepper.
Stir in clams and chopped
onion. Combine clam juice
and egg. Add to flour mixture
and stir until well blended.
3. Heat Crisco to 365° in a
deep saucepan or deep fryer.
Drop level tablespoons of
clam mixture into hot Crisco.
(Do not use fryer basket.) Fry
several fritters at a time for
3½ minutes or until browned.
Drain on paper towels.
4. Serve with *lemon wedges*
and Tartar Sauce, page 69.

4 servings

Clam Spaghetti Sauce

3 tablespoons Crisco
  shortening
¼ cup chopped celery
¼ cup chopped onion
2 cans (6½ ounces each)
  minced clams, drained
1 jar (48 ounces) spaghetti sauce

1. Melt Crisco in a large saucepan. Add celery and onion;
cook over medium-high heat
until tender (about 4 minutes).
2. Stir in clams and spaghetti
sauce; heat thoroughly. Serve
over *hot cooked spaghetti*.

1½ quarts sauce

Creamy Oyster Casserole

4 cans (8 ounces each)
  oysters*
1/4 cup Crisco shortening
1/4 cup chopped onion
1/4 cup all-purpose flour
1 1/4 teaspoons salt
1/4 teaspoon pepper
1/8 teaspoon ground nutmeg
1 cup milk
2 teaspoons grated lemon peel
2 teaspoons lemon juice
1 teaspoon Worcestershire
  sauce
2 tablespoons snipped parsley
2 cups cooked elbow macaroni
1/2 cup fine dry bread crumbs

1. Preheat oven to 350°.
2. Drain oysters, reserving 1
cup liquor. Set aside.
3. Melt Crisco in a heavy
skillet over medium heat. Add
onion; cook until crisp-tender,
stirring occasionally. Stir in
flour, salt, pepper, and
nutmeg; cook until bubbly.
Remove from heat. Gradually
stir in milk and reserved
oyster liquor, stirring until
smooth. Cook, stirring constantly, over medium heat
until sauce boils and thickens.
Cook and stir for 1 minute.
4. Remove from heat. Stir in
lemon peel, lemon juice,
Worcestershire sauce, parsley,
and oysters. Fold in cooked
macaroni and turn into a 2-
quart baking dish. Spoon
crumbs around edge.
5. Bake at 350° for 30 to 35
minutes or until heated and
crumbs are browned.

6 servings

*If fresh oysters are used, consistency
will be thinner. Salt may be increased
to 1 1/2 teaspoons.

Crispy Fried Oysters

3/4 cup dairy sour cream
2 eggs, beaten
3/4 teaspoon onion salt
1/2 teaspoon paprika
Crisco shortening for deep
  frying
1 pint select oysters, well
  drained
1/2 cup fine graham cracker
  crumbs
1 1/2 cups instant mashed
  potato buds or flakes

1. Combine sour cream, eggs,
onion salt, and paprika; mix
until blended. Set aside.
2. Heat Crisco to 365° in deep
saucepan or deep fryer.
3. Coat oysters with crumbs,
then dip into sour cream
mixture; drain well. Using a
small amount of potato buds
and adding more as needed,
coat oysters with potato buds.
4. Fry several oysters at a
time in hot Crisco for 1 1/2 to 2
minutes or until well browned.
5. Serve warm with *lemon
wedges*.

3 or 4 servings

Oysters à la King

1 pint fresh oysters or 2 cans
  (8 ounces each) whole
  oysters
Milk
1/4 cup Crisco shortening
1/2 pound fresh mushrooms,
  cleaned and sliced
1/2 cup chopped green pepper
1/4 cup all-purpose flour
1 1/2 teaspoons salt
1/8 teaspoon pepper
Dash ground nutmeg
1/4 cup minced pimiento
Buttered toast slices

1. (If fresh oysters are used,
heat them in their liquor just
until edges curl.) Drain
oysters thoroughly; reserve
liquid. Add enough milk to
liquid to make 2 1/2 cups.
2. Melt Crisco in a large
skillet, add mushrooms and
green pepper, and sauté for 5
minutes. Sprinkle flour, salt,
pepper, and nutmeg over
mushrooms; stir to coat
evenly. Add milk and oyster
liquid gradually while stirring.
Cook over medium-high heat,
stirring constantly, until sauce
boils and thickens. Gently mix
in oysters and pimiento.
3. Serve on buttered toast.

6 servings

VEGETABLES AND FRUITS

Fresh vegetables and fruits complement a meal in many ways. They add flavor, color, and texture... and valuable nutrients as well!

These surprising recipes are very tasty. Even children who dislike vegetables may learn to love them.

Harvard Beets

1/2 cup sugar
1 1/2 teaspoons cornstarch
1/4 cup cider vinegar
1/4 cup water
3 cups sliced or cubed cooked or canned beets
2 tablespoons Crisco shortening

1. Mix sugar and cornstarch in a large heavy saucepan. Add vinegar and water, blending until smooth. Cook over medium heat, stirring constantly, until sauce comes to boiling. Cook and stir for 2 minutes longer.
2. Remove from heat; add beets and toss well. Let stand for 30 minutes.
3. When ready to serve, melt Crisco in a saucepan, add beets, and heat thoroughly.

6 servings

Leek Mushroom Pie

8 leeks (about 3 pounds), halved lengthwise, washed, and patted dry
8 ounces fresh mushrooms, cleaned
1/4 cup Crisco shortening
5 tablespoons whipping cream, divided
1/2 teaspoon salt
Dash white pepper
Crisco pastry for a double-crust 9-inch pie, page 154

1. Remove the green part of the leeks and chop the white part coarsely. Remove tough stem tips of mushrooms. Chop mushrooms coarsely.
2. Melt Crisco in a 10-inch skillet. Add leeks and sauté for 5 minutes, stirring often. Add mushrooms and sauté for 5 more minutes, stirring often.
3. Add 4 tablespoons cream, 1 tablespoon at a time; stir and cook the mixture for 2 minutes after each addition.
4. Add the salt, white pepper, and remaining 1 tablespoon cream. Let mixture cool for 10 minutes.
5. Preheat oven to 425°.
6. Roll out half of pastry to a 13-inch circle. Line a 9-inch pie plate with pastry. Fill with leek mixture. Roll out remaining pastry to an 11-inch circle and place over filling. Trim edges and seal by pressing with a fork or fluting edge. Slit top.
7. Bake at 425° for 30 minutes or until lightly browned. Let stand for 15 minutes before serving.

8 servings

Fried Asparagus

1 pound fresh asparagus or 1 package (10 ounces) frozen asparagus spears
2 tablespoons Crisco shortening
1 tablespoon lemon juice
Dash salt
Dash pepper

1. If using fresh asparagus, wash and trim the bottoms.
2. Cut fresh or frozen asparagus in 1/2-inch diagonal slices.
3. Melt Crisco in a large heavy skillet and sauté asparagus for about 5 minutes, tossing frequently. Add lemon juice, salt, and pepper. Serve hot.

3 or 4 servings

Fried Tomatoes

4 very firm green tomatoes
1/2 cup yellow cornmeal
1 1/4 teaspoons salt
1/2 teaspoon sugar
1/8 teaspoon pepper
1/4 cup Crisco shortening

1. Cut out stem ends of tomatoes and slice 1/2 inch thick.
2. Mix cornmeal, salt, sugar, and pepper in a shallow dish. Coat both sides of tomato slices with the mixture.
3. Melt Crisco in a large heavy skillet over medium-high heat. Add as many tomato slices at one time as will lie flat in skillet. Lightly brown both sides, turning once; cook only until tender.

4 servings

Nutty Broccoli

1 large bunch broccoli, tough
  ends removed
1/4 cup Crisco shortening
2 tablespoons all-purpose flour
1 1/2 cups chicken broth
1/2 teaspoon salt
Dash pepper
2 tablespoons Crisco
  shortening
1/3 cup coarsely chopped
  walnuts
2 tablespoons fine bread
  crumbs

1. Cut tops off broccoli,
leaving 2-inch flowerettes.
Peel remaining stalks; cut into
2-inch pieces. (Cut large pieces
in halves or quarters lengthwise.) There should be about
3 cups stalk pieces and 6 cups
flowerettes.

2. Heat 1 quart of water to
boiling in a 3-quart saucepan.
Add stalk pieces; boil gently
for 5 to 7 minutes until crisp-
tender. Drain; rinse under
cold water.
3. Melt 1/4 cup Crisco in a
medium skillet over moderate
heat. Stir in flour. Cook for 1
minute. Gradually stir in
chicken broth; bring to boiling.
Cook and stir until sauce is
slightly thickened and smooth.
Add stalk pieces, flowerettes,
salt, and pepper. Partly cover
and simmer for 10 minutes or
until tender.
4. Melt remaining 2 tablespoons Crisco in a small skillet
over moderate heat. Stir in
walnuts and bread crumbs;
cook for 3 to 4 minutes or
until browned. Put vegetable
mixture into a serving bowl.
Sprinkle with walnut mixture.

6 servings

Squash Custard

2 tablespoons Crisco
  shortening, melted
3 cups mashed cooked
  butternut, hubbard, or
  buttercup squash
1/4 cup half-and-half or light
  cream
2 eggs, slightly beaten
2 tablespoons all-purpose flour
2 tablespoons brown sugar
1 teaspoon grated lemon peel
1/2 teaspoon salt
1/8 teaspoon pepper

1. Preheat oven to 350°.
2. Brush a 1-quart casserole
lightly with Crisco. Combine
melted Crisco, squash, half-
and-half, eggs, flour, brown
sugar, lemon peel, salt, and
pepper and turn into the
greased casserole. Place in a
pan of hot water.
3. Bake at 350° for 1 hour or
until firm in center.

6 servings

Squash with Apples

2 acorn squash, cut in half
  lengthwise
2 tart cooking apples, pared
  and cored
1 tablespoon lemon juice
1 1/2 teaspoons grated lemon
  peel
1/4 cup Crisco shortening,
  melted
1/2 cup packed brown sugar
1/2 teaspoon salt
1/8 teaspoon ground cinnamon

1. Preheat oven to 400°.
2. Scoop out seeds from squash
halves and place cut-side-down
in baking dish. Add 1/2 inch

boiling water. Bake at 400°
for 20 minutes.

3. Meanwhile, chop apples
and combine with lemon juice,
lemon peel, 2 tablespoons
melted Crisco, and brown sugar.

4. After baking for 20 minutes,
turn squash halves cut-side-up
and brush with remaining 2
tablespoons Crisco. Sprinkle
salt and cinnamon evenly over
the halves. Fill hollow centers
with apple mixture.

5. Add boiling water to ½-inch
level in a baking dish. Cover
squash with aluminum foil
and bake 30 minutes longer.
Garnish with apple slices or
lemon wedges, if desired.

4 servings

Special Spinach

*2 tablespoons Crisco
    shortening*
1 cup sliced green onions
*½ pound fresh spinach, sliced
    (about 8 cups)*
*½ pound bok choy or Swiss
    chard, sliced (about 3 cups)*
2 tablespoons sugar
2 tablespoons cider vinegar
*2 tablespoons Crisco
    shortening, melted*

1. Melt 2 tablespoons Crisco
in a large skillet. Add green
onions and cook over medium
heat for 3 minutes, stirring
occasionally.

2. Add spinach and bok choy.
Stir and cook for 3 minutes or
until vegetables are crisp-
tender.

3. Combine sugar and vinegar.
Add to melted Crisco and stir
to mix well. Pour over cooked
vegetables and stir. Serve
immediately.

4 servings

Bean and Rice Bake

*2 tablespoons Crisco
    shortening*
1½ cups chopped onion
¼ cup chopped green pepper
*2 cans (15½ ounces each) red
    kidney beans, drained*
1 cup cooked long grain rice
1 cup creamed cottage cheese
1 teaspoon salt
¼ teaspoon pepper
¼ teaspoon chili powder
*¼ cup shredded Cheddar
    cheese*
Green pepper rings

1. Preheat oven to 350°.

2. Melt Crisco in a medium
skillet. Sauté onion and
chopped green pepper until
tender (about 5 minutes).

3. Combine beans, rice, and
cottage cheese. Fold in onion,
green pepper, salt, pepper, and
chili powder.

4. Spoon into a lightly greased
2-quart casserole.

5. Bake at 350° for 35 minutes
or until bubbly. Garnish with
shredded Cheddar cheese and
green pepper rings.

5 or 6 servings

Corn Fritters

Crisco shortening for deep
    frying
1 cup sifted all-purpose flour
1 teaspoon baking powder
1 teaspoon sugar
1 teaspoon salt
1 package (10 ounces) frozen
    sweet whole kernel corn,
    thawed
Milk
2 eggs, well beaten
2 teaspoons Crisco shortening,
    melted

1. Fill a large skillet with
Crisco to one-half its depth
and heat to 365° while
preparing the fritter batter.
2. Combine flour, baking
powder, sugar, and salt in a
bowl and make a well in
center; set aside.
3. Drain thawed corn and
measure liquid. Add milk to
measure ½ cup liquid. Set
aside. Chop the corn and add
to beaten eggs, melted Crisco,
and the liquid mixture; mix
well. Add to dry ingredients
and stir until just blended.
4. Drop batter by teaspoonfuls
into hot Crisco to form a
layer. Fry for 3 to 4 minutes
or until golden brown, turning
once.
5. Remove fritters with a
slotted spoon and drain over
fat for a few seconds before
removing to paper towels.
6. Serve hot with *maple-
blended syrup.*

About 3 dozen fritters

Corn Scallop Fiesta

½ cup Crisco shortening
½ cup finely shredded carrot
½ cup chopped green pepper
2 tablespoons chopped celery
2 teaspoons chopped onion
2 cans (17 ounces each)
    cream-style corn
4 eggs, beaten
1 cup crushed soda crackers
½ cup undiluted evaporated
    milk
⅛ teaspoon Tabasco
1 teaspoon sugar
1½ teaspoons salt
1 cup shredded Cheddar
    cheese
Paprika
Parsley
Pimiento-stuffed green olives,
    sliced

1. Preheat oven to 350°.
2. Melt Crisco in a large heavy
skillet. Stir in carrot, green
pepper, celery, and onion.
Cook over medium heat until
vegetables are barely tender.
3. Stir in corn, eggs, cracker
crumbs, evaporated milk, and
Tabasco. Stir in sugar and
salt. Turn into a greased
8x8x2-inch baking dish. Top
with cheese and sprinkle with
paprika.
4. Bake at 350° for 30 minutes
or until center is set and top
is golden. Remove from oven;
garnish with parsley and
olives.

About 9 servings

Note: About 1½ cups of fresh parsley,
finely chopped, is needed to achieve
the checkerboard design as shown.
Sliced black olives may be substituted
for stuffed green olives.

Vegetables

Sautéed Cabbage Deluxe

1 head cabbage (about 2¹/₂ pounds)
¹/₃ cup Crisco shortening
1 teaspoon salt
2 tomatoes, peeled, seeded, and diced
¹/₄ teaspoon fennel seed
3 tablespoons chopped green onion tops

1. Remove tough outer leaves of cabbage; quarter, then core. Thinly slice each quarter.
2. Cook cabbage in Crisco and salt in a large skillet over low heat for 30 minutes or just until crisp-tender.
3. Stir in remaining ingredients. Heat thoroughly.

6 to 8 servings

Company Potato Cabbage Casserole

¹/₄ cup Crisco shortening
1 small head green cabbage, cored and coarsely chopped
2 large onions, chopped
6 potatoes, cooked, peeled, and thinly sliced
2 tablespoons snipped parsley
¹/₄ cup all-purpose flour
¹/₂ teaspoon salt
1¹/₂ cups chicken broth (at room temperature)
2 cups shredded cheese (bonbel or port salut)

1. Preheat oven to 350°.
2. Melt Crisco in a saucepan or Dutch oven. Sauté cabbage and onions until tender (about 10 minutes).
3. Lightly grease a shallow 3-quart casserole. Spoon half of the sautéed vegetables into casserole followed by half of the potatoes. Sprinkle with 1 tablespoon parsley. Repeat.
4. Mix flour with salt. Stir into broth in a saucepan. Stir over low heat until sauce bubbles and thickens.
5. Pour sauce over vegetables. Sprinkle shredded cheese over top of casserole.
6. Bake at 350° for 40 to 45 minutes or until bubbly.

10 to 12 servings

Spicy Oven Fries

3 tablespoons Crisco shortening
3 medium red potatoes (about 1¹/₄ pounds), pared and cut in lengthwise strips about ¹/₂ inch thick
1 tablespoon grated Parmesan cheese
¹/₄ teaspoon salt
¹/₈ teaspoon dried oregano, crushed
¹/₈ teaspoon onion salt
¹/₈ teaspoon garlic salt
¹/₈ teaspoon pepper
Dash hot chili powder

1. Preheat oven to 450°.
2. Melt Crisco in a 15¹/₂x10¹/₂x 1-inch jelly-roll pan by placing in oven for 1 to 2 minutes.
3. Spread potatoes in a single layer over melted Crisco, turning to coat strips evenly.
4. Combine Parmesan cheese, salt, oregano, onion salt, garlic salt, pepper, and chili powder. Sprinkle half of seasoning mixture over potatoes.
5. Bake at 450° for 12 minutes. Turn potatoes with spatula and sprinkle with remaining seasoning mixture. Bake for 15 minutes longer until tender in center and crisp on outside.

About 4 servings

Potato Pancakes

3 medium white potatoes (about 1 pound), pared and grated
¹/₄ cup finely chopped onion
1 tablespoon all-purpose flour
1 tablespoon milk
1 egg, slightly beaten
¹/₂ teaspoon salt
¹/₄ cup Crisco shortening

1. Preheat oven to 300°.
2. Place potatoes on a double thickness of paper towels, fold towels around, and squeeze to extract moisture. If necessary, repeat until potatoes are slightly dry.
3. Place the potatoes in a mixing bowl. Add onion, flour, milk, egg, and salt; mix well by hand.
4. Melt Crisco in a 10-inch skillet. Put 2 tablespoons of potato mixture into skillet and press flat with a spatula to about 4 inches in diameter. Repeat with more mixture until skillet is full but not crowded. Cook each pancake for 5 minutes on each side until brown and crisp. Repeat with remaining potato mixture and cook a total of 8 pancakes.
5. When pancakes are done, place on paper towels to blot and keep warm in a 300° oven. Garnish with applesauce or sour cream, if desired.

4 servings

Vegetables

French-Fried Potatoes

*Crisco shortening for deep
  frying*
*6 medium potatoes (about 2
  pounds)*

1. Heat Crisco to 360° in a
deep saucepan or deep fryer.
2. Wash and pare potatoes.
Cut lengthwise into strips
about ¹/₂x¹/₂ inch or ¹/₄x¹/₄ inch.
Pat dry with paper towels.
3. Fry a few at a time until
crisp and golden, about 10
minutes for the ¹/₂-inch strips
and about 6 minutes for the
¹/₄-inch strips.
4. Drain on paper towels.
Sprinkle with *salt.* Serve
immediately.

6 servings

French-Fried Sweet Potatoes

*Crisco shortening for deep
  frying*
*6 medium sweet potatoes
  (about 2 pounds)*

1. Heat Crisco to 360° in a
deep saucepan or deep fryer.
2. Wash and pare potatoes.
Cut lengthwise into strips
about ¹/₂x¹/₂ inch or ¹/₄x¹/₄ inch.
Pat dry with paper towels.
3. Fry a few at a time until
crisp and golden, about 3
minutes for the ¹/₂-inch strips
and about 1¹/₂ minutes for the
¹/₄-inch strips.
4. Drain on paper towels.
Sprinkle with *salt.* Serve
immediately.

6 servings

French-Fried Onion Rings

*2 large Bermuda onions,
  peeled and cut in ¹/₄-inch
  slices*
1 cup milk
1 cup all-purpose flour
¹/₈ teaspoon salt
*Crisco shortening for deep
  frying*

1. Separate onion slices into
rings. Put them in a shallow
dish and pour the milk over
them. Soak for 30 minutes,
turning twice.
2. Mix flour and salt in a
plastic bag. Add the onion
rings, a few at a time, and
shake to coat well.
3. Heat Crisco to 365° in a
deep saucepan or deep fryer.
Fry onion rings, several at a
time, for 2 to 3 minutes until
golden on both sides. Drain on
paper towels. Keep warm
while frying the remainder.
Sprinkle with *salt.*

8 servings

French-Fried Zucchini Slices

2 tablespoons milk
1 egg, slightly beaten
¹/₄ cup yellow cornmeal
¹/₄ cup all-purpose flour
¹/₄ teaspoon onion salt
¹/₈ teaspoon salt
*4 small (6 inches long)
  zucchini, cut in ¹/₃-inch slices*
*Crisco shortening for deep
  frying*

1. Combine milk and egg.
Combine cornmeal, flour,
onion salt, and salt.

2. Dip zucchini in milk and
egg, shaking off excess. Dip
in cornmeal mixture.
3. Heat Crisco to 365° in a
deep saucepan or deep fryer.
Fry zucchini slices in hot
Crisco for 1 to 2 minutes or
until golden. Serve hot.

4 servings

Variation: Substitute 1 pound fresh
whole mushrooms for the zucchini;
clean and pat dry.

Top of the Range Baked Beans

*2 tablespoons Crisco
  shortening*
¹/₂ cup chopped green pepper
¹/₂ cup chopped onion
*2 cans (16 ounces each) pork
  and beans*
*1 can (20 ounces) pineapple
  chunks, drained and chunks
  cut in half*
³/₄ cup catsup
¹/₄ cup dark molasses
*¹/₄ cup packed light brown
  sugar*
2 teaspoons prepared mustard

1. Melt Crisco in a large
saucepan or Dutch oven. Add
green pepper and onion. Sauté
for 5 minutes or until tender.
2. Stir in pork and beans,
pineapple, catsup, molasses,
brown sugar, and mustard.
Cover and cook over low heat
for 20 minutes, or until mixture comes just to boiling,
stirring frequently. Serve hot.

10 to 12 servings

Cranberry-Orange-Sauced Sweet Potatoes

6 medium sweet potatoes or
  yams
1/4 cup Crisco shortening
1/4 cup packed light brown
  sugar
1/2 teaspoon salt
1/4 cup fresh orange juice
1/4 cup water
1 1/4 cups fresh cranberries,
  rinsed
1/2 teaspoon cornstarch
2 tablespoons cold water

1. Preheat oven to 400°.
2. Wash sweet potatoes and
pat dry. Prick with a fork,
place in a shallow baking dish,
and bake at 400° for 40 to 50
minutes or until soft.
3. During the last 10 minutes
of baking, prepare sauce. Melt
Crisco in a medium saucepan.
Add brown sugar, salt, orange
juice, and 1/4 cup water, stirring over low heat until sugar
dissolves. Add cranberries and
bring to boiling. Reduce heat
and simmer covered for 5
minutes or until cranberries
start to pop.
4. Combine cornstarch with
2 tablespoons cold water
blending until smooth. Stir
into cranberries; cook, stirring
constantly, until sauce comes
to boiling. Reduce heat and
cook for 1 to 2 minutes or
until mixture is slightly
thickened.
5. Make a lengthwise cut in
the center of each potato;
press open from bottom. Place
sweet potatoes on a serving
platter. Top each with
cranberry sauce.

6 servings

Sweet Potato Fingers

6 medium sweet potatoes or
  yams, cooked and peeled
1/4 cup all-purpose flour
1/4 cup Crisco shortening
1/2 cup packed brown sugar
1 teaspoon salt
1/2 teaspoon ground nutmeg

1. Cut sweet potatoes into
fingers or strips. Dip each in
flour until well coated.
2. Melt Crisco in a medium
skillet. Fry potato fingers
until golden brown.
3. Combine brown sugar, salt,
and nutmeg; sprinkle over
sweet potato fingers and toss
lightly until sugar mixture
melts.

About 6 servings

Shredded Yams

2 teaspoons salt
1 gallon water
2 pounds sweet potatoes or
  yams
1/2 cup packed brown sugar
1/4 cup granulated sugar
1/2 cup light corn syrup
1/2 cup water
2 tablespoons Crisco
  shortening
2 cans (8 ounces each) sliced
  pineapple in pineapple juice

1. Preheat oven to 350°.
2. Dissolve salt in a gallon of
water. Peel and shred potatoes
into water. Drain; rinse well.
3. Place sweet potatoes in a
12x8-inch or 2-quart utility
dish.
4. Mix sugars, corn syrup, and
water in a saucepan. Heat to
boiling and cook for 2 to 3
minutes. Add Crisco and stir
until melted.

5. Drain pineapple and reserve
juice; set fruit aside. Add
enough water to reserved
pineapple juice to equal 1 cup.
Pour over sweet potatoes,
then pour on sugar syrup.
Garnish with pineapple slices.
6. Bake at 350° for 40 to 50
minutes or until tender. Serve
with a slotted spoon.

6 to 8 servings

Sweet Potato Pancakes

2 medium sweet potatoes
  (about 1 pound), pared and
  grated
1/3 cup finely chopped onion
2 tablespoons all-purpose flour
1 tablespoon milk
2 eggs, slightly beaten
3/4 teaspoon salt
1/4 cup plus 2 tablespoons
  Crisco shortening

1. Preheat oven to 300°.
2. Place potatoes in a mixing
bowl. Add onion, flour, milk,
eggs, and salt; mix well with
a spoon.
3. Melt 1/4 cup Crisco in a
10-inch skillet over low to
medium heat. Place about 2
tablespoons of potato mixture
in the skillet and press flat
with a spatula to about 4
inches in diameter. Repeat
with more mixture until the
skillet is full but not crowded.
Cook each pancake for 5
minutes on each side until
brown and crisp. After cooking 8 pancakes, add remaining
2 tablespoons of Crisco and
cook 4 more pancakes.
4. When pancakes are done,
place on paper towels to blot
and keep warm in a 300° oven.

6 servings

Vegetables

Crispy Carrots

1 pound carrots, cooked
3 tablespoons Crisco
  shortening, melted
³/₄ cup corn flakes, finely
  crushed
¹/₂ teaspoon salt
¹/₈ teaspoon pepper
¹/₈ teaspoon paprika

1. Drain carrots and roll in melted Crisco.
2. Combine crushed corn flakes, salt, pepper, and paprika; coat carrots.
3. Place carrots on broiler rack. Place under broiler with tops of carrots about 4 inches from heat. Broil for 2 minutes on each side.

4 servings

Green Bean Medley

¹/₄ cup Crisco shortening
¹/₂ pound fresh mushrooms,
  cleaned and thinly sliced
1 can (8 ounces) sliced water
  chestnuts, drained and
  slivered
3 tablespoons chopped onion
2 tablespoons lemon juice
1 teaspoon soy sauce
¹/₂ teaspoon salt
1 tablespoon chopped pimiento
1 pound fresh green beans,
  cooked and drained
1 can (3 ounces) french-fried
  onion rings

1. Melt Crisco in a large skillet. Add mushrooms, water chestnuts, and onion. Cook until lightly browned. Mix in lemon juice, soy sauce, salt, and pimiento; heat thoroughly.
2. Toss sauce with hot beans. Top with onion rings.

About 8 servings

Dilled Carrots

1 pound young carrots
3 tablespoons Crisco
  shortening, melted
1 tablespoon water
1 teaspoon lemon juice
¹/₂ teaspoon dried dill weed
¹/₂ teaspoon salt
¹/₈ teaspoon pepper

1. Preheat oven to 375°.
2. Pare carrots and cut into thin julienne strips. Place carrots in a greased 1¹/₂-quart casserole. Combine melted Crisco, water, lemon juice, dill weed, salt, and pepper and pour over carrots. Toss lightly to mix. Cover tightly.
3. Bake at 375° for 40 minutes or until carrots are crisp-tender. Carefully stir twice during baking.

6 servings

Carrot Ring with Green Beans

*3 tablespoons Crisco
 shortening*
1/3 cup finely chopped onion
*3 cups mashed cooked carrots
 (12 to 15 carrots)*
1 tablespoon sugar
1 teaspoon salt
1/8 teaspoon pepper
1/8 teaspoon ground nutmeg
2 eggs, slightly beaten
*Cooked green beans or other
 green vegetable*

1. Preheat oven to 350°.
2. Melt Crisco in a heavy skillet over medium heat. Add onion; cook until tender.
3. Combine onion-Crisco mixture, carrots, sugar, salt, pepper, nutmeg, and eggs in a bowl; mix until well blended. Pour into a well-greased 4-cup or 5½-cup ring mold.
4. Carefully place a shallow pan of hot water in oven, then set mold in pan.
5. Bake at 350° for 1 hour or until firm.
6. Immediately unmold onto serving platter. Fill center with cooked green beans or favorite green vegetable.

8 servings

Batter-Fried Parsnips

*8 medium parsnips (about 2
 pounds), pared*
2 quarts water
1/2 teaspoon salt
*3 tablespoons Crisco
 shortening, melted*
3 tablespoons lemon juice
1/2 teaspoon chervil
1/2 teaspoon tarragon
2 cups sifted all-purpose flour
*1 tablespoon Crisco
 shortening, melted*
3/4 cup apple cider
3/4 cup buttermilk
1/2 cup shredded Swiss cheese
*Crisco shortening for deep
 frying*
2 egg whites

1. Cut parsnips crosswise, then in half lengthwise. Cut large pieces in half lengthwise again. Put parsnips into boiling salted water. Boil for 8 to 10 minutes until crisp-tender. Rinse under cold water until cool; drain.
2. Mix parsnips, 3 tablespoons melted Crisco, lemon juice, chervil, and tarragon. Let stand for 1 hour.
3. Meanwhile, mix flour, 1 tablespoon melted Crisco, cider, buttermilk, and cheese until thick and smooth. Let stand for 1 hour.
4. Heat Crisco to 365° in a medium saucepan or deep fryer. Beat egg whites until stiff but not dry; fold into batter. Dip parsnips in batter. Fry, a few at a time, for 2 minutes until crisp and golden. (Do not use fryer basket.) Drain on paper towels. Garnish with *parsley* and *lemon wedges*. Serve hot.

8 servings

Vegetables

Stir-Fried Romaine

1 tablespoon Crisco shortening
9 green onions, sliced (about ¹/₂ cup)
5 white radishes, sliced (about ³/₄ cup)
1 large head romaine (about 1 pound), rinsed, dried, and sliced (8 cups)
2 tablespoons soy sauce
1 tablespoon sesame seed

1. Melt Crisco in a large skillet. Add sliced onions and radishes and cook over medium heat for 1 minute. Add romaine. Cook and stir over high heat for 2 to 3 minutes or just until it starts to wilt.
2. Stir in soy sauce and sesame seed. Serve at once.

4 to 6 servings

Creamed Peas

2 tablespoons Crisco shortening
2 tablespoons all-purpose flour
¹/₄ teaspoon salt
1¹/₄ cups milk
1 teaspoon instant minced onion
¹/₂ teaspoon basil, crushed
1 can (17 ounces) green peas, drained

1. Melt Crisco in a saucepan. Add flour and salt; blend well. Heat until bubbly. Add milk gradually, stirring constantly. Bring to boiling, add onion and basil, and cook for 1 to 2 minutes.
2. Mix in peas and heat.

About 6 servings

Mixed Vegetable Casserole

1 package (10 ounces) frozen mixed vegetables
1 package (10 ounces) frozen cauliflower
1 package (10 ounces) frozen green peas
¹/₄ cup Crisco shortening
¹/₄ cup all-purpose flour
1 cup half-and-half or light cream
1 cup chicken broth
1 tablespoon prepared horseradish
1 teaspoon prepared mustard
4 drops Tabasco
1 cup shredded sharp Cheddar cheese
¹/₄ cup soft bread crumbs

1. Cook each vegetable according to directions on package.
2. Preheat oven to 400°.
3. Melt Crisco in a saucepan, stir in flour, and cook until bubbly. Stir in half-and-half and broth and bring to boiling; stir and cook for 1 to 2 minutes. Blend in horseradish, mustard, and Tabasco.
4. Drain cooked vegetables. Combine vegetables and cheese; fold into cream sauce. Pour into an 11¹/₂x7¹/₂-inch baking dish. Sprinkle crumbs over top.
5. Bake at 400° for 20 to 25 minutes or until crumbs are golden brown and cheese is melted.

6 to 8 servings

Cheesy Vegetable Tarts

Pastry:
1¼ cups all-purpose flour
⅛ teaspoon salt
⅓ cup Crisco shortening
⅓ cup finely shredded
    Cheddar cheese
1 egg
1 to 2 tablespoons cold water

Filling:
1 bag (16 ounces) frozen
    vegetable blend (such as
    cauliflower, broccoli, and
    carrots)

Sauce:
2 tablespoons Crisco
    shortening
2 tablespoons all-purpose flour
1 cup milk
¼ teaspoon salt
Dash white pepper
2 tablespoons whipping cream
⅔ cup finely shredded
    Cheddar cheese

1. For Pastry, preheat oven to 425°. Combine flour and salt in a bowl. Cut in Crisco with a pastry blender or 2 knives until mixture resembles corn-meal. Stir in cheese, egg, and enough water to form dough.
2. Roll out pastry to ⅛-inch thickness on a lightly floured surface. Using the lid from a 3-pound Crisco can as a pattern, cut 8 circles (about 5¼ inches each). Place pastry circles over backs of inverted 2¾-inch muffin-pan cups or small custard cups. Pierce with a fork.
3. Bake at 425° for 15 minutes or until golden brown. Cool on a rack for 2 to 3 minutes, then carefully remove shells from muffin pans.
4. For Filling, prepare vegetables according to package directions. Reserve 8 vegetable pieces for garnish. Chop remaining vegetables to ½-inch pieces. Keep all vegetables warm while preparing sauce.
5. For Sauce, melt Crisco in a saucepan. Add flour and cook for 2 minutes. Add milk slowly, stirring constantly. Cook until mixture boils and thickens; stir constantly.
6. Remove from heat; stir in salt, pepper, cream, and Cheddar cheese.
7. Spoon vegetables into the baked tart shells. Spoon sauce over vegetables. Garnish with vegetable pieces. Serve hot.

8 tarts

Baked Onions

4 medium Spanish or Vidalia
    onions (about 1¾ pounds)
2 tablespoons Crisco
    shortening, melted
2 tablespoons Worcestershire
    sauce
½ teaspoon dried parsley
    flakes
⅛ teaspoon salt
Dash pepper

1. Preheat oven to 350°.
2. Remove ends and skins from onions. Cut an "X" halfway through each onion. Place onions cut-side-up in a 2-quart casserole.
3. Combine Crisco, Worcestershire sauce, dried parsley, salt, and pepper; pour over onions. Cover casserole.
4. Bake at 350° for 1½ hours or until tender.

4 servings

Vegetable Trio

3 hard-cooked eggs, finely
    chopped
2 cups mayonnaise
1 medium onion, chopped
¼ cup Crisco shortening,
    melted
1 tablespoon prepared
    mustard
2 teaspoons Worcestershire
    sauce
Dash Tabasco
1 can (17 ounces) whole green
    beans, drained
1 can (17 ounces) green lima
    beans, drained
1 can (17 ounces) sweet peas,
    drained

1. Preheat oven to 350°.
2. Reserve 3 tablespoons chopped egg for garnish. Combine remaining egg, mayonnaise, onion, melted Crisco, mustard, Worcestershire sauce, and Tabasco.
3. Layer green beans, lima beans, and peas in a 2-quart casserole, pouring sauce between each layer and then over the top.
4. Bake at 350° for 30 minutes or until hot and bubbly. Garnish top with reserved chopped egg.

10 to 12 servings

Sautéed Bananas

2 tablespoons Crisco
  shortening
2 tablespoons orange juice
4 firm ripe bananas
2 tablespoons confectioners'
  sugar

1. Melt Crisco in a large
heavy skillet over medium
heat. Stir in orange juice.
2. Peel bananas. Cut in half
crosswise, then cut each in
half lengthwise. Place in
skillet and cook over medium
heat for 5 minutes, turning
once.
3. Arrange bananas in a
serving dish. Sprinkle with
confectioners' sugar. Serve hot
for dessert or as an accompaniment to *veal, ham,* or
poultry.

4 servings

Baked Bananas

3 tablespoons Crisco
  shortening
2 teaspoons grated lemon peel
2 teaspoons lemon juice
6 firm ripe bananas
1/2 cup packed dark brown
  sugar

1. Preheat oven to 350°.
2. Place Crisco in a shallow 3-
quart utility dish. Set in oven
for 3 to 5 minutes or until
Crisco is melted. Remove from
oven; stir in lemon peel and
lemon juice.
3. Peel bananas; cut in half
crosswise and then lengthwise;
place in baking dish, turning
to coat with Crisco mixture.
4. Sprinkle brown sugar over
bananas.

5. Bake at 350° for 20 to 25
minutes or until brown sugar is
melted and bananas are tender.
Serve hot for dessert or as an
accompaniment to *chicken,
ham,* or *veal.*

8 servings

Banana Yam Casserole

4 large or 6 medium yams or
  sweet potatoes
1/3 cup Crisco shortening
1/3 cup chopped onion
1/2 cup orange juice
2 tablespoons light brown
  sugar
1/2 teaspoon ground cinnamon
1/4 teaspoon ground nutmeg
1/4 teaspoon ground cloves
1/2 teaspoon salt
2 medium firm-ripe bananas,
  peeled and cut in 1/2-inch
  slices
1/3 cup chopped pecans

1. Wash yams. Cover yams
with water, bring to boiling,
and cook for 20 minutes or
until soft. Cool, peel, and
mash.
2. Preheat oven to 350°.
3. Melt Crisco in a skillet.
Add onion and sauté until
tender (about 5 minutes).
4. Add mashed yams, orange
juice, brown sugar, cinnamon,
nutmeg, cloves, and salt; mix
thoroughly.
5. Turn half of mixture into
a greased 2-quart casserole.
Layer bananas over yam mixture. Top with remaining
yams. Sprinkle with pecans.
6. Bake at 350° for 30 to 35
minutes or until heated
through.

8 to 10 servings

Fruit Fritters

2/3 cup all-purpose flour
2 tablespoons sugar
1/8 teaspoon salt
1 egg, slightly beaten
1/4 cup milk
1/4 cup water
Crisco shortening for deep
  frying
1 can (20 ounces) pineapple
  chunks, drained
  OR 3 medium-size firm ripe
  bananas, peeled, cut in 1/2-
  inch slices
  OR 4 to 5 medium (2 1/2 inch)
  apples, pared, cored, and cut
  in 8 wedges
Confectioners' sugar
2 tablespoons sugar
1/4 teaspoon ground cinnamon

1. Mix flour, 2 tablespoons
sugar, and salt in a bowl. Add
egg, milk, and water beating
until smooth.
2. Heat Crisco to 365° in a
deep saucepan or deep fryer.
Coat each slice of fruit thor-
roughly with batter; drop into
hot Crisco.
3. For pineapple and bananas,
fry for 2 minutes or until
lightly browned. Sprinkle with
confectioners' sugar and serve
warm.
4. For apples, fry for 3 minutes or until medium browned.
Combine remaining 2 tablespoons sugar and cinnamon.
Sprinkle over apple fritters
and serve warm as an accompaniment to *pork, ham,* or
turkey.

4 servings

Golden Fruited Rice

1/2 cup golden raisins
1/4 cup chopped dried apricots
2 tablespoons Crisco shortening
1/2 cup chopped celery
3 tablespoons orange juice
1/4 teaspoon sugar
1/8 teaspoon curry powder
Dash ground ginger
1/4 teaspoon salt
Dash white pepper
3 cups cooked long grain rice
Orange slices

1. Cover raisins and apricots with warm water. Soak for 30 minutes; drain. Set aside.
2. Preheat oven to 375°.
3. Melt Crisco in a Dutch oven over low heat; add celery and cook for 8 to 10 minutes or until tender. Add raisins, apricots, orange juice, sugar, curry powder, ginger, salt, and pepper. Stir in rice.
4. Spoon mixture into a greased 1-quart casserole.
5. Bake at 375° for 10 to 20 minutes or until heated through. Garnish with orange slices.

6 servings

Delicious Sliced Apples

1/2 cup packed brown sugar
2 tablespoons all-purpose flour
Dash ground cloves
2 1/2 pounds apples, pared, cored, and sliced (about 8 cups slices)
1/4 cup Crisco shortening
1/4 cup water

1. Combine brown sugar, flour, and cloves in large bowl. Stir in apple slices and toss lightly.
2. Melt Crisco in a large skillet. Stir in apple mixture and cook over high heat for 5 minutes, stirring occasionally.
3. Stir in water. Bring mixture to boiling; cover and reduce heat. Simmer for 10 minutes or until apples are tender, stirring occasionally. Serve with *roast beef* or *turkey*.

6 to 8 servings

Deep-Fried Strawberries

1 quart fresh medium-size strawberries*
1 egg
2/3 cup milk
1 cup Homemade Crisco Quick Bread Mix, page 116
Crisco shortening for deep frying
Confectioners' sugar

1. Rinse strawberries; dry on paper towels.
2. Beat egg and milk in a bowl; add Crisco mix and beat with a beater until fairly smooth.
3. Heat Crisco to 365° in a deep saucepan or deep fryer.
4. Put 3 strawberries at a time into batter; remove berries, draining off excess batter. Fry

in hot Crisco for about 30 seconds or until light golden.

5. Remove berries with a slotted spoon and drain on paper towels. Repeat frying 3 coated berries at a time; be sure that temperature is 365°.

6. Dip in confectioners' sugar.

8 servings

*If berries are large, cut in half; if berries are small, reduce frying time.

Sweet 'n' Sour Cherries

2 tablespoons Crisco
* shortening*
1 medium green pepper, cored
* and cut in strips*
1 can (20 ounces) pineapple
* chunks in syrup*
¼ cup sugar
2 tablespoons cornstarch
3 tablespoons vinegar
½ teaspoon Worcestershire
* sauce*
2 cans (16 ounces each) pitted
* tart red cherries, drained*

1. Melt Crisco in a medium saucepan. Add green pepper and cook over medium heat until tender (about 2 minutes).

2. Drain pineapple, reserving syrup. Add enough water to syrup to measure 1½ cups liquid. Add to green pepper. Combine sugar and cornstarch; stir into liquid. Cook and stir over high heat for 2 to 3 minutes or until mixture boils and thickens. Stir in vinegar and Worcestershire sauce.

3. Stir in reserved pineapple and drained cherries; heat thoroughly. Serve with *roast pork* or *chicken*.

6 to 8 servings

Skillet-Fried Apple Rings

4 large tart cooking apples
3 tablespoons Crisco
* shortening*
¼ cup sugar
1½ teaspoons ground
* cinnamon*
⅛ teaspoon salt

1. Core but do not peel apples. Slice ½ inch thick to make rings.

2. Melt Crisco in a large heavy skillet over medium-high heat. Place apple rings in skillet.

3. Mix sugar, cinnamon, and salt. Sprinkle half of sugar mixture over apples. After 3 minutes carefully turn apple rings using a pancake turner to avoid breaking.

4. Sprinkle with remaining sugar mixture. Cook for 2 to 3 minutes longer or until apples are almost transparent. Serve hot as an accompaniment to *pork* or *poultry*.

4 servings

Curried Fruit

3 tablespoons Crisco
* shortening*
½ cup packed brown sugar
1 teaspoon curry powder
1 can (17 ounces) apricot
* halves in heavy syrup*
1 can (16 ounces) pear halves
* in heavy syrup*
1 can (20 ounces) pineapple
* chunks in pineapple juice*
6 maraschino cherries
2 medium bananas, peeled
* and cut in thick slices*

1. Preheat oven to 350°.

2. Melt Crisco in a small saucepan. Stir in brown sugar and curry powder. Set aside.

3. Drain apricot halves, pear halves, pineapple chunks, and cherries well; cut pear halves in half. Put fruit into a 1½-quart casserole. Stir in curry mixture.

4. Bake at 350° for 10 minutes.

5. Stir in banana slices. Bake for 25 minutes. Serve with *roast lamb* or *veal*.

6 to 8 servings

Scalloped Pineapple

1 can (20 ounces) crushed
* pineapple in pineapple juice*
2 tablespoons Crisco
* shortening*
⅛ teaspoon crushed dried
* mint flakes or wintergreen*
* extract*
4 bread slices, torn in small
* pieces*
Milk
2 tablespoons sugar
⅛ teaspoon salt
1 egg, beaten

1. Preheat oven to 375°.

2. Drain pineapple; reserve juice.

3. Melt Crisco in a saucepan; stir in mint. Remove from heat. Stir in pineapple and bread; mix. Turn into an ungreased 1-quart casserole.

4. Add enough milk to reserved juice to make 1 cup. Stir in sugar, salt, and egg. Pour over pineapple mixture; stir lightly.

5. Bake at 375° for 40 minutes or until a knife inserted in center comes out clean. Serve with *baked ham*.

6 servings

Bread baking is a joy not to be missed! There is the personal satisfaction of kneading the dough and shaping the loaves... the reward of watching the dough magically rise... and the mouth-watering aroma as the bread comes out of your oven.

Enjoy baking bread with Crisco Shortening!

Honey Batter Rolls

3 cups all-purpose flour
1 package active dry yeast
1 teaspoon salt
1 cup hot water (120 to 130°)
1/3 cup Crisco shortening, melted
1/3 cup honey
1 egg

1. Combine 2 cups flour, yeast, and salt in a mixer bowl. Add water, melted Crisco, honey, and egg; beat for 2 minutes on medium speed until dough is smooth.
2. Beat in remaining 1 cup flour with a spoon.
3. Cover with oiled waxed paper or plastic wrap; let rise until doubled (about 30 minutes).
4. Fill greased muffin cups one-half full with batter.
5. Cover; let rise until doubled (about 30 minutes).
6. Preheat oven to 400°.
7. Bake at 400° for 10 to 12 minutes or until golden brown.

2 dozen rolls

Sesame Loaf

2 1/2 to 3 cups all-purpose flour
1 package active dry yeast
1 1/2 teaspoons salt
1 cup hot tap water (120 to 130°)
1/4 cup Crisco shortening, melted
1 egg white
1 tablespoon water
1 teaspoon sesame seed

1. Combine 1 cup flour, yeast, and salt in a large mixer bowl. Stir in hot water and melted Crisco; beat until smooth (about 3 minutes) on high speed of electric mixer. Stir in enough additional flour to make a soft dough.
2. Turn dough onto a floured surface and knead until smooth and elastic. Cover with a bowl; let rest for 20 minutes.
3. Shape dough into a round loaf and place on a greased cookie sheet. Slash top, if desired.
4. Cover; let rise until doubled (about 45 minutes).
5. Preheat oven to 400°.
6. Brush loaf with a mixture of egg white and water; sprinkle with sesame seed.
7. Bake at 400° for 20 minutes or until golden brown. For a crisper crust, put a pan of boiling water on lower rack of oven during baking.

1 loaf bread

Sesame Hard Rolls

2 1/2 to 3 cups all-purpose flour
1 package active dry yeast
1 1/2 teaspoons salt
1 cup hot tap water (120 to 130°)
1/4 cup Crisco shortening, melted
1 egg white
1 tablespoon water
1 teaspoon sesame seed

1. Combine 1 cup flour, yeast, and salt in a large mixer bowl. Stir in hot water and melted Crisco; beat until smooth (about 3 minutes) on high speed of electric mixer. Stir in enough additional flour to make a soft dough.
2. Turn dough onto a floured surface and knead until smooth and elastic. Cover with a bowl; let rest for 20 minutes.
3. Divide dough into 12 equal pieces. Shape each into a smooth oval and place on a greased cookie sheet. Slash tops lengthwise about 1/4 inch deep.
4. Cover; let rise until doubled (about 45 minutes).
5. Preheat oven to 400°.
6. Brush rolls with a mixture of egg white and water; sprinkle with sesame seed.
7. Bake at 400° for 20 minutes or until golden brown. For a crisper crust, put a pan of boiling water on lower rack of oven during baking.

1 dozen rolls

Bread and Rolls

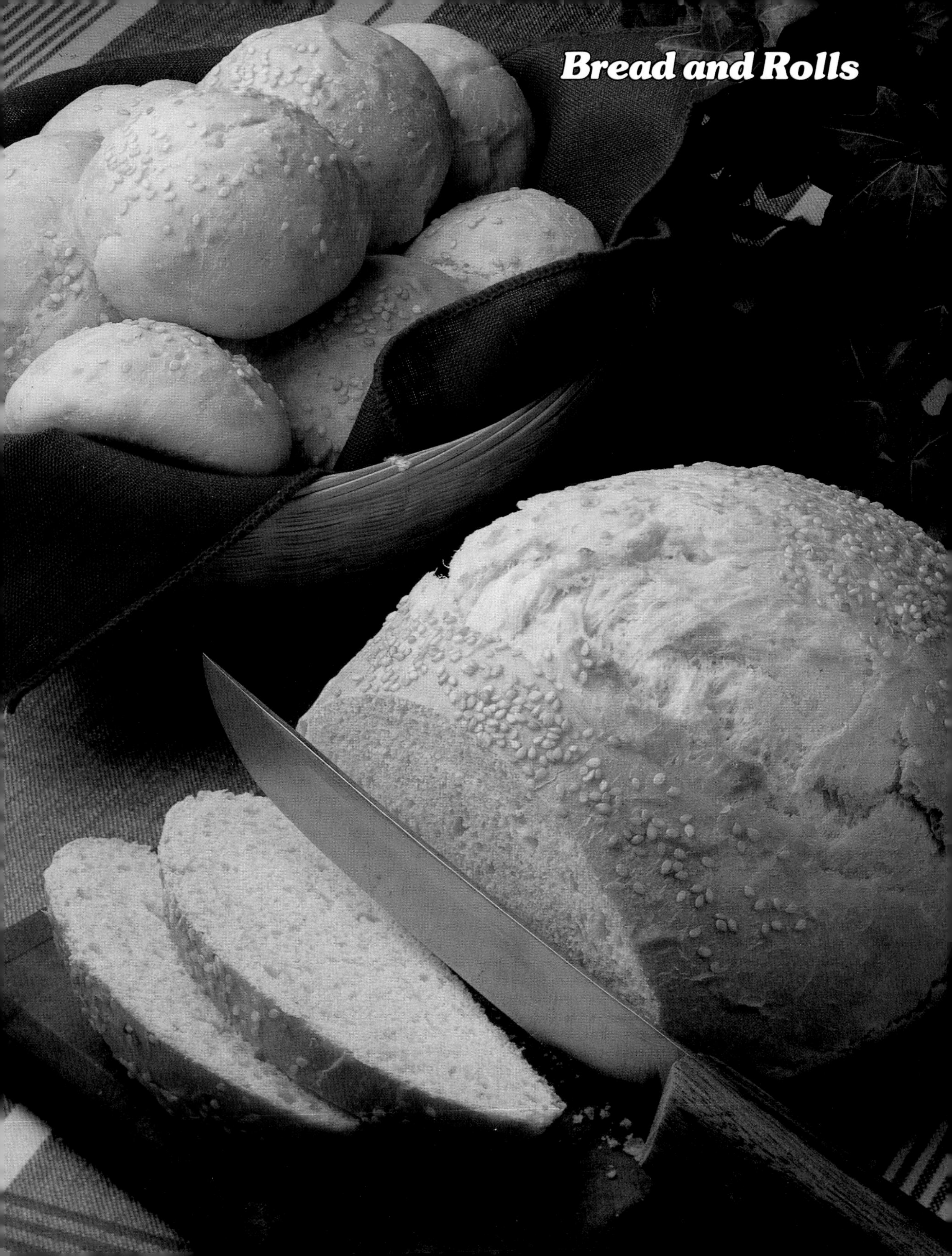

Bread and Rolls

Whole Wheat Bread

3 cups whole wheat flour
3 to 3¹/₂ cups all-purpose flour
¹/₄ cup sugar
1 tablespoon salt
2 packages active dry yeast
1¹/₄ cups water
1 cup milk
¹/₄ cup molasses
¹/₃ cup Crisco shortening

1. Combine 3 cups whole wheat flour and 3 cups all-purpose flour, stirring well. Put 2¹/₂ cups flour mixture into a large mixer bowl. Add sugar, salt, and undissolved yeast; mix well.
2. Combine water, milk, molasses, and Crisco in a saucepan. Place over low heat until liquid is warm (not over 130°); Crisco need not be melted. Add liquid gradually to dry ingredients, beating for 2 minutes at medium speed. Add 1 cup flour mixture and beat for 2 minutes at high speed. Stir in enough remaining flour to make a soft dough. (If more flour is needed, use all-purpose flour.)
3. Turn dough onto a lightly floured surface and knead until smooth and elastic.
4. Place dough in a greased deep bowl and turn to bring greased surface to top. Cover; let rise until doubled (about 1 hour).
5. Punch down dough and divide in half. Shape into loaves. Place in 2 greased 9x5x3-inch or 8¹/₂x4¹/₂x2¹/₂-inch loaf pans. Cover; let rise again until doubled (about 45 minutes).

6. Preheat oven to 375°.
7. Bake at 375° for 35 to 40 minutes or until bread sounds hollow when tapped. Remove from pans and cool on racks.

2 loaves bread

Whole Wheat Rolls

3 cups whole wheat flour
3 to 3¹/₂ cups all-purpose flour
¹/₄ cup sugar
1 tablespoon salt
2 packages active dry yeast
1¹/₄ cups water
1 cup milk
¹/₄ cup molasses
¹/₃ cup Crisco shortening

1. Combine 3 cups whole wheat flour and 3 cups all-purpose flour, stirring well. Put 2¹/₂ cups flour mixture into a large mixer bowl. Add sugar, salt, and undissolved yeast; mix well.
2. Combine water, milk, molasses, and Crisco in a saucepan. Place over low heat until liquid is warm (not over 130°); Crisco need not be melted. Add liquid gradually to dry ingredients, beating for 2 minutes at medium speed. Add 1 cup flour mixture and beat for 2 minutes at high speed. Stir in enough remaining flour to make a soft dough. (If more flour is needed, use all-purpose flour.)
3. Turn dough onto a lightly floured surface and knead until smooth and elastic.
4. Place dough in a greased deep bowl and turn to bring greased surface to top. Cover; let rise until doubled (about 1 hour).

5. Punch down dough; shape dough as desired for 36 rolls. Place on ungreased cookie sheets or in greased muffin cups. Cover; let rise in a warm place until doubled (30 to 45 minutes).
6. Preheat oven to 400°.
7. Bake at 400° for 10 to 12 minutes or until lightly browned.

3 dozen rolls

Pan Rolls

2 packages active dry yeast
2 cups warm water (110 to 115°)
¹/₂ cup instant nonfat dry milk
3 tablespoons sugar
1 tablespoon salt
¹/₃ cup Crisco shortening, melted
5¹/₂ to 6 cups all-purpose flour

1. Sprinkle yeast over warm water in a large mixer bowl. Add dry milk, sugar, salt, melted Crisco, and 3 cups flour. Blend at low speed until moistened, then beat for 3 minutes at medium speed. Using a spoon, stir in enough remaining flour to make a soft dough.
2. Turn dough onto a lightly floured surface and knead until smooth and elastic. Divide dough into 24 pieces; shape into balls. Place in 2 greased 8-inch round cake pans. Cover; let rise until doubled (about 30 minutes).
3. Preheat oven to 400°.
4. Bake at 400° for 15 to 20 minutes or until golden brown.

2 dozen rolls

Anadama Bread

1 cup yellow cornmeal
1/3 cup Crisco shortening
1/2 cup molasses
2 teaspoons salt
2 cups boiling water
1 package active dry yeast
1/4 cup warm water (110 to 115°)
5 to 6 cups all-purpose flour

1. Combine cornmeal, Crisco, molasses, and salt in a large bowl. Stir in boiling water. Let cool to lukewarm.
2. Meanwhile, sprinkle yeast over warm water; let stand until softened.
3. Add 1 cup flour to lukewarm mixture; beat until very smooth. Mix in softened yeast. Add about half of remaining flour and beat until very smooth. Mix in enough remaining flour to make a soft dough.
4. Turn dough onto a lightly floured surface. Cover; let rest for 10 minutes. Knead dough until smooth and elastic.
5. Place dough in a greased deep bowl and turn to bring greased surface to top. Cover; let rise in a warm place until doubled (about 1 hour).
6. Punch down dough; divide in half. Shape into loaves. Place in 2 greased 9x5x3-inch loaf pans. Cover; let rise again until doubled (about 1 hour).
7. Preheat oven to 375°.
8. Bake at 375° for 30 to 35 minutes or until bread tests done. Remove from pans and cool on racks.

2 loaves bread

Oatmeal Raisin Bread

1 1/2 cups boiling water
1 1/2 cups uncooked oats
1/4 cup dark molasses
1/3 cup Crisco shortening
1/4 cup sugar
1 tablespoon salt
1 cup raisins
2 packages active dry yeast
1/2 cup warm water (110 to 115°)
2 eggs
4 1/2 cups all-purpose flour

1. Pour boiling water over oats, molasses, Crisco, sugar, and salt in a large bowl; stir until Crisco is melted. Stir in raisins. Cool to warm (110 to 115°).
2. Sprinkle yeast over warm water; let stand until softened. Add to warm mixture in bowl. Add eggs, one at a time, beating well after each addition. Add about one-half of flour, 1/2 cup at a time, beating vigorously after each addition. Beat in remaining flour (dough will be soft).
3. Place dough in a greased deep bowl and turn to bring greased surface to top. Cover; let rise in a warm place until doubled (45 minutes to 1 hour).
4. Beat down dough with a spoon and divide in half. Spread each half evenly in a greased 9x5x3-inch loaf pan. Cover; let rise again until doubled (about 45 minutes).
5. Preheat oven to 350°.
6. Bake at 350° for 40 to 45 minutes. Let cool for 10 minutes in pans on a rack; remove from pans.

2 loaves bread

French Bread

*1³/₄ cups warm water (110 to
   115°)*
2 packages active dry yeast
2 tablespoons sugar
2 teaspoons salt
*2 tablespoons Crisco
   shortening, melted*
*4³/₄ to 5¹/₄ cups sifted all-
   purpose flour*
1 egg white, beaten until frothy

1. Pour warm water into a
large bowl. Sprinkle yeast
over water and stir until
dissolved. Blend in sugar, salt,
and melted Crisco. Add 3 cups
flour. Beat with a wooden
spoon until smooth.
2. Stir in enough additional
flour to make a soft dough.
Turn dough out on a lightly
floured surface. Knead until
smooth and elastic. Shape
into a ball.
3. Place in a greased bowl and
turn to grease top of dough.
Cover; let rise in a warm place
until doubled (about 1 hour).
4. Punch down dough. Divide
in half. Roll each half on a
lightly floured surface to form
a 15x8-inch rectangle. Roll up
tightly as for a jelly roll. Place
loaves seam-side-down on a
large greased cookie sheet;
fold ends under.
5. With a sharp knife, slash
dough diagonally down length
of loaf at 1-inch intervals.
Brush with beaten egg white.
Let rise uncovered 20 minutes.
6. Preheat oven to 400°.
7. Place a large shallow pan
on lower oven rack and fill
with boiling water. Place
bread on center rack.
8. Bake at 400° for 30 minutes
or until golden. Cool on racks.

2 loaves bread

Limpa

2 cups boiling water
¹/₄ cup light molasses
¹/₄ cup Crisco shortening
¹/₂ teaspoon anise seed
¹/₂ teaspoon fennel seed
¹/₄ teaspoon caraway seed
*¹/₄ teaspoon grated orange
   peel*
1 package active dry yeast
1¹/₄ cups rye flour
1¹/₄ cups whole wheat flour
¹/₂ cup sugar
1 teaspoon salt
*¹/₂ teaspoon crushed
   cardamom seed*
1 egg, beaten
3¹/₂ to 4 cups all-purpose flour

1. Pour boiling water over
molasses, Crisco, anise seed,
fennel seed, caraway seed, and
orange peel in a bowl. Cool
slightly (should not be
warmer than 130°).
2. Combine yeast, rye flour,
wheat flour, sugar, salt, and
crushed cardamom in a large
bowl. Stir in molasses mixture
and egg until well blended.

Stir in enough remaining all-
purpose flour until dough no
longer clings to sides of bowl.
3. Turn dough onto a lightly
floured surface and knead for
5 minutes or until smooth and
elastic.
4. Place dough in a greased
large bowl and turn to bring
greased surface to top. Cover;
let rise in a warm place until
doubled (about 45 minutes).
5. Punch down dough and
turn onto lightly floured
surface. Divide in half; shape
into round loaves. Place each
on a greased cookie sheet.
Cover with oiled waxed paper
or plastic wrap; let rise again
until doubled (about 45
minutes).
6. Preheat oven to 375°.
7. With a sharp knife, cut an
X on top of each doubled loaf.
8. Bake at 375° for 30 to 35
minutes or until bread sounds
hollow when tapped. Cool on
racks.

2 loaves bread

Easy Mixer Bread

2 packages active dry yeast
2 cups warm water (110 to
  115°)
¹/₂ cup instant nonfat dry milk
3 tablespoons sugar
1 tablespoon salt
¹/₃ cup Crisco shortening,
  melted
5¹/₂ to 6 cups all-purpose flour

1. Sprinkle yeast over warm
water in a large mixer bowl.
Add dry milk, sugar, salt,
melted Crisco, and 3 cups
flour. Blend at low speed until
moistened, then beat for 3
minutes at medium speed.
Using a spoon, stir in enough
remaining flour to make a soft
dough.
2. Turn dough onto a lightly
floured surface and knead until
smooth and elastic. Divide
dough in half. Roll each half
into a 12x6-inch rectangle.
Roll up, starting with 6-inch
side. Place seam-side-down in
2 greased 9x5x3-inch loaf
pans.
3. Cover; let rise in a warm
place until doubled (about 45
minutes).
4. Preheat oven to 400°.
5. Bake at 400° for 30 minutes.
Remove from pans and cool
on racks.

2 loaves bread

Cinnamon Bread

2 packages active dry yeast
2 cups warm water (110 to
  115°)
¹/₂ cup instant nonfat dry milk
3 tablespoons sugar
1 tablespoon salt
¹/₃ cup Crisco shortening,
  melted
5¹/₂ to 6 cups all-purpose flour
1 tablespoon Crisco
  shortening, melted
¹/₄ cup sugar
2 teaspoons ground cinnamon

1. Sprinkle yeast over warm
water in a large mixer bowl.
Add dry milk, 3 tablespoons
sugar, salt, ¹/₃ cup melted
Crisco, and 3 cups flour. Blend
at low speed until moistened,
then beat for 3 minutes at
medium speed. Using a spoon,
stir in enough remaining flour
to make a soft dough.
2. Turn dough onto a lightly
floured surface and knead
until smooth and elastic.
Divide dough in half. Roll
each half into a 12x6-inch
rectangle; spread each with
half of the remaining melted
Crisco. Combine ¹/₄ cup sugar
and cinnamon; sprinkle half of
mixture over each rectangle.
Roll up, starting with 6-inch
side. Place seam-side-down in
2 greased 9x5x3-inch loaf
pans.
3. Cover; let rise in a warm
place until doubled (about 45
minutes).
4. Preheat oven to 400°.
5. Bake at 400° for 30
minutes. Remove from pans
and cool on racks.

2 loaves bread

Easy Mixer Rolls

3 Different Ways to Shape Rolls

Crescents: Roll dough into two 12-inch circles. Brush with melted butter. Cut each into 16 wedges. Roll up wedge toward point. Place point-down on cookie sheet; curve ends.

Twists: Roll dough into 18x10-inch rectangle. Cut into 10x3/4-inch strips. Form a circle with each strip; twist and seal edges.

Pinwheels: Roll dough into two 12x8-inch rectangles. Sprinkle with cinnamon sugar and roll up as for a jelly roll. Cut each roll into twelve 1-inch slices. Place cut-side-up in muffin cups.

Easy Mixer Rolls

2 packages active dry yeast
2 cups warm water (110 to 115°)
1/2 cup instant nonfat dry milk
3 tablespoons sugar
1 tablespoon salt
1/3 cup Crisco shortening, melted
5 1/2 to 6 cups all-purpose flour

1. Sprinkle yeast over warm water in a large mixer bowl. Add dry milk, sugar, salt, melted Crisco, and 3 cups flour. Blend at low speed until moistened, then beat for 3 minutes at medium speed. Using a spoon, stir in enough remaining flour to make a soft dough.

2. Turn dough onto a lightly floured surface and knead until smooth and elastic. Roll out dough and shape into crescents, twists, or pinwheels (see detailed instructions for shaping). Arrange crescents and twists on ungreased cookie sheets and put pinwheels into greased muffin pans.

3. Cover; let rise in a warm place until doubled (about 45 minutes).

4. Preheat oven to 400°.

5. Bake at 400° until golden brown; crescents and twists for 10 to 12 minutes, pinwheels for 15 to 20 minutes.

24 twists or pinwheels or 32 crescents

103

Basil Pinwheels

1 package active dry yeast
1/4 cup warm water (110 to
  115°)
3 tablespoons Crisco
  shortening
1 tablespoon sugar
1 1/2 teaspoons salt
3/4 cup milk, scalded
2 1/2 to 3 cups sifted all-purpose
  flour
2 tablespoons butter or
  margarine, melted
2 teaspoons dried basil
1/2 teaspoon onion powder

1. Sprinkle yeast over warm water; set aside.
2. Put Crisco, sugar, and salt into a large mixer bowl. Add scalded milk and blend; cool to warm (not over 130°). Stir in softened yeast. Add 1 cup flour. Blend at low speed until moistened, then beat for 3 minutes at medium speed. Using a spoon, stir in enough remaining flour to make a soft dough.
3. Turn dough onto a lightly floured surface and knead until smooth and elastic. Shape into a ball. Place dough in a greased deep bowl and turn to grease top. Cover; let rise in a warm place until doubled (about 1 hour).
4. Punch down dough. Roll dough into a 12-inch square on a lightly floured surface. Combine melted butter, basil, and onion powder. Spoon onto dough and spread evenly. Roll up as for a jelly roll.
5. Using a sharp knife, cut into 12 equal slices. Arrange cut-side-up in a greased 9x1 1/2-inch round pan, placing 9 rolls around edge of pan and 3 rolls in center. Cover; let rise until doubled (45 to 60 minutes).
6. Preheat oven to 375°.
7. Bake at 375° for 25 minutes or until golden brown.

1 dozen rolls

Refrigerator Rolls

1 package active dry yeast
1/2 cup warm water (110 to 115°)
1 cup milk, scalded
2/3 cup Crisco shortening
1/2 cup sugar
2 teaspoons salt
1 cup mashed potatoes
2 eggs
6 to 6 1/2 cups all-purpose flour

1. Sprinkle yeast over warm water; let stand until softened.
2. Pour scalded milk over Crisco, sugar, and salt in a bowl; stir until Crisco is melted. Stir in mashed potatoes. Add eggs, one at a time; stir well after each addition. Stir in 1 cup flour. Add softened yeast and mix well. Stir in enough remaining flour to make a soft dough.
3. Turn dough onto a lightly floured surface. Cover; let rest for 10 minutes. Knead dough until smooth and elastic.
4. Place dough in a greased deep bowl and turn to bring greased surface to top. Cover tightly and set in refrigerator. Dough can be refrigerated for 1 to 3 days.
5. Shape dough into rolls 2 hours before baking. Cover; let rise until doubled.
6. Preheat oven to 425°.
7. Bake at 425° for 15 minutes or until golden brown. Brush with melted butter, if desired.

3 dozen rolls

Poppy Seed Breadsticks

1 cup hot milk (about 120°)
1/4 cup Crisco shortening
1 tablespoon sugar
1 teaspoon salt
1 package active dry yeast
3 to 3 1/2 cups all-purpose flour
1 egg
2 tablespoons water
Poppy seed

1. Combine milk, Crisco, sugar, and salt. Cool slightly.
2. Combine yeast and 2 1/2 cups flour in a large bowl. Stir in milk mixture until well blended. Beat in enough remaining flour to make a stiff dough.
3. Turn onto a lightly floured surface. Knead for 5 minutes or until smooth and elastic. Let rest for 5 minutes.
4. With a sharp knife, cut dough into 72 equal pieces. Roll out each piece between palms of hands or on a flat surface to make a 6-inch strip. Place on greased cookie sheets.
5. Combine egg and water. Brush breadsticks with egg mixture and sprinkle with poppy seed. Cover; let rest for 20 minutes.
6. Preheat oven to 300°.
7. Bake at 300° for 45 to 50 minutes or until golden brown. Cool on racks.

72 breadsticks

Sugared Doughnuts

1 cup milk, scalded
¹/₃ cup Crisco shortening
¹/₃ cup sugar
1 teaspoon salt
2 eggs
2¹/₂ to 3 cups all-purpose flour
1 package active dry yeast
Crisco shortening for deep
  frying
Granulated sugar for coating

1. Pour scalded milk over Crisco, sugar, and salt in a bowl; stir until Crisco is melted. Add eggs, one at a time; beat well after each addition.

2. Combine 2 cups flour and yeast in a large bowl, add milk mixture, and beat with a spoon until smooth. Stir in enough remaining flour to make a soft dough.

3. Turn dough onto a lightly floured surface and knead until smooth and elastic.

4. Place dough in a greased deep bowl and turn to bring greased surface to top.

5. Cover; let rise in a warm place until doubled (about 1 hour).

6. Punch down dough. Roll to ¹/₂-inch thickness on a lightly floured surface. Cut with a floured 3-inch doughnut cutter.

Place doughnuts and holes on a cookie sheet; cover and let rise until doubled (about 30 minutes).

7. Heat Crisco to 365° in a large saucepan or deep fryer.

8. Fry doughnuts and holes, 4 or 5 at a time, in hot Crisco for 2 minutes or until golden brown; turn several times during frying.

9. Remove and drain on paper towels.

10. Shake a few doughnuts and holes at a time with sugar in a paper bag.

About 18 doughnuts and holes

Deep-Fried Treats

Bismarcks

1 cup milk, scalded
1/3 cup Crisco shortening
1/3 cup sugar
1 teaspoon salt
2 eggs
2 1/2 to 3 cups all-purpose flour
1 package active dry yeast
Crisco shortening for deep
   frying
Jelly or jam
Granulated sugar for coating

1. Pour scalded milk over Crisco, sugar, and salt in a bowl; stir until Crisco is melted. Add eggs, one at a time, beating well after each addition.
2. Combine 2 cups flour and yeast in a large bowl, add milk mixture, and beat with a spoon until smooth. Stir in enough remaining flour to make a soft dough.
3. Turn dough onto a lightly floured surface and knead until smooth and elastic.
4. Place dough in a greased deep bowl and turn to bring greased surface to top.
5. Cover; let rise in a warm place until doubled (1 1/4 to 1 1/2 hours).
6. Punch down dough. Roll to 1/2-inch thickness on a lightly floured surface. Cut with a floured 3-inch round cutter. Place on a cookie sheet; cover and let rise until doubled (about 30 minutes).
7. Heat Crisco to 365° in a large deep saucepan or deep fryer.
8. Fry bismarcks uncrowded in hot Crisco for 2 minutes or until golden brown; turn several times during frying.
9. Remove and drain on paper towels.

10. Cut a slit through side of each to center. Force about 1 teaspoon or more jam or jelly into center and press lightly to close slit.
11. Shake 2 or 3 bismarcks at a time with sugar in a bag.

18 bismarcks

Fried Bread

1 package active dry yeast
1 cup warm water (110° to 115°)
2 tablespoons sugar
1 1/2 teaspoons salt
2 tablespoons Crisco
   shortening
2 1/2 to 3 cups sifted all-purpose
   flour
Crisco shortening for deep
   frying

1. Sprinkle yeast over warm water in a large mixer bowl. Add sugar, salt, 2 tablespoons Crisco, and 1 1/2 cups flour. Blend at low speed until moistened, then beat for 3 minutes at medium speed. Using a spoon, stir in enough remaining flour to make a soft dough.
2. Turn dough onto a lightly floured surface and knead until smooth and elastic. Place dough in a greased deep bowl and turn to grease top. Cover; let rise in a warm place until doubled (about 1 hour).
3. Heat Crisco to 365° in deep saucepan or deep fryer.
4. Cut yeast dough into 1-inch pieces; stretch pieces slightly and fry in hot Crisco for 1 1/2 minutes or until golden brown; turn over once.
5. Drain on paper towels. Shake in a bag with *cinnamon sugar*. Serve warm.

About 4 dozen pieces

Cinnamon Puffs

1 package active dry yeast
1 teaspoon sugar
1/4 cup warm water (110 to
   115°)
1 egg
1 tablespoon Crisco
   shortening, melted
1/2 cup milk, scalded
1/2 cup water
1/4 teaspoon salt
2 cups all-purpose flour
Crisco shortening for deep
   frying
1/2 cup honey
1/2 teaspoon ground cinnamon

1. Sprinkle yeast and sugar over warm water; let stand until softened.
2. Beat egg and melted Crisco with a fork in a bowl. Stir in milk, water, salt, and 1 cup flour; beat with a spoon until smooth. Stir in softened yeast, then remaining flour.
3. Cover; let rise in a warm place until doubled (about 1 hour).
4. Heat Crisco to 365° in a large saucepan or deep fryer.
5. Stir down batter with a spoon. Drop rounded measuring tablespoons of batter into hot Crisco. (Do not use a fryer basket.) Fry puffs, 6 to 8 at a time, for 3 minutes or until golden brown.
6. Remove and drain on paper towels. Keep warm while frying remaining puffs.
7. Combine and heat honey and cinnamon in a small saucepan. Dip warm puffs in warm honey mixture. Drain on a rack.

2 to 2 1/2 dozen puffs

Crisscross Coffeecake

Coffeecake:
4 to 4¹/₂ cups all-purpose flour
2 packages active dry yeast
1¹/₂ teaspoons salt
1 cup milk
¹/₄ cup water
¹/₂ cup Crisco shortening
¹/₂ cup sugar
1 egg

Cream Filling:
¹/₄ cup Crisco shortening
2 tablespoons powdered
  non-dairy creamer
1¹/₂ cups confectioners' sugar
¹/₈ teaspoon salt
1 teaspoon vanilla extract
1 tablespoon water
1 cup chopped walnuts or
  pecans

1. For Coffeecake, combine 2 cups flour, yeast, and salt in a large mixer bowl.
2. Heat milk, water, Crisco, and sugar in a saucepan over low heat just until Crisco is melted. If temperature goes above 130°, mixture should be cooled to 130° before adding to dry ingredients.
3. Add liquid to dry ingredients; beat until smooth (about 2 minutes at medium speed). Add egg and ¹/₂ cup flour; beat for 2 minutes at medium speed. Beat in enough remaining flour to make a soft dough.
4. Turn dough out onto a floured surface and knead until smooth and elastic.
5. Place dough in a greased deep bowl and turn to bring greased surface to top. Cover; let rise in a warm place until doubled (about 1 hour).
6. While dough is rising, prepare Cream Filling.

7. For Cream Filling, put all ingredients except nuts into a small mixer bowl. Blend at low speed, then beat 2 minutes at medium speed.
8. Punch down dough; divide in half. Roll each half into a 12x8-inch rectangle. Transfer rectangle to a greased baking sheet with sides. Spread half the Cream Filling lengthwise down center of each rectangle, leaving 2 inches on either side plain. Sprinkle with half the nuts. Make about 12 slashes, each 2 inches long, down long sides of each coffeecake. Fold strips alternately over filling, herringbone fashion.
9. Cover; let rise again until doubled (about 45 to 60 minutes).
10. Preheat oven to 350°.
11. Bake at 350° for 30 minutes or until golden brown. Remove from baking sheets and cool on racks.
12. Frost with a confectioners' sugar icing, if desired.

2 coffeecakes

Filled Coffeecake

Coffeecake:
¹/₂ cup milk
¹/₂ cup Crisco shortening
¹/₂ cup sugar
1¹/₂ teaspoons salt
2 packages active dry yeast
¹/₂ cup warm water (110 to 115°)
4 to 5 cups all-purpose flour
2 eggs

Cottage Cheese Date Filling:
1¹/₂ cups finely chopped pitted
  dates
1 cup small-curd cottage cheese
¹/₄ cup sugar
2 egg yolks, slightly beaten
2 teaspoons grated lemon peel

1. For Coffeecake, heat milk, Crisco, sugar, and salt in a small saucepan over low heat; stir occasionally until Crisco is melted. Pour into a large bowl. Cool to lukewarm.
2. Sprinkle yeast over warm water; let stand until softened.
3. Beat 1 cup flour into milk mixture. Beat in eggs, then softened yeast. Beat in enough remaining flour to make a soft dough.
4. Turn dough onto a lightly floured surface and knead until smooth and elastic.
5. Place dough in a greased deep bowl and turn to bring greased surface to top. Cover; let rise in a warm place until doubled (1 to 1¹/₂ hours).
6. Prepare filling while dough is rising. For Cottage Cheese Date Filling, combine all ingredients.
7. Punch down dough; divide in half. Roll each half into an 18x10-inch rectangle on a lightly floured surface. Spread half of filling over each rectangle; cut into three 10x6-inch strips. Starting with a long side, roll up each strip and twist slightly. Braid 3 rolls together and place in a greased 9x5x3-inch loaf pan, tucking ends under.
8. Cover pans with plastic wrap. Refrigerate for 2 to 24 hours.
9. When ready to bake, preheat oven to 350°.
10. Meanwhile, remove loaves from refrigerator, uncover, and let stand at room temperature for 15 minutes.
11. Bake at 350° for 45 to 50 minutes or until bread tests done. Immediately remove from pans and cool on racks.

2 filled coffeecakes

Breakfast Treat

Caramel Pecan Rolls

1 package active dry yeast
¼ cup warm water (110 to 115°)
1 cup milk, scalded
⅓ cup Crisco shortening
⅓ cup sugar
1½ teaspoons salt
2 eggs
4 to 4½ cups all-purpose flour
3 tablespoons butter or margarine

¾ cup dark corn syrup
⅓ cup plus ½ cup packed brown sugar
1 cup raisins
½ cup coarsely chopped pecans
1 tablespoon ground cinnamon
2 tablespoons Crisco shortening, melted

1. Sprinkle yeast over warm water; let stand until softened.

2. Pour scalded milk over ⅓ cup Crisco, sugar, and salt in a large bowl; stir until Crisco is melted. Add eggs, one at a time, beating until smooth after each addition. Stir in 1 cup flour, then softened yeast. Add enough remaining flour to make a soft dough.

3. Turn dough onto a lightly floured surface and knead until smooth and elastic.

4. Place dough in a greased deep bowl and turn to bring greased surface to top. Cover; let rise in a warm place until doubled (about 1 hour).

5. Melt butter in a small saucepan; stir in corn syrup and ⅓ cup brown sugar. Spread mixture evenly over bottom of a 13x9x2-inch baking pan.

6. Combine raisins, pecans, ½ cup brown sugar, and cinnamon; set aside.

7. Punch down dough. Roll out to a 16x12-inch rectangle on a lightly floured surface. Spread with melted Crisco. Sprinkle raisin mixture evenly over dough. Roll up as for a jelly roll, starting with a longer side. Cut into 15 slices. Place slices cut-side-up in pan.

8. Cover pan tightly with plastic wrap and refrigerate for 2 to 24 hours.

9. When ready to bake, remove from refrigerator, uncover, and let stand at room temperature for 15 minutes.

10. Preheat oven to 350°.

11. Bake at 350° for 35 to 40 minutes. Invert pan immediately on a large platter or tray; shake to loosen rolls. Serve hot.

15 pecan rolls

Basic Bread Making

An electric mixer makes beating easy. Mix yeast with part of the flour; add warm liquid and beat with mixer. Stir in remaining flour.

On floured board, knead dough until smooth and elastic. Fold dough over and push down with heel of hand; give dough quarter turn. Repeat method.

Place dough in greased bowl. Cover and let rise in warm place. An unheated oven may be used; place pan of hot water on lower rack and covered bowl of dough on top rack.

Dough is ready for shaping when doubled in size. When dough has reached the top of the bowl, check to see if two fingers pressed ½ inch into dough will leave indentations.

Punch down dough to release air bubbles to give a firmer texture to the bread. Divide dough in half.

On floured board, roll each half of dough to 12x8-inch rectangle of uniform thickness. Break any air bubbles with rolling pin.

Roll dough tightly as for jelly roll from narrow edge to form loaf; seal edge and ends. Place seam-side-down in greased loaf dish.

Brush top of loaf with mixture of 1 beaten egg and 1 tablespoon milk to achieve a shiny, golden crust.

Tap top of baked loaf to test for doneness. If loaf sounds hollow, bread is properly baked. Remove loaf from dish at once. Cool before slicing.

"Quick breads" are made without yeast and are easy and fast to prepare. For the quickest breads, check the recipes using Homemade Quick Bread Mix. This mix can be prepared in advance for your busy days.

Besides delicious breads, this chapter also includes quick recipes for muffins and doughnuts, coffeecakes, pancakes and waffles.

Ginger Bran Loaf

1 1/2 cups sifted all-purpose flour
2/3 cup sugar
1 tablespoon baking powder
1 teaspoon ground ginger
1/2 teaspoon salt
1 egg
1 cup milk
1/4 cup Crisco shortening, melted and cooled
1 1/2 cups ready-to-eat bran flakes

1. Preheat oven to 350°.
2. Combine flour, sugar, baking powder, ginger, and salt in a bowl.
3. Beat egg in a bowl until thick. Add milk and melted Crisco, continuing to beat until blended. Add to dry ingredients and mix just enough to moisten flour. Add bran flakes and with not more than 15 strokes, quickly and lightly stir until bran flakes are just moistened.
4. Turn batter into a greased 8 1/2x4 1/2x2 1/2-inch loaf pan.

5. Bake at 350° for 45 to 50 minutes or until a toothpick inserted in center comes out clean.
6. Cool for 5 minutes in pan on a rack, remove from pan, and cool thoroughly on rack.

1 loaf bread

Blueberry Bread

3 cups all-purpose flour
1/4 cup sugar
4 teaspoons baking powder
1 teaspoon salt
1/2 teaspoon baking soda
1/4 cup Crisco shortening
1 tablespoon grated orange peel
2 eggs
1 1/4 cups milk
1 cup fresh or dry-pack frozen blueberries

1. Preheat oven to 375°.
2. Combine flour, sugar, baking powder, salt, and baking soda in a large bowl. Cut Crisco into dry ingredients with a pastry blender or 2 knives until mixture resembles coarse crumbs. Stir in orange peel. Beat eggs and milk together with a fork; add to bowl and stir only until dry ingredients are moistened. Rinse and drain blueberries and fold in carefully.
3. Turn batter into a greased 9x5x3-inch loaf pan.
4. Bake at 375° for 50 to 55 minutes or until golden brown.
5. Cool for 10 minutes in pan on a rack. Remove from pan and cool slightly on a rack before slicing.

1 loaf bread

Orange Nut Bread

1 large orange
1/2 cup dark seedless raisins
3/4 cup canned applesauce
1 egg, slightly beaten
3 tablespoons Crisco shortening, melted
2 1/2 cups all-purpose flour
1 cup sugar
2 teaspoons baking powder
1 teaspoon baking soda
1 teaspoon salt
3/4 cup chopped walnuts

1. Preheat oven to 350°.
2. Cut orange in half, juice, and reserve 1 orange shell. Add water if needed to make 1/2 cup liquid; reserve. Grind reserved orange shell and raisins through medium blade of food chopper. Add the reserved liquid, applesauce, egg, and melted Crisco; mix well.
3. Combine flour, sugar, baking powder, baking soda, and salt in a bowl. Mix in walnuts. Add orange mixture and stir until blended.
4. Turn batter into a greased 9x5x3-inch loaf pan.
5. Bake at 350° for 60 to 70 minutes or until a toothpick inserted in center comes out clean.
6. Cool for 10 minutes in pan on a rack, remove from pan, and cool on rack. Cool completely before slicing.

1 loaf bread

Vegetable Quick Bread

2 cups all-purpose flour
1 cup whole wheat flour
1 cup sugar
1 tablespoon baking powder
1¹/₂ teaspoons ground
 cinnamon
1 teaspoon salt
¹/₂ teaspoon baking soda
¹/₄ teaspoon ground ginger
¹/₃ cup Crisco shortening
2 cups shredded carrots or
 squash such as zucchini
¹/₂ cup finely chopped nuts
¹/₂ cup chopped dates or
 raisins
2 eggs
³/₄ cup milk

1. Preheat oven to 350°.
2. Combine flours, sugar, baking powder, cinnamon, salt, baking soda, and ginger in a large bowl. Cut Crisco into dry ingredients with a pastry blender or 2 knives until mixture resembles coarse crumbs. Stir in carrots, nuts, and dates. Beat eggs and milk together with a fork; add to bowl and stir only until dry ingredients are moistened. Batter will be stiff.
3. Divide batter evenly in 2 greased 8¹/₂x4¹/₂x1¹/₂-inch loaf pans.
4. Bake at 350° for 1 hour or until a toothpick inserted in center comes out clean.
5. Cool for 10 minutes in pan on a rack. Remove from pan and cool on a rack before slicing.

2 loaves bread

Oatmeal Soda Bread

3 cups sifted all-purpose flour
¹/₃ cup sugar
2¹/₂ teaspoons baking soda
1¹/₂ teaspoons salt
3 tablespoons Crisco shortening
1³/₄ cups uncooked old-
 fashioned oats
1 egg, beaten
1³/₄ cups buttermilk

1. Preheat oven to 375°.
2. Combine flour, sugar, baking soda, and salt in a bowl. Cut in Crisco with a pastry blender or 2 knives. Mix in oats. Gradually add a mixture of egg and buttermilk, stirring until well blended.
3. Turn mixture into a greased 9x1¹/₂-inch round layer cake pan; spread evenly. Cut a deep cross into top.
4. Bake at 375° for 45 to 50 minutes or until a toothpick inserted in center comes out clean.

1 loaf bread

Onion Bread

7 tablespoons Crisco
 shortening, divided
1 cup chopped onion
¹/₄ teaspoon salt
Dash ground red pepper
2 cups sifted all-purpose flour
4 teaspoons baking powder
1 teaspoon salt
³/₄ cup milk
¹/₂ cup shredded Cheddar cheese

1. Preheat oven to 450°.
2. Melt 2 tablespoons Crisco in a skillet over medium heat. Stir in onion. Cook and stir for 10 minutes or until tender. Stir in salt and red pepper.
3. Combine flour, baking powder, and salt in a large bowl. Cut 5 tablespoons Crisco into dry ingredients with a pastry blender or 2 knives until mixture resembles coarse crumbs. Stir in milk until dry ingredients are moistened.
4. Spread batter into greased 8x8x2-inch pan. Spread onions over top. Sprinkle with cheese.
5. Bake at 450° for 20 minutes or until toothpick inserted in center comes out clean. Serve warm.

12 servings

Chocolate Banana Bread

1¹/₂ cups sifted all-purpose flour
¹/₂ cup unsweetened cocoa
²/₃ cup sugar
1 teaspoon baking powder
¹/₂ teaspoon baking soda
¹/₂ teaspoon salt
¹/₂ cup Crisco shortening
1 cup mashed ripe bananas
 (about 2 medium bananas)
2 eggs, slightly beaten

1. Preheat oven to 350°.
2. Combine flour, cocoa, sugar, baking powder, baking soda, and salt in a large bowl. Cut in Crisco with pastry blender or two knives until mixture resembles coarse meal. Add bananas and eggs; stir with a fork just until blended.
3. Spread batter evenly in a greased and floured 9x5x3-inch loaf pan.
4. Bake at 350° for 55 minutes or until a toothpick inserted in center comes out clean. Cool for 10 minutes in pan on a rack. Remove from pan.

1 loaf bread

Crisco Quick Bread Mix

Homemade Crisco Quick Bread Mix

10 cups sifted all-purpose flour
1/3 cup baking powder
1/4 cup sugar
1 tablespoon salt
2 cups Crisco shortening

1. Combine flour, baking powder, sugar, and salt in a large bowl. Cut in Crisco with pastry blender or 2 knives until mixture resembles coarse meal.
2. Store in covered container up to 6 weeks at room temperature. For longer storage, place in freezer.
3. To measure, spoon mix into measuring cup and level with spatula.

12 cups mix

Honey Blueberry Bread

3 cups Homemade Crisco Quick Bread Mix (above)
1/4 cup sugar
1/2 cup chopped pecans
1 1/2 teaspoons grated lemon peel
2 eggs
1/2 cup water
1/3 cup honey
1 tablespoon instant coffee powder
1 1/2 cups fresh or dry-pack frozen blueberries

1. Preheat oven to 350°.
2. Combine Crisco mix, sugar, pecans, and lemon peel in a large bowl.
3. Beat eggs, water, honey, and coffee powder. Add to bowl and stir only until dry ingredients are moistened. Rinse and drain blueberries and fold in carefully.
4. Turn batter into a greased 9x5x3-inch loaf pan.
5. Bake at 350° for 1 hour and 10 minutes to 1 hour and 20 minutes or until golden and a toothpick inserted in center comes out clean.
6. Cool for 10 minutes in pan on a rack. Remove from pan and cool thoroughly on rack before slicing.
7. Slice bread with a serrated knife. If desired, spread slices with butter or cream cheese.

1 loaf bread

Date Nut Bread

2 1/2 cups Homemade Crisco Quick Bread Mix (on this page)
1/4 cup sugar
1 cup chopped walnuts
1 package (8 ounces) diced dates
1 egg, beaten
3/4 cup milk

1. Preheat oven to 350°.
2. Combine Crisco mix, sugar, walnuts, and dates in a bowl. Combine egg and milk. Add to dry mixture and stir only until moistened.
3. Wash, dry, and grease two 1-pound Crisco cans. Divide batter evenly in cans.
4. Bake at 350° for 65 to 70 minutes or until a toothpick inserted in center comes out clean. Cool for 10 minutes in cans on a rack. Invert and remove bread from cans and cool thoroughly on rack.

2 loaves bread

Olive Quick Bread

2 1/2 cups Homemade Crisco Quick Bread Mix (on this page)
1/4 cup sugar
1 cup chopped nuts
1 cup shredded Colby or mild Cheddar cheese
1 cup chopped pimiento-stuffed green olives
1 egg
3/4 cup milk

1. Preheat oven to 350°.
2. Combine Crisco mix, sugar, nuts, cheese, and olives in a bowl.
3. Mix egg and milk with a fork. Add to bowl and stir only until dry ingredients are moistened.
4. Spoon batter into a greased 9x5x3-inch loaf pan.
5. Bake at 350° for 55 to 60 minutes or until a toothpick inserted in center comes out clean.
6. Cool for 10 minutes on a rack, remove from pan, and cool completely on rack. Slice and serve with *cream cheese*.

1 loaf bread

Crisco Quick Bread Mix

Pineapple Coconut Loaf

2 cups Homemade Crisco
  Quick Bread Mix
  (opposite page)
1/2 cup packed light brown
  sugar
1 egg
1 can (8 ounces) crushed
  pineapple (undrained)
1/2 cup coarsely chopped
  pecans
1/2 cup flaked coconut
1/4 cup semisweet chocolate
  pieces

Topping:
2 tablespoons sugar
1/2 teaspoon ground cinnamon
2 tablespoons flaked coconut

1. Preheat oven to 350°.
2. Combine Crisco mix and
brown sugar in a bowl. Beat
egg with a fork; stir in
undrained pineapple. Add to
bowl and stir only until dry
ingredients are moistened.
Mix in pecans, coconut, and
chocolate pieces.
3. Turn batter into a greased
9x5x3-inch loaf pan and
spread to corners.
4. For Topping, mix
ingredients and spoon evenly
over batter.
5. Bake at 350° for 50 to 60
minutes or until a toothpick
inserted in center comes out
clean. Cool for 10 minutes in
pan on a rack. Remove from
pan and cool thoroughly on
rack.

1 loaf bread

Nutty Applesauce Bread

2 cups Homemade Crisco
  Quick Bread Mix
  (opposite page)
1/2 cup sugar
1/2 teaspoon baking soda
1/2 teaspoon ground cinnamon
1/4 teaspoon ground nutmeg
1 cup finely chopped nuts
1 egg
1 cup unsweetened applesauce

1. Preheat oven to 350°.
2. Combine Crisco mix, sugar,
baking soda, cinnamon,
nutmeg, and nuts in a large
bowl. Beat egg with a fork;
stir in applesauce. Add to
bowl and stir only until dry
ingredients are moistened.
3. Turn batter into a greased
9x5x3-inch loaf pan.
4. Bake at 350° for 45 to 50
minutes or until golden
brown.
5. Cool for 10 minutes in pan
on a rack. Remove from pan
and cool slightly on a rack
before slicing. Serve with
cream cheese.

1 loaf bread

Apricot Nut Bread

1½ cups coarsely chopped
  dried apricots
1 cup water
2½ cups all-purpose flour
¾ cup sugar
4 teaspoons baking powder
1 teaspoon salt
½ teaspoon baking soda
⅔ cup chopped nuts
1 egg, slightly beaten
1 cup buttermilk
3 tablespoons Crisco
  shortening, melted

1. Preheat oven to 350°.
2. Combine apricots and water
in a heavy saucepan. Bring
to boiling, reduce heat and
simmer, uncovered, for 10
minutes or until water is
absorbed. Cool.
3. Combine flour, sugar,
baking powder, salt, and
baking soda in a large bowl.
Stir in nuts.
4. Combine apricots, egg,
buttermilk, and Crisco. Add
to dry ingredients and stir
only until dry ingredients are
moistened.
5. Turn batter into a greased
(bottom only) 9x5x3-inch loaf
pan.
6. Bake at 350° for 55 to 60
minutes or until a toothpick
inserted in center comes out
clean.
7. Cool for 10 minutes in pan
on rack. Remove from pan;
cool completely before slicing.

1 loaf bread

Glazed Pear Loaf

1 can (16 ounces) Bartlett
  pear halves
2½ cups all-purpose flour
½ cup sugar
1 tablespoon baking powder
1 teaspoon salt
⅛ teaspoon ground cardamom
  or ground mace
½ cup chopped pecans
¼ cup Crisco shortening, melted
1 egg, slightly beaten
2 teaspoons grated lemon peel

Lemon Glaze:
2 teaspoons lemon juice
½ cup confectioners' sugar

1. Preheat oven to 350°.
2. Drain pears, reserving liquid.
Reserve 1 pear half for garnish.
Puree remaining pear halves;
add reserved pear liquid to
pureed pears to equal 1 cup.
3. Combine flour, sugar, baking
powder, salt, and cardamom
in a bowl. Mix in pecans.
4. Combine pureed pear mixture with melted Crisco, egg,
and lemon peel; stir into dry
ingredients until mixed.
5. Turn batter into a greased
8½x4½x2½-inch loaf pan.
6. Slice reserved pear half into
sixths; arrange slices over top
of batter in pan.
7. Bake at 350° for 60 to 65
minutes or until a toothpick
inserted in center comes out
clean. Cool for 10 minutes in
pan on a rack and turn out
onto a rack.
8. Meanwhile, for Lemon
Glaze, blend enough lemon
juice into confectioners' sugar
to make a thin glaze. Spoon
over top of warm bread. Cool.
Wrap in foil and let stand
overnight before slicing.

1 loaf bread

Boston Brown Bread

1 cup whole wheat flour
1 cup rye flour
1 cup yellow cornmeal
1½ teaspoons baking powder
1 teaspoon salt
½ teaspoon baking soda
2 cups buttermilk
¾ cup molasses
2 tablespoons Crisco
  shortening, melted
1 cup dark seedless raisins

1. Mix flours, cornmeal, baking
powder, salt, and baking soda
in a large bowl. Stir in
buttermilk, molasses, melted
Crisco, and raisins until well
mixed.
2. Spoon batter into 4 well-
greased 1-pound vegetable or
fruit cans. Cover with aluminum foil and tie with string.
3. Place cans on a rack in a
large kettle. Pour in boiling
water to come halfway up
sides of cans. Cover and simmer for 2½ to 3 hours. Pour
in more boiling water if
necessary to keep cans in
boiling water to the halfway
point.
4. Remove from kettle and
remove foil. Cool in cans for
10 minutes on a rack. Invert
loaves onto rack. Serve warm.

4 loaves bread

Serving suggestion: For a
nutritious lunch, spread softened
cream cheese between slices of cooled
Boston Brown Bread to make
sandwiches. Cut each sandwich in
half and serve with *fresh fruit*.

Cranberry Orange Muffins

*3 cups Homemade Crisco
   Quick Bread Mix, page 116*
1/2 cup sugar
*1 tablespoon grated orange
   peel*
1 egg
1/2 cup milk
1/2 cup orange juice
*1 cup fresh or dry-pack frozen
   cranberries, rinsed, drained,
   and cut in halves*

1. Preheat oven to 400°.
2. Combine Crisco mix, sugar, and orange peel in a bowl.
3. Beat egg, milk, and orange juice together with a fork. Add to bowl; stir only until dry ingredients are moistened. Carefully fold in cranberries.
4. Spoon batter into 18 greased medium-size muffin cups.
5. Bake at 400° for 18 to 22 minutes or until lightly browned.

18 muffins

Blueberry Sugar Cakes

*3 cups Homemade Crisco
   Quick Bread Mix, page 116*
*1/2 cup plus 1 tablespoon
   sugar, divided*
2 eggs
1 cup milk
*3/4 cup fresh or dry-pack
   frozen blueberries*
1/4 teaspoon ground cinnamon

1. Preheat oven to 400°.
2. Combine Crisco mix and 1/2 cup sugar in a bowl.

3. Beat eggs and milk together with a fork. Add to bowl; stir only until dry ingredients are moistened. Rinse and drain blueberries and fold in carefully.
4. Spoon batter into 18 greased medium-size muffin cups.
5. Combine remaining 1 tablespoon sugar and the cinnamon. Sprinkle over batter.
6. Bake at 400° for 18 to 20 minutes or until lightly browned.

18 muffins

Blueberry Orange Muffins

*2 1/2 cups Homemade Crisco
   Quick Bread Mix, page 116*
3 tablespoons sugar
*1 tablespoon grated orange
   peel*
1 egg
1/2 cup milk
1/4 cup orange juice
*3/4 cup fresh or dry-pack
   frozen blueberries*

1. Preheat oven to 400°.
2. Combine Crisco mix, sugar, and orange peel in a bowl.
3. Beat egg, milk, and orange juice together with a fork. Add to bowl; stir only until dry ingredients are moistened. Rinse and drain blueberries and fold in carefully.
4. Spoon batter into 12 greased medium-size muffin cups.
5. Bake at 400° for 20 minutes or until lightly browned.

12 muffins

Spicy Fruit Muffins

*1 1/2 cups sifted all-purpose
   flour*
1/2 cup sugar
2 teaspoons baking powder
3/4 teaspoon salt
1/2 teaspoon ground cinnamon
1/4 teaspoon ground nutmeg
*1/2 cup chopped mixed dried
   fruit*
1/2 cup finely chopped walnuts
1 egg, slightly beaten
1 cup milk
*1/4 cup Crisco shortening,
   melted*

1. Preheat oven to 425°.
2. Sift flour, sugar, baking powder, salt, cinnamon, and nutmeg together into a large bowl. Mix in dried fruit and walnuts.
3. Beat egg, milk, and Crisco together with a fork in a small bowl. Add to large bowl; stir only until dry ingredients are moistened.
4. Spoon about 2 rounded tablespoons of batter into each of 12 greased 2 3/4-inch muffin cups.
5. Bake at 425° for 20 to 25 minutes or until a toothpick inserted in center comes out clean. Serve warm with *butter*.

12 muffins

Pineapple Oatmeal Muffins

1 can (8 ounces) crushed
  pineapple (undrained)
1 cup uncooked oats
1/2 cup dairy sour cream
1/3 cup Crisco shortening
1/3 cup packed brown sugar
1 teaspoon grated lemon peel
1 egg, beaten
1 1/4 cups all-purpose flour
1 teaspoon salt
1 teaspoon baking powder
1/2 teaspoon baking soda

1. Preheat oven to 400°.
2. Combine undrained pine-apple, oats, and sour cream; let stand 15 minutes.
3. Cream Crisco, brown sugar, and lemon peel thoroughly in a mixer bowl. Beat in egg. Blend in pineapple mixture at low speed.
4. Combine flour, salt, baking powder, and baking soda. Add to pineapple mixture; stir with a spoon just until dry ingredients are moistened.
5. Spoon batter into 18 greased medium-size muffin cups.
6. Bake at 400° for 18 minutes or until golden brown.

18 muffins

Pineapple Oatmeal Nut Muffins

Follow recipe above; stir *1/2 cup chopped walnuts* into dry ingredients in step 4. Bake as directed.

Cheese Fans

2 cups all-purpose flour
1 tablespoon baking powder
1 teaspoon salt
1/2 cup Crisco shortening
1/2 cup milk
1 cup finely shredded sharp
  Cheddar cheese

1. Preheat oven to 450°.
2. Combine flour, baking pow-der, and salt in a bowl. Cut Crisco into dry ingredients with pastry blender or 2 knives until mixture resembles coarse meal. Make a well in center and add milk; stir with fork until dough follows fork.
3. Form dough into a ball and knead lightly with fingertips 10 to 15 times on a lightly floured surface. Roll dough into a 12x10-inch rectangle about 1/4 inch thick. Cut into 5 lengthwise strips.
4. Sprinkle 4 dough strips with cheese, stack strips, and top with remaining strip. Cut into 12 equal sections. Place sections cut-side-up in greased muffin cups.
5. Bake at 450° for 10 to 15 minutes or until golden brown.

1 dozen rolls

Deep-Fried Treats

Fried Bread Puffs

1 cup all-purpose flour
1 cup whole wheat flour
6 tablespoons sugar, divided
1 teaspoon salt
3 teaspoons ground cinnamon, divided
2 tablespoons Crisco shortening
³/₄ cup plus 2 tablespoons cold water
Crisco shortening for deep frying

1. Combine flours, 2 tablespoons sugar, salt, and 1 teaspoon cinnamon in a bowl.
2. Cut in Crisco with a pastry blender or 2 knives.
3. Add water, 1 to 2 tablespoons at a time, mixing until dry ingredients are moistened and a soft dough is formed.
4. Pinch off pieces of dough and shape into 1-inch balls.
5. Roll each on a lightly floured surface into a 3-inch round.
6. Heat Crisco to 365° in a deep saucepan or deep fryer.
7. Fry, one at a time, in hot Crisco for 1 minute. Turn and fry for 1 minute longer (will be puffed and lightly browned).
8. Drain on paper towels.
9. Blend remaining 4 tablespoons sugar and 2 teaspoons cinnamon. Sprinkle over warm puffs.

About 2 dozen puffs

Note: To make larger puffs, shape 2-inch balls and roll into 5-inch rounds. Fry as directed.

Mini Doughnuts

1¹/₂ cups all-purpose flour
1 teaspoon baking powder
¹/₂ teaspoon salt
1 egg
¹/₃ cup sugar
1 teaspoon vanilla extract
1¹/₂ teaspoons grated lemon peel
1 teaspoon lemon juice
¹/₃ cup half-and-half or light cream
2 tablespoons butter or margarine, melted
Crisco shortening for deep frying

1. Combine flour, baking powder, and salt.
2. Beat egg, sugar, extract, lemon peel, and lemon juice until very thick in a bowl.
3. Blend half-and-half and melted butter; add dry ingredients alternately with half-and-half mixture to beaten egg, beating until blended after each addition.
4. Chill dough if necessary until easy to handle.
5. Roll dough to ¹/₄-inch thickness on a floured surface. Cut dough with a lightly floured 2¹/₄-inch scalloped cutter and use a 1-inch round cutter to cut out centers.
6. Heat Crisco to 375° in a deep saucepan or deep fryer.
7. Fry doughnuts, a layer at a time, for 2 minutes or until golden brown; turn doughnuts as they rise to surface and several times during frying.
8. Remove with a slotted spoon; drain on paper towels.
9. Coat doughnuts with *sugar*.

20 doughnuts

Nutmeg Crullers

2 cups sifted all-purpose flour
1 teaspoon baking powder
¹/₂ teaspoon salt
¹/₄ teaspoon ground nutmeg
1 egg
¹/₃ cup packed brown sugar
¹/₃ cup milk
¹/₂ teaspoon vanilla extract
2 tablespoons Crisco shortening, melted
Crisco shortening for deep frying
Sugar for coating

1. Combine flour, baking powder, salt, and nutmeg.
2. Beat egg, brown sugar, milk, and vanilla extract together. Stir in flour mixture and 2 tablespoons melted Crisco; mix well.
3. Turn dough onto a lightly floured surface. Roll into a 15x12-inch rectangle. Cut into 4x1-inch strips.
4. Heat Crisco to 365° in a deep saucepan or deep fryer.
5. Twist each dough strip tightly. Fry 6 at a time for about 1 minute or until golden brown; turn over once.
6. Remove with a slotted spoon and drain on paper towels.
7. Coat crullers with sugar. Serve warm.

45 crullers

Coffeecakes

Quick Raisin Ring

Ring:
2½ cups Homemade Crisco
   Quick Bread Mix, page 116
½ cup milk
3 tablespoons butter, melted
⅓ cup packed brown sugar
½ teaspoon ground cinnamon
1 cup seedless raisins
¼ cup chopped nuts

Glaze:
½ cup confectioners' sugar
1 tablespoon milk

1. Preheat oven to 375°.
2. For Ring, combine Crisco mix and milk in a bowl, stirring until dry ingredients are moistened.
3. Roll out dough to a 14x10-inch rectangle on a lightly floured surface.
4. Brush dough with 2 table-spoons melted butter. Combine brown sugar, cinnamon, raisins, and nuts; sprinkle over dough. Roll up as for a jelly roll.
5. Place sealed-edge-down on a lightly greased cookie sheet. Join ends to form a ring; seal. With scissors, make 12 cuts two-thirds of the way through ring at 1-inch intervals.
6. Turn each section on its side. Brush with remaining 1 tablespoon melted butter.
7. Bake at 375° for 25 to 30 minutes or until golden brown.
8. For Glaze, stir sugar and milk together until smooth. Spoon over hot raisin ring.

1 coffeecake

Streusel Coffeecake

Batter:
1½ cups all-purpose flour
½ cup sugar
2 teaspoons baking powder
½ teaspoon salt
½ cup Crisco shortening
⅔ cup milk
1 egg, slightly beaten
¼ teaspoon almond extract

Topping:
⅓ cup sugar
¼ cup all-purpose flour
2 tablespoons butter or
   margarine

1. Preheat oven to 350°.
2. For Batter, combine flour, sugar, baking powder, and salt in a large bowl. Cut in Crisco with pastry blender or 2 knives until mixture resembles coarse crumbs. Beat milk, egg, and almond extract together; add to dry ingredients and stir just to moisten.
3. Pour batter into a greased 8x8x2-inch pan.
4. For Topping, mix sugar and flour in a bowl. Cut in butter with a pastry blender or 2 knives until mixture resembles fine crumbs. Sprinkle over batter in pan.
5. Bake at 350° for 45 minutes or until a toothpick inserted in center comes out clean.

9 servings

Sour Cream Coffeecake

2 cups sugar, divided
2 teaspoons ground cinnamon
¾ cup finely chopped walnuts
¾ cup Crisco shortening
1 teaspoon vanilla extract
3 eggs
3 cups all-purpose flour
1½ teaspoons baking powder
1½ teaspoons baking soda
1 teaspoon salt
1½ cups dairy sour cream

1. Preheat oven to 350°.
2. Combine ¾ cup sugar, cinnamon, and walnuts.
3. Cream Crisco, remaining 1¼ cups sugar, and vanilla extract in a large mixer bowl. Add eggs, one at a time, beating well after each addition.
4. Combine flour, baking powder, baking soda, and salt. Add alternately with sour cream to creamed mixture, mixing until blended after each addition (batter will be thick).
5. Spread one-half of batter in a greased 10-inch tube pan. Spoon three-fourths of nut mixture over batter. Repeat with remaining batter and nut mixture.
6. Bake at 350° for 1 hour or until a toothpick inserted in center comes out clean.
7. Cool cake for 20 minutes in pan on a rack. Loosen from sides; place an inverted plate on cake and invert both. Remove pan; turn cake top-side-up placing on rack. Cool completely. To serve, slide onto a cake plate.

About 12 servings

Coffeecakes

Apple Kuchen

2 cups Homemade Crisco
   Quick Bread Mix, page 116
1/2 cup plus 2 tablespoons
   sugar, divided
2 eggs
2/3 cup milk
1 teaspoon vanilla extract
2 cups thinly sliced pared
   apples
1/2 teaspoon ground cinnamon
1/2 cup apricot preserves

1. Preheat oven to 375°.
2. Combine Crisco mix and 1/2
cup sugar in a bowl.
3. Beat eggs, milk, and vanilla
extract together with a fork.
Add to dry ingredients and
stir until well mixed.
4. Spread batter in a greased
9x9x2-inch pan.
5. Arrange apple slices, slightly overlapping, in rows on
batter.
6. Blend remaining 2 tablespoons sugar and cinnamon.
Sprinkle over apples. Spoon
preserves on top.
7. Bake at 375° for 40 to 45
minutes or until apples are
tender and top is golden
brown.
8. Serve slightly warm or
completely cooled. Cut into
squares.

9 servings

Blueberry Buckle

Topping:
1/2 cup sugar
1/3 cup all-purpose flour
1/2 teaspoon ground cinnamon
1/4 teaspoon salt
1/4 cup Crisco shortening

Batter:
1/4 cup Crisco shortening
3/4 cup sugar
2 eggs
1 1/2 cups all-purpose flour
2 teaspoons baking powder
1/2 teaspoon salt
1/2 teaspoon ground nutmeg
1/4 teaspoon ground cloves
1/2 cup milk
1 1/2 cups fresh or dry-pack
   frozen blueberries

1. Preheat oven to 375°.
2. For Topping, combine sugar,
flour, cinnamon, and salt in a
bowl. Cut in Crisco with a
pastry blender or 2 knives
until mixture resembles coarse
crumbs.
3. For Batter, cream Crisco
and sugar in a mixer bowl.
Add eggs, one at a time, beating well after each addition.
Combine flour, baking powder,
salt, nutmeg, and cloves; add
alternately with milk to
creamed mixture, beating until
blended after each addition.
Rinse and drain blueberries;
fold in.
4. Turn batter into a greased
9x9x2-inch pan. Sprinkle
Topping over batter.
5. Bake at 375° for 45 to 50
minutes or until a toothpick
inserted in center comes out
clean. Cut into squares.

9 servings

Blueberry Maple Squares

Topping:
1/4 cup packed brown sugar
3 tablespoons all-purpose flour
1/2 teaspoon ground cinnamon
1/4 teaspoon salt
2 tablespoons Crisco
    shortening
1/4 cup chopped nuts

Batter:
2 cups all-purpose flour
2/3 cup sugar
1 tablespoon baking powder
1/2 teaspoon salt
2 eggs
2/3 cup milk
1/2 cup Crisco shortening,
    melted
1 1/2 teaspoons maple flavor
1 1/2 cups fresh or dry-pack
    frozen blueberries

1. Preheat oven to 350°.
2. For Topping, combine brown sugar, flour, cinnamon, and salt in a bowl. Cut in Crisco with a pastry blender or 2 knives. Stir in nuts.
3. For Batter, combine flour, sugar, baking powder, and salt in a bowl.
4. Beat eggs, milk, Crisco, and flavor with a fork. Add to dry ingredients and stir only until dry ingredients are moistened. Rinse and drain blueberries and fold in carefully.
5. Spread batter in a greased 9x9x2-inch pan. Sprinkle Topping evenly over batter.
6. Bake at 350° for 45 to 50 minutes or until a toothpick inserted in center comes out clean. Cut into squares. Serve warm with *butter pats* and *honey*.

9 servings

Sesame Rounds

1 3/4 cups all-purpose flour
1/2 cup yellow cornmeal
2 tablespoons sugar
1 teaspoon salt
1/2 teaspoon baking soda
1/4 cup Crisco shortening
1/2 cup water
2 tablespoons vinegar
2 tablespoons melted butter
2 tablespoons sesame seed

1. Preheat oven to 375°.
2. Combine flour, cornmeal, sugar, salt, and baking soda in a large bowl. With pastry blender or 2 knives, cut Crisco into flour mixture until mixture resembles coarse crumbs. Stir in water and vinegar.
3. Turn dough onto lightly floured surface; knead gently a few times. Divide dough into 32 balls. Roll each ball into a 4 1/2-inch round.
4. With turner, transfer 6 rounds to ungreased cookie sheet, placing rounds 1 inch apart.
5. Brush rounds with melted butter, sprinkle with sesame seed, and firmly press seeds into dough with turner.
6. Bake at 375° for 8 to 10 minutes or until lightly browned. With turner, transfer baked rounds to a rack.
7. Cool thoroughly before storing in a tightly covered container.

32 rounds

Pancakes

Quick Pancakes

²/₃ cup milk
1 egg, beaten
¹/₄ cup Crisco shortening,
  melted
1 cup all-purpose flour
¹/₂ cup sifted confectioners'
  sugar
2 teaspoons baking powder
¹/₄ teaspoon salt
Crisco shortening for brushing

1. Mix milk, egg, and Crisco.
2. Combine flour, confectioners' sugar, baking powder, and salt; add to milk mixture and stir until dry ingredients are just moistened.
3. Heat a griddle or skillet and brush with Crisco.
4. For each pancake, pour about 3 tablespoons batter onto griddle. Cook until bubbles appear evenly over top. Turn over and brown second side.

8 (4-inch) pancakes

Easy Waffles

2 cups all-purpose flour
1 tablespoon sugar
1 tablespoon baking powder
1 teaspoon salt
3 eggs, well beaten
2 cups milk
¹/₂ cup Crisco shortening,
  melted

1. Combine flour, sugar, baking powder, and salt in a bowl.
2. Beat eggs and milk until blended. Add egg mixture and Crisco to dry ingredients; beat just until smooth.
3. Bake in waffle baker following manufacturer's directions.

3 (9-inch) waffles

Apple Breakfast

¹/₄ cup Crisco shortening
3 medium apples, pared,
  cored, and sliced (about 4
  cups sliced)
3 eggs
¹/₂ cup milk
¹/₂ cup all-purpose flour
¹/₄ cup plus 1 teaspoon sugar,
  divided
¹/₄ teaspoon salt
1 teaspoon ground cinnamon
Lemon juice (optional)

1. Melt Crisco in a heavy skillet. Add apples and cook over medium heat until soft.
2. Preheat oven to 500°.
3. Combine eggs, milk, flour, 1 teaspoon sugar, and salt. Pour over apples in skillet. Continue to cook over medium heat for 6 to 7 minutes or until bottom is golden brown.
4. Mix remaining ¹/₄ cup sugar and the cinnamon; sprinkle over apples.
5. Bake at 500° for 8 to 9 minutes or until top is golden brown.
6. Drizzle with lemon juice, if desired, and serve hot.

4 servings

128

Deluxe Waffles

2 cups all-purpose flour
1 tablespoon sugar
1 tablespoon baking powder
1/2 teaspoon salt
2 eggs, separated
1 1/4 cups milk
5 tablespoons Crisco
  shortening, melted

1. Combine flour, sugar, baking powder, and salt in a bowl.
2. Beat egg yolks until thick, add milk and melted Crisco, and beat until blended. Add to dry ingredients and stir until just blended.
3. Beat egg whites to stiff, not dry, peaks. Gently fold egg whites into batter. Turn batter into a pitcher for easy pouring.
4. Bake in waffle baker following manufacturer's directions.

3 cups batter or 2 (9-inch) square waffles

Apple Waffles

Follow recipe for Deluxe Waffles. Mix *1 small apple, pared, cored, and finely chopped,* into batter. Serve with *applesauce.*

Blueberry Waffles

Follow recipe for Deluxe Waffles. Bake waffles and while still warm sprinkle with *confectioners' sugar* and decorate with *1 cup fresh or frozen blueberries.*

Pecan Waffles

Follow recipe for Deluxe Waffles. Mix *3/4 cup chopped pecans* into batter. Serve with *maple syrup* and decorate with *pecan halves.*

Strawberry Waffles

Follow recipe for Deluxe Waffles. Bake waffles and while still warm sprinkle with *confectioners' sugar* and decorate with *strawberry halves.* Serve with *strawberry syrup* or *jam.*

Cheese Waffles

Follow recipe for Deluxe Waffles. Mix *1 1/2 cups shredded sharp Cheddar cheese* into batter. Serve with *cheese sauce* and decorate with *shredded cheese.*

Chocolate Waffles

Follow recipe for Deluxe Waffles. Mix *3/4 cup semisweet chocolate pieces* into batter. Serve with *whipped cream* and decorate with *shaved chocolate.*

A home-baked cake is a personal gift from your kitchen that makes every meal a special occasion. It's fun, too! . . . a creative adventure limited only by your imagination.

Made with Crisco, your cake will be deliciously moist and tasty. And a Crisco frosting will make it even tastier.

Golden Tube Cake

2¾ cups sifted cake flour
1½ cups sugar
2 teaspoons baking powder
1¼ teaspoons salt
1 cup Crisco shortening
¾ cup milk
1 teaspoon orange extract
1 teaspoon lemon extract
3 eggs
1 egg yolk

1. Preheat oven to 375°.
2. Combine cake flour, sugar, baking powder, and salt in a large mixer bowl. Add Crisco, about ½ cup milk, and extracts. Beat for 2 minutes at medium speed; scrape down sides of bowl occasionally. Add remaining milk, eggs, and egg yolk; continue beating for 2 minutes.
3. Turn batter into a greased and floured 9-inch tube pan.
4. Bake at 375° for 45 minutes or until a toothpick inserted in center comes out clean.
5. Cool cake for 30 minutes in pan on a rack, remove from pan, and cool on rack. Frost as desired or serve with *fresh fruit*.

10 to 12 servings

Double-Filled Jelly Roll

2 tablespoons Crisco shortening
½ cup sifted cake flour
⅛ teaspoon salt
3 eggs, separated
½ cup sugar
1 teaspoon vanilla extract
½ cup Crisco shortening
¼ cup warm water
3 cups confectioners' sugar
⅔ cup currant jelly

1. Preheat oven to 400°.
2. Grease a 15½x10½x1-inch jelly-roll pan with 1 tablespoon Crisco. Line with waxed paper, then grease paper with 1 tablespoon Crisco. Set aside.
3. Sift cake flour and salt together and set aside.
4. Beat egg yolks in a mixer bowl until thick and lemon colored (about 5 minutes).
5. Beat egg whites until soft peaks form. Gradually add sugar and beat until stiff peaks form. Pour beaten yolks over beaten whites; add extract and then fold in. Sift flour mixture over top and fold in carefully and thoroughly. Pour batter into pan.
6. Bake at 400° for 13 to 15 minutes or until cake pulls away from sides of pan.
7. Loosen edges of cake with a knife. Turn pan upside-down onto clean towel dusted with *confectioners' sugar*. Gently peel off waxed paper. Trim edges. While cake is still warm, roll up cake, starting with narrow end. Cool thoroughly.

8. Combine ½ cup Crisco, water, and confectioners' sugar. Beat for 5 minutes or until smooth. (Mixture should be soft and spreadable. If necessary, add more water.) Chill mixture for 1 hour.
9. When cake is cool, unroll and spread with jelly. Spread chilled mixture on jelly. Reroll cake. Dust with confectioners' sugar, if desired. Cover and store refrigerated overnight.

6 to 8 servings

Lunch Box Quickie

2¼ cups sifted all-purpose flour
2 teaspoons baking soda
1 teaspoon salt
1 cup packed brown sugar
2 eggs
¼ cup Crisco shortening
1 can (17 ounces) fruit cocktail (undrained)
¾ cup semisweet chocolate pieces
½ cup chopped nuts

1. Preheat oven to 350°.
2. Combine all ingredients except chocolate and nuts in a large mixer bowl. Blend at low speed until moistened; beat for 2 minutes at medium speed, scraping bowl occasionally. Pour batter into a greased and floured 13x9x2-inch pan; sprinkle with chocolate pieces and nuts.
3. Bake at 350° for 35 to 40 minutes or until a toothpick inserted in center comes out clean.

12 to 14 servings

Golden Nut Cake

3½ cups sifted all-purpose
   flour
2 teaspoons baking powder
1 teaspoon salt
1½ cups Crisco shortening
2 cups sugar
6 eggs
1½ teaspoons rum extract
1 cup milk
4 cups coarsely chopped
   pecans or walnuts

1. Preheat oven to 300°.
2. Lightly grease bottom and sides of a 10-inch tube pan. Line with brown paper; grease paper.
3. Sift flour, baking powder, and salt together; set aside.
4. Put Crisco into a large mixer bowl. Gradually add sugar, beating at medium speed until light and fluffy. Add eggs, one at a time, beating well after each addition. Blend in rum extract. At low speed, blend in flour mixture in fourths, alternately with milk, beginning and ending with flour mixture. Fold in nuts.
5. Spoon batter into prepared pan, spreading evenly.
6. Bake at 300° for 1 hour 50 minutes to 2 hours or until a toothpick inserted near center comes out clean. Let cake cool in pan on wire rack for 30 minutes. Turn out onto rack; gently remove paper. Invert cake again and cool cake completely. Wrap in aluminum foil or plastic wrap.
7. To serve, cut into thin slices. Top with whipped cream or ice cream, if desired.

16 to 20 servings

Lemon Yogurt Pound Cake

2¼ cups sifted all-purpose
   flour
1¼ cups sugar
1 teaspoon salt
½ teaspoon baking soda
1½ teaspoons grated lemon
   peel
1 teaspoon vanilla extract
1 cup Crisco shortening
1 container (8 ounces) lemon
   yogurt
3 eggs

1. Preheat oven to 325°.
2. Put all ingredients into a large mixer bowl and blend at low speed. Beat for 3 minutes at medium speed.
3. Pour batter into a greased and floured 10-inch tube pan.
4. Bake at 325° for 65 to 75 minutes or until a toothpick inserted in center comes out clean.
5. Cool cake for 30 minutes in pan on a rack, remove from pan, and cool completely on a rack. Sprinkle with *confectioners' sugar*.

12 to 16 servings

Yellow Cakes

Cupcake Twinkles

2¹/₂ cups sifted cake flour
1²/₃ cups sugar
1 tablespoon baking powder
1 teaspoon salt
1¹/₄ cups milk
²/₃ cup Crisco shortening
3 eggs
1 teaspoon vanilla extract

Filling:
¹/₄ cup butter or margarine
2 cups sifted confectioners' sugar
2 tablespoons water

1. Preheat oven to 350°.
2. Combine cake flour, sugar, baking powder, and salt in a large mixer bowl. Add ³/₄ cup milk and Crisco. Beat for 2 minutes at medium speed (or beat vigorously by hand about 300 strokes). Add eggs, ¹/₂ cup milk, and extract. Beat for 2 minutes.
3. Pour batter into paper-lined muffin cups, filling each two-thirds full.
4. Bake at 350° for 20 to 25 minutes or until a toothpick inserted in center comes out clean.
5. Cool for 15 minutes in pans on racks. Remove cupcakes from pans and peel off paper liners.
6. For Filling, beat butter until softened in a small mixer bowl. Add confectioners' sugar and beat until blended. Add water; beat until smooth.
7. Cut a thin slice from bottom of each cupcake. Carefully hollow out center and spoon 2 teaspoons of Filling into cupcake. Replace bottom slice.

2 to 3 dozen cupcakes

Ribbon Layer Cake

2¹/₄ cups sifted all-purpose flour
1¹/₂ cups sugar
1 tablespoon baking powder
1 teaspoon salt
¹/₂ cup Crisco shortening
1 cup milk
1 teaspoon vanilla extract
2 eggs
Yellow, green, and red food coloring (4 drops of each)
1 jar (10 ounces) strawberry jelly

Frosting:
³/₄ cup Crisco shortening
2¹/₂ cups confectioners' sugar
1¹/₂ teaspoons vanilla extract
2 to 3 tablespoons milk
Green food coloring (6 drops)

1. Preheat oven to 350°.
2. Combine flour, sugar, baking powder, salt, Crisco, milk, and vanilla extract in a large mixer bowl. Blend at low speed. Beat for 2 minutes at medium speed. Add eggs and beat for 3 minutes at high speed.
3. Divide batter into thirds. Color each third with food coloring to make pale yellow, pale green, and pale pink batters. Pour batter into 3 greased and floured 8-inch square pans.
4. Bake at 350° for 20 to 25 minutes or until a toothpick inserted in center comes out clean.
5. Cool for 10 minutes in pans on racks, remove from pans, and cool completely on racks. Trim edges and cut each layer in half to make 6 rectangles.
6. Spread 5 sections of cake with strawberry jelly. Stack layers alternating colors. Top with remaining section; turn so layers are up and down.
7. For Frosting, combine all ingredients except food coloring. Beat until creamy. Blend in food coloring to color frosting a pale green. Frost cake.
8. Be sure to slice cake so there is a ribbon effect.

16 servings

Strawberry Shortcake

1 quart fresh strawberries
Sugar
2¼ cups sifted all-purpose
*   flour*
2 tablespoons sugar
1 tablespoon baking powder
½ teaspoon salt
½ cup Crisco shortening
1 egg, beaten
¾ cup milk
Milk for brushing
½ cup strawberry jam
2 cups whipping cream,
*   whipped*

1. Reserve 1 whole strawberry. Slice remaining berries and reserve 5 slices. Sweeten remaining sliced berries with sugar to taste.
2. Preheat oven to 425°.
3. Combine flour, 2 tablespoons sugar, baking powder, and salt in a bowl. Cut in Crisco with a pastry blender or 2 knives until mixture resembles coarse crumbs. Make a well in center. Combine egg and ¾ cup milk, add to well, and stir with a fork 20 to 30 strokes.
4. Turn dough out onto a lightly floured surface and shape into a ball. Knead lightly with fingertips about 15 times. Divide dough in thirds. Grease three 8x1½-inch layer cake pans, line bottoms with waxed paper, and grease paper. Put a third of dough in each pan. Pat out evenly to fit bottom of pans. Brush tops with milk.
5. Bake at 425° for 15 to 18 minutes or until tops are lightly browned. Loosen edges of shortcake rounds. Remove from pans and peel off waxed paper. Set right-side-up on racks.
6. Spread each of two shortcake layers with ¼ cup strawberry jam. Place one shortcake layer on a serving plate. Arrange half of the sweetened strawberry slices over bottom layer. Spoon 1½ cups whipped cream over berries. Cover with second shortcake layer and arrange remaining sweetened sliced berries over it. Spread with 1½ cups whipped cream. Top with plain shortcake layer. Spread with 1 cup whipped cream. Decorate with reserved whole strawberry and slices.

6 servings

Cinnamon Cupcakes

Cupcakes:
2¼ cups sifted cake flour
2 teaspoons baking powder
½ teaspoon salt
¾ cup Crisco shortening
1 teaspoon vanilla extract
1½ cups sugar
¾ cup milk
4 egg whites
2 tablespoons sugar
½ teaspoon ground cinnamon

Frosting:
¼ cup Crisco shortening
2½ cups sifted confectioners'
*   sugar*
2 egg whites
1 teaspoon vanilla extract
¼ teaspoon ground cinnamon

1. Preheat oven to 350°.
2. For Cupcakes, combine cake flour, baking powder, and salt; set aside.
3. Cream Crisco and vanilla extract. Add 1½ cups sugar gradually, creaming until fluffy.
4. Alternately add dry ingredients in fourths and milk in thirds, beating only until smooth after each addition.
5. Add unbeaten egg whites to batter and mix at medium speed until blended.
6. Spoon batter into paper-lined muffin cups, filling each about two-thirds full. Combine 2 tablespoons sugar and cinnamon. Sprinkle ¼ teaspoon cinnamon sugar over batter in each cup. Lightly swirl into batter with knife.
7. Bake at 350° for 20 to 25 minutes or until golden brown and a toothpick inserted in center comes out clean. Cool.
8. For Frosting, put Crisco into a mixer bowl. Gradually beat in 1 cup confectioners' sugar; set aside.
9. Beat egg whites until soft peaks are formed. Gradually add remaining 1½ cups confectioners' sugar, beating until mixture holds soft peaks. Gradually add Crisco mixture, beating until smooth and creamy. Blend in vanilla extract and cinnamon.
10. Spread frosting on cooled cupcakes.

24 cupcakes

White Cakes

Ice Cream Cakes

2³/₄ cups sifted cake flour
1²/₃ cups sugar
4¹/₂ teaspoons baking powder
1 teaspoon salt
1¹/₃ cups milk, divided
²/₃ cup Crisco shortening
5 egg whites
1 teaspoon vanilla extract
¹/₂ gallon chocolate ice cream, softened
2 jars (8 ounces each) maraschino cherries, drained and cut in halves
1 cup chopped walnuts
6 cups whipped dessert topping

1. Preheat oven to 350°.
2. For cake, combine cake flour, sugar, baking powder, and salt in a large mixer bowl. Add 1 cup milk and Crisco. Blend at low speed. Beat for 2 minutes at medium speed (or beat vigorously by hand about 300 strokes). Add egg whites, remaining ¹/₃ cup milk, and vanilla extract. Continue beating for 2 minutes.
3. Pour batter into 2 greased and floured 9x1¹/₂-inch round layer cake pans.
4. Bake at 350° for 25 to 30 minutes or until a toothpick inserted in center comes out clean.
5. Cool for 10 minutes in pans on racks, remove from pans, and cool on racks.
6. Mix ice cream, cherries, and nuts. Divide evenly in 2 aluminum-foil-lined 9-inch round pans. Freeze until firm.
7. For each cake, place one cooled cake layer on a foil-covered cardboard round. Remove one ice cream layer from pan, peel off foil, and place ice cream on cake. Frost sides and top with half of whipped dessert topping.
8. Freeze until firm. Let soften slightly before serving.

Two 9-inch ice cream cakes

Frosted Cake Fingers

2³/₄ cups sifted cake flour
1²/₃ cups sugar
4¹/₂ teaspoons baking powder
1 teaspoon salt
1¹/₃ cups milk
²/₃ cup Crisco shortening
5 egg whites
1 teaspoon vanilla extract

Choco Pecan Frosting:
1 package (12 ounces) semisweet chocolate pieces
1 can (14 ounces) sweetened condensed milk
³/₄ cup chopped pecans

1. Preheat oven to 350°.
2. Combine cake flour, sugar, baking powder, and salt in a large mixer bowl. Add 1 cup milk and Crisco. Blend at low speed. Beat for 2 minutes at medium speed (or beat vigorously by hand about 300 strokes). Add egg whites, remaining ¹/₃ cup milk, and vanilla extract. Continue beating for 2 minutes.
3. Pour batter into a greased and floured 15¹/₂x10¹/₂x1-inch jelly-roll pan.
4. Bake at 350° for 35 minutes or until a toothpick inserted in center comes out clean.
5. Cool for 10 minutes in pan on a rack, remove from pan, and cool on rack.
6. For Choco Pecan Frosting, melt chocolate pieces in a small saucepan over low heat. Remove from heat. Stir in sweetened condensed milk until well blended. Let stand for 4 minutes, then stir well.
7. Spread frosting on cooled cake and sprinkle with pecans. Cut into fingers.

24 cake fingers

White Cakes

Pistachio Company Cake

2¹/₄ cups sifted cake flour
2 teaspoons baking powder
¹/₂ teaspoon salt
³/₄ cup Crisco shortening
1 teaspoon vanilla extract
1¹/₂ cups sugar
2³/₄ cups milk, divided
4 egg whites, beaten to stiff, not dry, peaks
1 package (4-serving-size) pistachio instant pudding and pie filling mix
1 cup coarsely chopped nuts

1. Preheat oven to 350°.
2. Sift cake flour, baking powder, and salt together; set aside.
3. Cream Crisco with vanilla extract. Add sugar, creaming until fluffy. Add dry ingredients alternately with ³/₄ cup milk, beating until smooth.
4. Gently fold egg whites into batter until thoroughly blended. Divide batter evenly in 2 greased and floured 9x1¹/₂-inch round layer cake pans.
5. Bake at 350° for 25 to 30 minutes or until a toothpick inserted in center comes out clean. Cool for 15 minutes on racks, remove from pans, and cool on racks.
6. Prepare pistachio pudding using 2 cups milk as directed on package. Set aside.
7. Place one cake layer on serving plate, spread half of pistachio pudding on bottom layer, and sprinkle with ¹/₂ cup nuts. Place second layer on top of bottom layer, spread remaining pudding over top, and sprinkle with remaining nuts. Keep refrigerated.

12 servings

Cocoa Mocha Cake

2³/₄ cups sifted cake flour
1²/₃ cups sugar
4¹/₂ teaspoons baking powder
1 teaspoon salt
1¹/₃ cups milk, divided
²/₃ cup Crisco shortening
5 egg whites
1 teaspoon vanilla extract

Cocoa Mocha:

³/₄ cup Crisco shortening
1 tablespoon vanilla extract
¹/₂ teaspoon salt
1 tablespoon unsweetened cocoa
4 to 4¹/₂ cups confectioners' sugar
5 tablespoons black coffee
1 cup raisins
2 tablespoons orange marmalade

1. Preheat oven to 350°.
2. Combine cake flour, sugar, baking powder, and salt in a mixer bowl. Add 1 cup milk and Crisco. Blend at low speed. Beat for 2 minutes at medium speed (or beat vigorously by hand about 300 strokes). Add egg whites, ¹/₃ cup milk, and extract. Beat for 2 minutes.
3. Pour batter into 2 greased and floured 9x1¹/₂-inch round layer cake pans.
4. Bake at 350° for 25 to 30 minutes or until a toothpick inserted in center comes out clean.
5. Cool for 15 minutes in pans on racks, remove and cool.
6. For Cocoa Mocha, cream Crisco, extract, salt, and cocoa. Add sugar and coffee alternately, beating until smooth.
7. Combine 1 cup frosting, raisins, and marmalade. Fill cake. Frost with remaining Cocoa Mocha.

16 servings

Poppy Seed Cake

1¹/₃ cups milk, divided
¹/₃ cup poppy seed
2³/₄ cups sifted cake flour
1²/₃ cups sugar
4¹/₂ teaspoons baking powder
1 teaspoon salt
²/₃ cup Crisco shortening
5 egg whites
1 teaspoon vanilla extract

Chocolate Velvet Frosting:

¹/₄ cup Crisco shortening
1¹/₂ teaspoons vanilla extract
¹/₄ teaspoon salt
2 egg yolks
2 envelopes (1 ounce each) premelted unsweetened chocolate
3 cups confectioners' sugar
3 to 4 tablespoons milk

1. Mix ¹/₃ cup milk and poppy seed; let soak for 1 hour.
2. Preheat oven to 350°.
3. Combine cake flour, sugar, baking powder, and salt in a large mixer bowl. Add remaining 1 cup milk and Crisco. Blend at low speed. Beat for 2 minutes at medium speed (or beat vigorously by hand about 300 strokes). Add egg whites, poppy seed, and vanilla extract. Continue beating for 2 minutes.
4. Pour batter into 2 greased and floured 9x1¹/₂-inch round layer cake pans.
5. Bake at 350° for 25 to 30 minutes or until a toothpick inserted in center comes out clean.
6. Cool for 10 minutes in pans on racks, remove from pans, and cool on racks.
7. For Chocolate Velvet Frosting, cream Crisco, vanilla extract, salt, and egg yolks in

White Cakes

a bowl. Beat in premelted chocolate. Alternately add confectioners' sugar and milk, beating until smooth after each addition. Beat until of spreading consistency. Fill and frost cake.

16 servings

Blueberry Cone Cakes

1/2 cup fresh or dry-pack
  frozen blueberries
1/4 cup Crisco shortening
3/4 cup sugar
1 egg, slightly beaten
1/2 teaspoon lemon extract
1 cup sifted cake flour
1 teaspoon baking powder
1/8 teaspoon salt
1/4 cup milk
1 dozen large flat-bottom
  *cones**
1 package white frosting mix

1. Preheat oven to 350°.
2. Rinse and drain blueberries and let dry on paper towels.
3. Cream Crisco and sugar in a mixer bowl. Add egg and lemon extract; mix well.
4. Combine cake flour, baking powder, and salt. Add to egg mixture alternately with milk, mixing thoroughly after each addition. Carefully fold in the blueberries. Divide batter into cones. Set cones in muffin cups or on a baking sheet.
5. Bake at 350° for 30 to 35 minutes; cool.
6. Prepare frosting mix and frost cakes. Decorate with *assorted candies, sprinkles, coconut, and marshmallows.*

12 cone cakes

*Fresh cones with straight sides work best.

137

Chocolate Cakes

Magnificent Chocolate Cake

6 ounces (6 squares)
   unsweetened chocolate
4 cups sifted all-purpose flour
3 cups sugar
1 tablespoon baking powder
2 teaspoons salt
1⅓ cups Crisco shortening
2 cups milk
6 eggs, well beaten
2½ teaspoons vanilla extract
¾ cup finely chopped walnuts
Confectioners' sugar

1. Preheat oven to 325°.
2. Melt chocolate and set aside to cool.
3. Combine flour, sugar, baking powder, and salt in a large mixer bowl. Add Crisco, cooled chocolate, and 1½ cups milk. Blend on low speed. Beat for 2 minutes at medium speed (or beat vigorously by hand about 300 strokes); scrape sides of bowl frequently.
4. Blend in beaten eggs, remaining milk, and vanilla extract. Continue beating for 2 minutes; stir in walnuts.
5. Turn batter into a greased and floured 10-inch tube pan; spread evenly. Tap pan lightly on a table or counter top to break up any large air bubbles.
6. Bake at 325° for 1 hour and 45 minutes or until a toothpick inserted in center comes out clean.
7. Cool cake for 20 minutes in pan on a rack, remove from pan, and cool cake completely on rack.
8. Sprinkle cake with confectioners' sugar.

24 servings

Semisweet Chocolate Cake

4 ounces (4 squares) semisweet
   chocolate
½ cup boiling water
1 cup Crisco shortening
1 teaspoon vanilla extract
2 cups sugar
4 egg yolks
2¼ cups sifted all-purpose flour
1 teaspoon baking soda
½ teaspoon salt
1 cup buttermilk
4 egg whites

Coconut Pecan Frosting:
1 cup undiluted evaporated
   milk
1 cup sugar
3 egg yolks
½ cup Crisco shortening
⅛ teaspoon salt
1 teaspoon vanilla extract
1 cup flaked coconut
1 cup chopped pecans

1. Preheat oven to 350°.
2. Melt chocolate and stir in water; cool.
3. Cream Crisco with extract; add sugar, creaming until fluffy after each addition. Add egg yolks and beat well. Stir in melted chocolate.
4. Combine flour, baking soda, and salt; add alternately in thirds with buttermilk, starting and ending with dry ingredients.
5. Beat egg whites to stiff, not dry, peaks in a small mixer bowl. Fold into cake batter. Spoon into 3 greased and waxed-paper-lined 8x1½-inch round layer cake pans.
6. Bake at 350° for 30 to 35 minutes or until a toothpick inserted in center comes out clean. Cool for 15 minutes in pans on racks. Remove and cool right-side-up on racks.
7. For Coconut Pecan Frosting, combine evaporated milk, sugar, egg yolks, Crisco, and salt in a medium saucepan. Cook and stir over medium heat until thickened (about 10 minutes). Remove from heat. Stir in vanilla extract, coconut, and pecans. Cool for 15 to 20 minutes, stirring occasionally. When cool, spread over tops of cake layers; stack.

12 to 16 servings

Quick 'n' Rich Chocolaty Cake

⅓ cup Crisco shortening
1½ cups sifted all-purpose
   flour
1 cup sugar
⅓ cup unsweetened cocoa
1 teaspoon baking soda
½ teaspoon salt
1 cup water
2 teaspoons vanilla extract
2 tablespoons white vinegar
Confectioners' sugar

1. Preheat oven to 375°.
2. Melt Crisco in a saucepan over medium heat.
3. Grease and flour a 9x1½-inch round layer cake pan.
4. Combine flour, sugar, cocoa, baking soda, and salt in a large bowl. Add water, vanilla extract, and melted Crisco, stirring until blended. Stir in vinegar quickly but carefully until blended. Immediately turn batter into pan and set in oven.
5. Bake at 375° for 30 to 35 minutes or until a toothpick inserted in center comes out clean. Cool completely in pan.
6. Dust lightly with confectioners' sugar.

About 8 servings

Double Fudge Cake

1¼ cups sifted all-purpose
    flour
1 cup sugar
1¼ teaspoons baking powder
½ teaspoon salt
¼ teaspoon baking soda
3 tablespoons Crisco
    shortening
1 cup milk
1 egg
3 envelopes (1 ounce each)
    premelted unsweetened
    chocolate
1 teaspoon vanilla extract
½ cup semisweet chocolate
    pieces (see Note)
¼ cup chopped nuts

1. Preheat oven to 350°.
2. Combine flour, sugar, baking powder, salt, and baking soda in a large mixer bowl. Add Crisco, milk, egg, premelted chocolate, and vanilla extract. Blend on low speed. Beat for 3 minutes on high speed. Mix in chocolate pieces and nuts.
3. Turn batter into a greased and lightly floured 9x9x2-inch pan.
4. Bake at 350° for 35 minutes or until a toothpick inserted in center comes out clean. Cool in pan on a rack.

8 to 10 servings

Note: If desired, reserve chocolate pieces for topping. As soon as cake is removed from oven, sprinkle chocolate pieces over top. Let stand until chocolate is glossy, then spread evenly.

Quick and Easy Cocoa Cake

1⅓ cups sifted cake flour
1¼ cups sugar
½ cup unsweetened cocoa
1 teaspoon baking powder
½ teaspoon baking soda
½ teaspoon salt
½ cup Crisco shortening
2 eggs
¾ cup milk
1½ teaspoons vanilla extract
2 teaspoons vinegar

**Easy Milk Chocolate
Frosting:**
2 tablespoons Crisco
    shortening
2 tablespoons unsweetened
    cocoa
⅛ teaspoon salt
1¾ cups confectioners' sugar
2 to 3 tablespoons milk
1 teaspoon vanilla extract

1. Preheat oven to 350°.
2. Sift cake flour, sugar, cocoa, baking powder, baking soda, and salt together into a large mixer bowl. Blend to distribute cocoa. Add Crisco.
3. Add a mixture of eggs, ¼ cup milk, and vanilla extract to dry ingredients. Beat for 2 minutes at medium speed (or beat vigorously by hand about 300 strokes); scrape sides and bottom of bowl occasionally.
4. Add mixture of remaining ½ cup milk and the vinegar to batter. Beat for 1 minute at medium speed (or beat vigorously by hand about 150 strokes). Turn batter into a greased 9x9x2-inch pan.
5. Bake at 350° for 35 to 40 minutes or until a toothpick inserted in center comes out clean.

6. Remove from oven to a rack and cool completely in pan.
7. For Easy Milk Chocolate Frosting, combine ingredients in a small mixer bowl. Beat for 1 minute or until smooth and creamy. Spread frosting over cooled cake.

9 servings

Chocolate Cupcakes

⅓ cup Crisco shortening
1 cup sugar
1 egg
1 egg yolk
1 teaspoon vanilla extract
2 ounces (2 squares)
    unsweetened chocolate,
    melted
1⅔ cups sifted cake flour
2 teaspoons baking powder
½ teaspoon salt
½ cup milk

1. Preheat oven to 350°.
2. Cream shortening and sugar until light and fluffy in a large mixer bowl. Add egg, egg yolk, and vanilla extract; beat thoroughly. Blend in melted chocolate.
3. Combine cake flour, baking powder, and salt. Add dry ingredients alternately to creamed mixture, beating until smooth after each addition.
4. Fill paper-lined muffin cups about half full.
5. Bake at 350° for 20 to 25 minutes. Cool on racks. If desired, frost with Easy Milk Chocolate Frosting (above).

20 medium cupcakes

Chocolate Cakes

Chocolate Cake with Caramel Frosting

1/2 cup Crisco shortening
2 cups packed brown sugar
3 eggs
1 teaspoon vanilla extract
2 ounces (2 squares)
   unsweetened chocolate,
   melted and cooled
2 cups sifted all-purpose flour
1 teaspoon baking soda
3/4 teaspoon salt
1 cup buttermilk

Caramel Frosting:
3 tablespoons milk
3 tablespoons butter or
   margarine
1/2 cup packed brown sugar
1 2/3 cups sifted confectioners'
   sugar

1. Preheat oven to 350°.
2. Cream Crisco and brown sugar in a large mixer bowl. Add eggs, one at a time, and beat well after each addition. Mix in vanilla extract and melted chocolate until blended.
3. Combine flour, baking soda, and salt. Add dry ingredients alternately with buttermilk to creamed mixture, mixing until blended after each addition.

4. Turn batter into a greased and floured 13x9x2-inch pan and spread evenly.
5. Bake at 350° for 40 to 45 minutes or until a toothpick inserted in center comes out clean. Cool completely in pan.
6. For Caramel Frosting, combine milk, butter, and brown sugar in a saucepan. Heat until sugar is dissolved. Cool to room temperature. Stir in confectioners' sugar. Beat until frosting is of spreading consistency.
7. Spread frosting over cooled cake.

12 to 16 servings

Spicy Buttermilk Cake

1/2 cup Crisco shortening
1 cup packed brown sugar
2 eggs
2 cups sifted all-purpose flour
1 teaspoon baking powder
1 teaspoon salt
1/2 teaspoon baking soda
1 teaspoon ground cinnamon
1/2 teaspoon ground allspice
1/4 teaspoon ground cloves
3/4 cup buttermilk

Raisin Frosting:
2 tablespoons Crisco shortening
2 cups confectioners' sugar
1/2 teaspoon salt
3 to 4 tablespoons half-and-half or light cream, warmed
1/2 cup chopped raisins

1. Preheat oven to 350°.
2. Cream Crisco and brown sugar in a large mixer bowl. Add eggs, one at a time, beating well after each addition.
3. Combine flour, baking powder, salt, baking soda, and spices; add to creamed mixture alternately with buttermilk, mixing until blended after each addition.
4. Turn batter into a greased and floured 13x9x2-inch pan.
5. Bake at 350° for 35 minutes or until a toothpick inserted in center comes out clean. Cool in pan on a rack.
6. For Raisin Frosting, cream Crisco, 1/2 cup confectioners' sugar, and salt. Add remaining confectioners' sugar to creamed mixture alternately with warmed half-and-half, beating well after each addition. Stir in raisins. Spread over cooled cake. Decorate with *pecan halves.*

12 to 16 servings

Fruit-Topped Molasses Spice Cake

2/3 cup Crisco shortening
1/2 cup sugar
1/2 cup dark molasses
1 1/2 teaspoons pumpkin pie spice
2 eggs
2 1/2 cups sifted all-purpose flour
1 teaspoon baking powder
1 teaspoon baking soda
1/2 teaspoon salt
1 cup buttermilk
1 can (16 ounces) pear halves, drained and sliced
1 cup whipping cream
2 tablespoons confectioners' sugar
1/4 teaspoon vanilla extract

1. Preheat oven to 350°.
2. Cream Crisco, sugar, molasses, and spice in a large mixer bowl. Add eggs, one at a time, beating well after each addition.
3. Combine flour, baking powder, baking soda, and salt; alternately add to creamed mixture with buttermilk, mixing only until blended after each addition.
4. Turn batter into 2 greased and floured 9x1 1/2-inch round layer cake pans.
5. Bake at 350° for 20 to 25 minutes or until a toothpick inserted in center comes out clean.
6. Cool for 10 minutes in pans on racks, remove from pans, and cool completely on racks.
7. Pat pear slices dry with paper towels.
8. When ready to serve, beat whipping cream to soft peaks,

Spice Cakes

then beat in confectioners' sugar and vanilla extract.

9. Spread 1 cup whipped cream over one layer and arrange some pear slices on whipped cream. Put second layer in place; spread with remaining whipped cream. Decorate with remaining pear slices.

8 servings

Coffee-Raisin-Frosted Spice Cake

²/₃ cup Crisco shortening
1 cup packed brown sugar
1 teaspoon ground cinnamon
½ teaspoon ground allspice
½ teaspoon ground nutmeg
¼ teaspoon ground cloves
3 eggs
2 cups sifted all-purpose flour
1½ teaspoons baking powder
¾ teaspoon salt
½ teaspoon baking soda
¾ cup buttermilk

Coffee Raisin Frosting:
2 tablespoons Crisco
* shortening*
1 tablespoon butter or
* margarine*
3 cups sifted confectioners'
* sugar*
¼ teaspoon salt
3 tablespoons hot strong coffee
1 tablespoon hot half-and-half
⅓ cup chopped (or whole)
* raisins*

1. Preheat oven to 350°.
2. Cream Crisco, brown sugar, and spices. Add eggs, one at a time, beating well after each addition.
3. Combine flour, baking powder, salt, and baking soda; add to creamed mixture alternately with buttermilk, mixing until blended after each addition.
4. Pour into a greased 13x9x2-inch pan.
5. Bake at 350° for 30 to 35 minutes or until a toothpick inserted in center comes out clean. Cool completely in pan on a rack.
6. For Coffee Raisin Frosting, cream Crisco, butter, 1 cup confectioners' sugar, and salt in a bowl. Blend hot coffee and half-and-half; add to creamed mixture alternately with remaining confectioners' sugar, beating well after each addition. Add additional liquid if needed for desired spreading consistency. Stir in raisins. Spread on cooled cake.

12 to 16 servings

Harvest Pumpkin Spice Cake

½ cup Crisco shortening
1⅓ cups sugar
2 eggs
2 cups sifted all-purpose flour
2 teaspoons baking powder
1 teaspoon baking soda
1 teaspoon salt
2 teaspoons ground cinnamon
½ teaspoon ground nutmeg
¼ teaspoon ground allspice
¼ teaspoon ground ginger
1 cup canned pumpkin
1 cup buttermilk
½ cup finely chopped dates
½ cup chopped walnuts

Almond Spice Frosting:
4 egg whites
5 cups sifted confectioners'
* sugar*
½ cup Crisco shortening
2 teaspoons almond extract
½ teaspoon ground cinnamon

1. Preheat oven to 350°.
2. Cream Crisco and sugar in a large mixer bowl. Add eggs, one at a time, beating well after each addition.
3. Combine flour, baking powder, baking soda, salt, and spices. Blend pumpkin and buttermilk together. Alternately add dry ingredients and pumpkin mixture to creamed mixture, beating until smooth after each addition. Beat on medium speed for 2 minutes.
4. Stir in dates and nuts.
5. Pour into 2 greased and floured 9x1½-inch round layer cake pans.
6. Bake at 350° for 30 to 35 minutes or until a toothpick inserted in center comes out clean. Cool for 10 minutes in pans on racks. Turn cake out of pans and cool completely.
7. For Almond Spice Frosting, beat egg whites until shape begins to hold. Gradually add 3 cups sugar, beating constantly until mixture stands in firm, shiny peaks. Cream Crisco in a small mixer bowl. Gradually add remaining 2 cups sugar, beating well. Beat Crisco mixture into egg white mixture until smooth and creamy. Stir in almond extract and cinnamon.
8. Frost cake and refrigerate several hours.

12 to 16 servings

Spice Cakes

Spice Cake with Broiled Topping

1/2 cup Crisco shortening
1 1/4 cups packed brown sugar
2 eggs
2 1/2 cups sifted all-purpose flour
2 teaspoons baking powder
1/2 teaspoon baking soda
1/4 teaspoon salt
1 teaspoon ground cinnamon
1/4 teaspoon ground cloves
1/4 teaspoon ground mace
1/4 teaspoon ground nutmeg
1 cup buttermilk

Broiled Topping:
1/3 cup Crisco shortening
3/4 cup packed brown sugar
3 tablespoons milk
1/4 teaspoon salt
1 1/3 cups flaked coconut

1. Preheat oven to 350°.
2. Cream Crisco and brown sugar in a large mixer bowl. Add eggs, one at a time, beating after each addition.
3. Combine flour, baking powder, baking soda, salt, and spices. Add dry ingredients to creamed mixture alternately with buttermilk, mixing well after each addition.
4. Pour batter into a greased 13x9x2-inch pan.
5. Bake at 350° for 40 to 50 minutes or until a toothpick inserted in center comes out clean.
6. For Broiled Topping, put Crisco, brown sugar, milk, and salt into a saucepan. Bring to boiling; stir. Remove from heat and stir in coconut. Cool. Spread topping over warm cake. Put under broiler so top is 6 to 8 inches from heat; broil for 3 to 5 minutes or until coconut is golden brown.

12 to 16 servings

Spicy Date Nut Cake

1 cup Crisco shortening
3 eggs
1 teaspoon vanilla extract
1 1/4 cups sugar
2 cups sifted all-purpose flour
1 teaspoon baking soda
1 teaspoon salt
1 teaspoon ground allspice
1 teaspoon ground cinnamon
1 cup finely snipped dates
1 cup chopped walnuts
1 cup soured milk*

1. Preheat oven to 300°.
2. Cream Crisco, eggs, vanilla extract, and sugar in a large mixer bowl.
3. Combine flour, baking soda, salt, and spices; add 2 tablespoons mixture to dates and nuts in a bowl; toss to coat.
4. Add remaining dry ingredients alternately with soured milk to creamed mixture, beating only until smooth after each addition. Stir in date-nut mixture. Spread evenly in a greased 13x9x2-inch pan.
5. Bake at 300° for 60 to 75 minutes or until a toothpick inserted in center comes out clean. Cool completely in pan and frost as desired.

12 to 16 servings

* Put 1 tablespoon lemon juice or cider vinegar into a 1-cup glass measure and fill with milk to the 1-cup line; stir well.

Cinnamon Banana Favorites

1/2 cup Crisco shortening
1 1/2 teaspoons vanilla extract
1 cup sugar
2 eggs
1 cup mashed ripe bananas (about 2 medium bananas)
2 cups sifted cake flour
1 1/2 teaspoons salt
1 teaspoon baking soda
1/4 cup dairy sour cream

Cream Cheese Cinnamon Frosting:
3 tablespoons Crisco shortening
1 package (3 ounces) cream cheese, softened
1 teaspoon ground cinnamon
2 teaspoons vanilla extract
2 cups sifted confectioners' sugar

1. Preheat oven to 350°.
2. Cream Crisco and vanilla extract. Add sugar gradually, beating thoroughly. Add eggs, one at a time, beating until light and fluffy after each addition. Blend in bananas.
3. Combine cake flour, salt, and baking soda; add to creamed mixture alternately with sour cream, beating well after each addition.
4. Spoon batter into paper-lined muffin cups, filling each about two-thirds full.
5. Bake at 350° for 25 minutes or until a toothpick inserted in center comes out clean. Remove from pans to cool.
6. For frosting, cream Crisco, cream cheese, cinnamon, and extract in a bowl. Gradually add confectioners' sugar, beating until smooth and creamy. Frost cooled cupcakes.

24 cupcakes

Honey Walnut Cake

³/₄ cup Crisco shortening
1 teaspoon vanilla extract
¹/₂ cup sugar
1 egg
2¹/₂ cups sifted all-purpose flour
1¹/₂ teaspoons baking soda
1 teaspoon salt
³/₄ teaspoon ground cinnamon
¹/₄ teaspoon ground cloves
³/₄ cup honey
1 cup walnuts, chopped medium fine
1 cup hot water
Thawed frozen whipped dessert topping

Topping:
3 tablespoons butter or margarine, melted
¹/₃ cup honey
³/₄ cup walnuts, chopped medium

1. Preheat oven to 325°.
2. Grease a 12x8x1³/₄-inch baking dish.
3. Cream Crisco and vanilla extract; add sugar gradually, beating until well mixed. Add egg and beat until light and fluffy.
4. Combine flour, baking soda, salt, and spices. Stir into creamed mixture in order the dry ingredients, honey, and walnuts; mix thoroughly. Quickly and thoroughly stir in hot water. Turn into dish.

5. Bake at 325° for 35 to 40 minutes or until a toothpick inserted in center comes out clean.
6. Meanwhile, for Topping, blend ingredients and set aside.
7. Immediately spoon Topping over hot cake and spread evenly.
8. Set under broiler with top about 8 inches from heat; broil just until bubbly and lightly browned. (Watch carefully to avoid scorching.)
9. Serve warm or cold and accompany with a bowl of whipped dessert topping.

12 servings

Unfrosted Cakes

Upside-Down Cranberry Cake

Topping:
1/4 cup Crisco shortening, melted
1 cup sugar
1/2 teaspoon vanilla extract
2 cups cranberries, rinsed and coarsely chopped

Cake:
1/4 cup Crisco shortening
1/2 cup sugar
1 egg
1/2 teaspoon vanilla extract
1 cup sifted cake flour
1 1/2 teaspoons baking powder
1/2 teaspoon salt
1/3 cup milk

1. Preheat oven to 350°.
2. For Topping, combine melted Crisco, 2/3 cup sugar, and vanilla extract. Spread mixture evenly in a greased 8x8x2-inch pan. Top with chopped cranberries. Sprinkle remaining 1/3 cup sugar over cranberries.
3. For Cake, blend Crisco, sugar, egg, and vanilla extract in a large mixer bowl.
4. Combine cake flour, baking powder, and salt; add to creamed mixture alternately with milk, mixing until blended after each addition. Pour batter evenly over cranberries.
5. Bake at 350° for 40 minutes or until a toothpick inserted in center comes out clean. Cool for 5 minutes in pan. Invert onto a serving plate and remove pan.

9 servings

Choco Cherry Cake

1 ounce (1 square) unsweetened chocolate
2 cups sifted all-purpose flour
1 cup sugar
1 teaspoon baking soda
1/4 teaspoon salt
3/4 cup milk
1/2 cup Crisco shortening
1/4 cup maraschino cherry juice
2 eggs
1/3 cup chopped maraschino cherries
1/3 cup chopped pecans

Cherry Chocolate Sauce:
1 ounce (1 square) unsweetened chocolate
1/4 cup butter or margarine
2 cups sifted confectioners' sugar
1/3 cup maraschino cherry juice

1. Preheat oven to 350°.
2. Melt chocolate; set aside.
3. Combine flour, sugar, baking soda, and salt in a large mixer bowl. Make a well in center. Add milk, Crisco, cherry juice, and eggs. Blend at low speed until moistened. Beat for 2 minutes at medium speed. Add melted chocolate, cherries, and pecans; beat until mixed.
4. Pour into a greased and floured 13x9x2-inch pan.
5. Bake at 350° for 25 to 30 minutes or until a toothpick inserted in center comes out clean. Set pan on a rack.

6. For Cherry Chocolate Sauce, melt chocolate and butter in a saucepan. Beat in confectioners' sugar alternately with cherry juice until smooth.
7. To serve, cut cake into squares and top with sauce.

16 servings

Chocolate Pudding Cake

1 cup all-purpose flour
3/4 cup sugar
2 teaspoons baking powder
1/2 teaspoon salt
6 tablespoons unsweetened cocoa, divided
1/2 cup milk
3 tablespoons Crisco shortening, melted
1 teaspoon vanilla extract
3/4 cup packed brown sugar
1 2/3 cups hot water

1. Preheat oven to 350°.
2. Combine flour, sugar, baking powder, salt, and 3 tablespoons cocoa in a bowl. Add milk, melted Crisco, and vanilla extract; stir until blended.
3. Turn batter into an ungreased 8x8x2-inch baking dish. Combine remaining 3 tablespoons cocoa and the brown sugar. Sprinkle over batter. Pour hot water over all (do not stir).
4. Bake at 350° for 35 to 40 minutes or until a toothpick inserted in center about halfway to the bottom of pan comes out clean. Serve warm. Spoon out each serving of pudding cake and invert with sauce on top on dessert plate.

About 8 servings

Apricot Upside-Down Skillet Cake

Topping:
1 package (6 ounces) dried
*   apricots*
2 cups water
3 tablespoons Crisco
*   shortening, melted*
1/3 cup packed brown sugar
1/3 cup drained canned
*   crushed pineapple*

Cake:
1/2 cup Crisco shortening
1 cup sugar
2 eggs
1 teaspoon vanilla extract
2 cups sifted cake flour
1 tablespoon baking powder
1 teaspoon salt
2/3 cup milk

1. Preheat oven to 350°.
2. Grease a 10-inch skillet with Crisco. If the skillet handle is not heat-resistant, wrap handle with four thicknesses of aluminum foil.

3. For Topping, simmer apricots in water in a large saucepan for 30 minutes or until plump and tender. Cool and drain well.
4. Mix melted Crisco, brown sugar, and pineapple thoroughly. Arrange apricots in bottom of skillet. Spoon pineapple mixture over apricots.
5. For Cake, cream Crisco, sugar, eggs, and vanilla extract in a large mixer bowl. Combine cake flour, baking powder, and salt; add to creamed mixture alternately with milk, mixing until blended after each addition. Pour batter evenly over fruit.
6. Bake at 350° for 45 to 50 minutes or until a toothpick inserted in center comes out clean. Cool for 5 minutes in pan. Invert onto a serving plate and remove pan.

12 to 14 servings

Upside-Down Peach Cake

Topping:
1/2 pound dried peaches
2 cups water
3 tablespoons Crisco
*   shortening, melted*
1/2 cup packed brown sugar
1/3 cup drained canned
*   crushed pineapple*
Pecan halves

Cake:
1/4 cup Crisco shortening
1/2 cup sugar
1 egg
1/2 teaspoon vanilla extract
1 cup sifted cake flour
1 1/2 teaspoons baking powder
1/2 teaspoon salt
1/3 cup milk

1. Preheat oven to 350°.
2. For Topping, simmer peaches in water in a saucepan until plump and tender. Cool; drain well.
3. Mix melted Crisco, brown sugar, and pineapple thoroughly. Arrange peaches and pecan halves in bottom of a lightly greased 8x8x2-inch pan. Spoon pineapple mixture over all.
4. For Cake, cream Crisco, sugar, egg, and vanilla extract in a large mixer bowl. Combine cake flour, baking powder, and salt; add to creamed mixture alternately with milk, mixing until blended after each addition. Pour batter evenly over fruit.
5. Bake at 350° for 40 minutes or until a toothpick inserted in center comes out clean. Cool for 5 minutes in pan. Invert onto a serving plate.

9 servings

Unfrosted Cakes

Upside-Down Peach Cupcakes

2¼ cups sifted cake flour
1½ cups sugar
2 teaspoons baking powder
½ teaspoon salt
1 cup milk
¾ cup Crisco shortening
4 egg whites
1 teaspoon vanilla extract
1 cup packed brown sugar
  (2 teaspoons per muffin cup)
¼ cup Crisco shortening,
  melted (½ teaspoon per
  muffin cup)
1 can (16 ounces) sliced
  peaches, drained

1. Preheat oven to 350°.
2. Combine cake flour, sugar, baking powder, and salt in a large mixer bowl. Add ⅔ cup milk and Crisco. Blend at low speed. Beat for 2 minutes at medium speed (or beat vigorously by hand about 300 strokes). Add egg whites, remaining ⅓ cup milk, and vanilla extract. Continue beating for 2 minutes.
3. Using 2 dozen well-greased 2⅞-inch muffin cups, press 2 teaspoons brown sugar into bottom of each. Add ½ teaspoon melted Crisco. Cut peach slices in half lengthwise, if necessary, to make 24 slices. Place a sliced peach in each cup. Spoon batter into muffin cups, filling each about two-thirds full.
4. Bake at 350° for 25 to 30 minutes or until a toothpick inserted in center comes out clean. Run a pointed knife around each cupcake to loosen. Invert cakes onto racks to cool.

24 cupcakes

Upside-Down Pecan Cupcakes

Topping:
3 tablespoons packed brown
  sugar
2 tablespoons Crisco
  shortening, melted
1 tablespoon water
54 pecan halves (about ¾ cup)

Cake:
⅓ cup Crisco shortening
¾ cup sugar
2 eggs
½ teaspoon vanilla extract
1½ cups sifted cake flour
2 teaspoons baking powder
¾ teaspoon salt
½ cup milk

1. Preheat oven to 350°.
2. For Topping, combine brown sugar, Crisco, and water in a small mixer bowl. Spoon 1 teaspoon of mixture into each of 18 well-greased 2⅞-inch muffin cups. Arrange 3 pecan halves top-side-down in each cup.
3. For Cake, cream Crisco, sugar, eggs, and vanilla extract in a large mixer bowl. Combine cake flour, baking powder, and salt; add to creamed mixture alternately with milk, mixing until blended after each addition. Spoon batter into muffin cups filling each about two-thirds full.
4. Bake at 350° for 15 to 20 minutes, or until a toothpick inserted in center comes out clean. Run a pointed knife around each cupcake to loosen. Invert cakes onto racks to cool.

18 cupcakes

Everyone loves a great homemade pie. . . a delicious pie with tender, flaky pie crust that melts in your mouth. That's why pies are America's favorite dessert.

Crisco Shortening makes perfect pastry for pies, as generations of piemakers have discoved.

Blushing Pear Cranberry Pie

1¹/₂ pounds fresh winter pears, pared, quartered, cored, and sliced (about 4 cups)
2 tablespoons orange juice
1¹/₂ cups fresh or dry-pack frozen cranberries, rinsed and drained
1 cup sugar
3 tablespoons quick-cooking tapioca
1 teaspoon grated orange peel
¹/₄ teaspoon salt
Crisco pastry for a double-crust 9-inch pie, page 154
2 tablespoons butter or margarine

1. Combine pear slices and orange juice in a large bowl; toss lightly. Stir in cranberries. Combine sugar, tapioca, orange peel, and salt. Add to fruit and mix lightly. Set aside while preparing pastry.
2. Preheat oven to 425°.
3. Divide pastry almost in half. Roll out larger half to a 13-inch circle on a lightly floured surface. Line a 9-inch pie plate with pastry. Trim edge to ¹/₂ inch beyond rim of pie plate.
4. Turn filling into unbaked pie shell. Dot with butter.
5. Roll out remaining pastry to an 11-inch circle. Place top crust over fruit and trim edge to 1 inch beyond rim of pie plate. Fold top crust under lower crust and form a ridge. Flute edge. Cut slits for steam to escape.
6. Bake at 425° for 40 to 45 minutes or until pears are tender and crust is golden brown.
7. Cool on a rack before cutting. Serve with ice cream, if desired.

One 9-inch pie

Apple Pie in Cheddar Crust

Cheddar Cheese Pastry:
2 cups sifted all-purpose flour
1 cup shredded Cheddar cheese
¹/₂ teaspoon salt
²/₃ cup Crisco shortening
6 tablespoons cold water
1 egg yolk, beaten
1 tablespoon water

Apple Filling:
9 cups sliced pared tart cooking apples
¹/₃ cup packed light brown sugar
¹/₃ cup granulated sugar
2 tablespoons all-purpose flour
1 teaspoon ground cinnamon
¹/₄ teaspoon ground nutmeg
¹/₄ teaspoon salt
2 tablespoons butter or margarine

1. Preheat oven to 400°.
2. For Cheddar Cheese Pastry, combine flour, Cheddar cheese, and salt in a large bowl. Cut in Crisco with pastry blender or 2 knives until mixture resembles coarse crumbs. Add cold water, 1 tablespoon at a time, mixing until dry ingredients are moistened and dough can be gathered into a ball. Reserve egg yolk and water.
3. Divide dough almost in half. Roll out larger half to a 13-inch circle on a lightly floured surface. Line a 9-inch pie plate with pastry. Trim edge to ¹/₂ inch beyond rim of pie plate.
4. For Apple Filling, combine apples, sugars, flour, cinnamon, nutmeg, and salt in a large bowl; mix well. Arrange in the unbaked pie shell. Dot with butter.
5. Roll out remaining pastry to an 11-inch circle. Place top crust over apples and trim edge to 1 inch beyond rim of pie plate. Fold top crust under lower crust and form a ridge. Flute edge. Cut slits for steam to escape. Combine egg yolk and water. Brush over crust.
6. Bake at 400° for 40 minutes or until apples are tender and crust is golden brown. Cool on a rack.
7. Serve warm or cold with *scoops of ice cream* or *slices of Cheddar cheese.*

One 9-inch pie

Double-Crust Pies

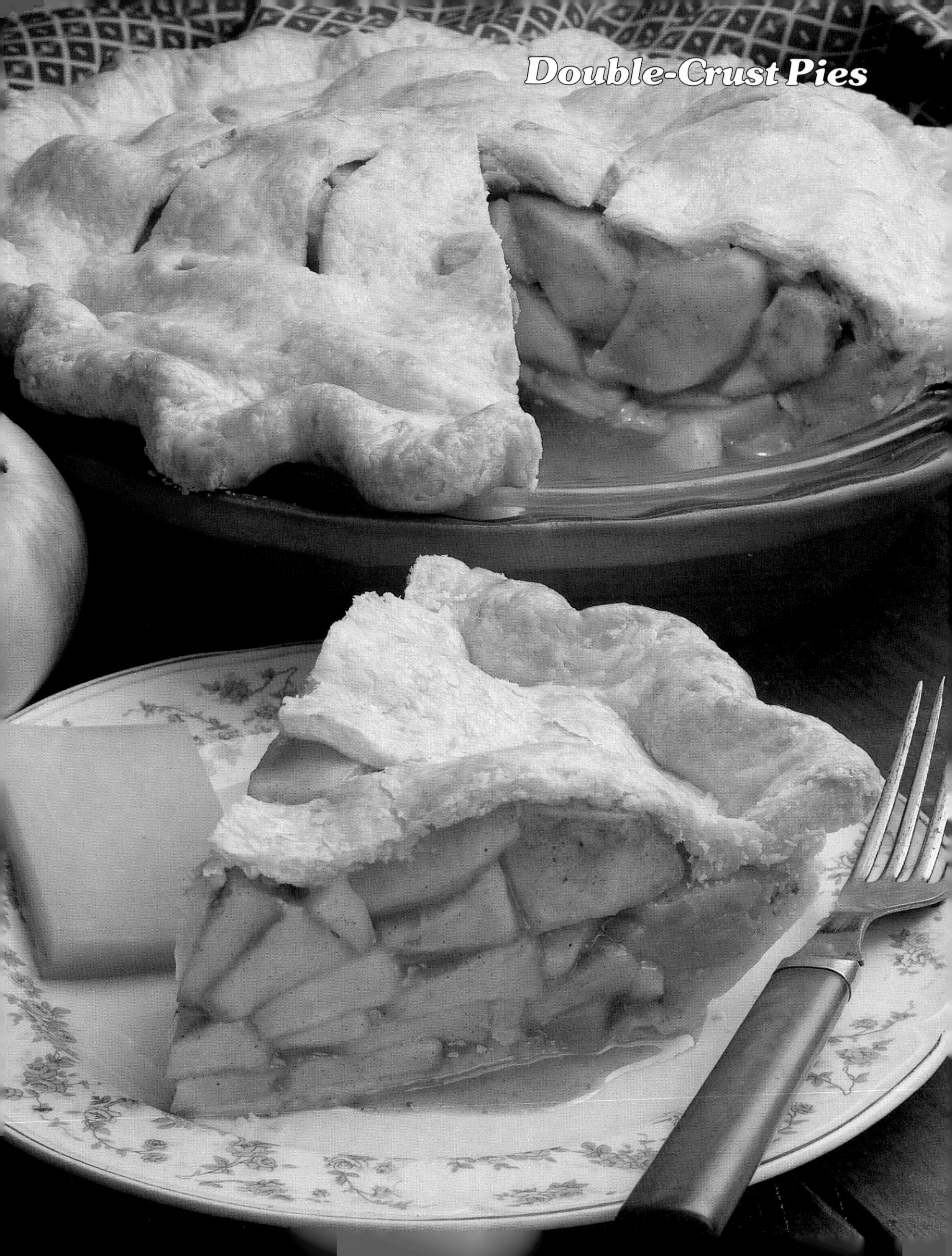

Fresh Peach Pie

4 cups sliced peeled fresh
  peaches*
1 tablespoon lemon juice
1¼ cups sugar
3 tablespoons quick-cooking
  tapioca
⅛ teaspoon salt
⅛ teaspoon ground nutmeg
Crisco pastry for a double-
crust 9-inch pie, page 154
2 tablespoons butter or
  margarine

1. Gently toss peach slices
with lemon juice. Combine
sugar, tapioca, salt, and
nutmeg. Add to peaches and
mix lightly. Set aside while
preparing pastry.
2. Preheat oven to 425°.
3. Divide pastry almost in
half. Roll out larger half to a
13-inch circle on a lightly
floured surface. Line a 9-inch
pie plate with pastry. Trim
edge to ½ inch beyond rim
of pie plate.
4. Turn filling into unbaked
pie shell; dot with butter.
5. Roll out remaining pastry
to an 11-inch circle. Place top
crust over fruit and trim edge
to 1 inch beyond rim of pie
plate. Fold top crust under
lower crust and form a ridge.
Flute edge. Cut slits for steam
to escape.
6. Bake at 425° for 40 to 50
minutes or until fruit is
tender and crust is golden
brown.
7. Cool slightly on a rack
before cutting. Serve with ice
cream, if desired.

One 9-inch pie

*If fresh peaches are not available, 1
package (20 ounces) dry-pack frozen
sliced peaches may be used.

Lattice-Top Blueberry Pie

Crisco pastry for a double-
crust 9-inch pie, page 154
5 cups fresh blueberries or 1
  package (20 ounces) frozen
  blueberries, thawed
1 cup sugar
¼ cup all-purpose flour*
¼ teaspoon salt
1 teaspoon grated lemon peel
1 tablespoon lemon juice
2 tablespoons butter or
  margarine

1. Preheat oven to 400°.
2. Divide pastry almost in
half. Roll larger half to a 13-
inch circle on a lightly floured
surface. Line a 9-inch pie plate
with pastry. Trim edge to ½
inch beyond rim of pie plate.
3. Rinse and drain blueberries;
put into a bowl. Add sugar,
flour, salt, and lemon peel;
toss lightly. Turn into the
unbaked pie shell. Drizzle
lemon juice over filling; dot
with butter.
4. Roll out remaining pastry;
cut into strips about ½ inch
wide. Place 4 to 5 strips across
filling in pie plate. Angle 4
to 5 strips across first ones.
Weave strips in crisscross
fashion to form lattice top.
Trim ends. Fold trimmed edge
of lower crust over ends of
strips. Seal and flute.
5. Bake at 400° for 40 minutes
until crust is golden. Cool on
a rack.
6. Serve with scoops of ice
cream or dollops of whipped
cream, if desired.

One 9-inch pie

* If using frozen blueberries, increase
flour to ⅓ cup.

Double-Crust Pies

Tropical Pineapple Pie

1/3 cup sugar
1/4 cup cornstarch
1/4 teaspoon salt
2 cans (20 ounces each) crushed pineapple in heavy syrup (undrained)
2 tablespoons butter or margarine
Crisco pastry for a double-crust 9-inch pie, page 154
1/4 cup finely chopped blanched almonds

1. Combine sugar, cornstarch, and salt in a heavy saucepan. Stir in undrained pineapple. Cook over medium-high heat, stirring constantly, until mixture comes to boiling. Cook and stir for 2 minutes. Add butter; stir until melted. Set filling aside while preparing pastry.
2. Preheat oven to 425°.
3. Prepare Crisco pastry adding chopped almonds before water.
4. Divide pastry almost in half. Roll larger half to a 13-inch circle on a lightly floured surface. Line a 9-inch pie plate with pastry. Trim edge to 1/2 inch beyond edge of pie plate.
5. Turn filling into unbaked pie shell.
6. Roll out remaining pastry to an 11-inch circle. Place top crust over filling and trim edge to 1 inch beyond rim of pie plate. Fold top crust under lower crust and form a ridge. Flute edge. Cut slits for steam to escape.
7. Bake at 425° for 35 minutes or until golden brown.
8. Cool on a rack before cutting. Serve with *ice cream*.

One 9-inch pie

Old-Fashioned Apple Slices

2 pounds tart cooking apples, pared, quartered, cored, and sliced (6 cups apple slices)
1 tablespoon lemon juice
3/4 cup hot water
3/4 cup sugar
1/4 teaspoon salt
2 tablespoons cornstarch
1/4 cup cold water
Crisco pastry for a double-crust 9-inch pie, page 154
2 tablespoons fine dry bread crumbs
1/2 teaspoon ground cinnamon
1/8 teaspoon ground nutmeg
1 tablespoon butter or margarine
Milk for brushing

Glaze:
3/4 cup confectioners' sugar
Dash salt
1/4 teaspoon vanilla extract
3 to 4 teaspoons hot milk

1. Put apple slices and lemon juice into a bowl and toss lightly to mix. Set aside.
2. Combine hot water, sugar, and salt in a large heavy saucepan. Cook over medium-high heat, stirring occasionally, until syrup comes to boiling. Add apple slices. Cover and cook over low heat for 15 minutes or until apples are tender, but not soft; stir carefully twice during cooking.
3. Carefully remove apple slices from syrup with slotted spoon. Combine cornstarch and cold water and blend into the hot syrup. Cook over medium-high heat, stirring constantly, until syrup comes to boiling. Cook and stir for 2 minutes. Add to apple slices and mix gently. Set aside while preparing pastry.
4. Preheat oven to 425°.
5. Roll out two-thirds of the pastry to a 10-inch square on a lightly floured surface. Carefully ease into an 8-inch square pan, pressing pastry against bottom and sides of pan.
6. Sprinkle bread crumbs over pastry. Spoon filling into crust; sprinkle with cinnamon and nutmeg, then dot with butter.
7. Roll out remaining pastry to an 8-inch square. Place over filling, sealing to bottom crust by pressing with fingers. Brush with milk. Cut several slits for steam to escape.
8. Bake at 425° for 40 minutes or until golden brown. Cool on a rack.
9. For Glaze, combine ingredients, blending until smooth and of spreading consistency. Spread Glaze evenly over top. Cut into slices.

12 slices

Decoration Idea: Make a double-crust pie special by cutting out designs with small cookie cutters before top crust is placed over filling. Vary cutter to suit the occasion. Bake cutouts separately; place atop baked pie.

Flaky Crisco Pastry

Crisco Pastry for Double-Crust Pie

2 cups sifted all-purpose flour
1 teaspoon salt
3/4 cup Crisco shortening
3 to 4 tablespoons cold water

1. Combine flour and salt in a mixing bowl. Cut in Crisco with pastry blender or 2 knives until mixture is uniform (mixture should be fairly coarse).
2. Sprinkle with water, 1 tablespoon at a time; toss lightly with fork. When all water has been added, work dough into a firm ball. Divide dough into two parts.
3. On a lightly floured surface, press dough into flat circles with smooth edges. Roll bottom crust to a circle 1/8 inch thick and about 1 1/2 inches larger than inverted pie plate. Gently ease dough into pie plate, being careful not to stretch the dough. Trim edge even with pie plate.
4. Add filling to shell. Moisten pastry edge with water. Roll top crust the same way and lift onto filled pie. Trim 1/2 inch beyond edge of pie plate. Fold top edge under bottom crust; flute edge. Cut slits or design in top crust or prick with fork for escape of steam.

One double-crust or lattice-top 9-inch pie or 8 to 12 tart shells

Crisco Pastry for Single-Crust Pie

1 1/3 cups sifted all-purpose flour
1/2 teaspoon salt
1/2 cup Crisco shortening
2 to 3 tablespoons cold water

1. Combine flour and salt in a mixing bowl. Cut in Crisco with pastry blender or 2 knives until mixture is uniform (mixture should be fairly coarse).
2. Sprinkle with water, 1 tablespoon at a time; toss lightly with fork. When all water has been added, work dough into a firm ball.
3. Press dough into a flat circle with smooth edges. On a lightly floured surface, roll dough to a circle 1/8 inch thick and about 1 1/2 inches larger than inverted pie plate.
4. Gently ease dough into the pie plate, being careful not to stretch the dough. Trim 1/2 inch beyond edge of pie plate. Fold under to make double thickness around rim. Flute edge of pastry as desired.

One 8- or 9-inch pie shell

To bake without filling: Preheat oven to 425°. Prick bottom and sides of shell with fork. Bake for 10 to 15 minutes or until lightly browned.

To bake with filling: Preheat oven to temperature directed in recipe. Do not prick shell. Bake as directed in recipe.

Homemade Crisco Pie Crust Mix

6 cups sifted all-purpose flour
1 tablespoon salt
1 pound (2 1/3 cups) Crisco shortening

1. Mix flour and salt in a large mixing bowl. Cut in Crisco with pastry blender or 2 knives until mixture is uniform and very fine.
2. Store in a covered container, such as an empty 3-pound Crisco can. No refrigeration is needed.
3. To use, measure mix into a bowl. Sprinkle water over mix, 1 tablespoon at a time; toss lightly with a fork. When all water has been added, work dough into a firm ball.

About 8 cups mix

For single-crust pie: Use 1 1/2 cups of the Crisco Pie Crust Mix and 3 tablespoons water.

For double-crust or lattice-top pie: Use 2 1/4 cups of the Crisco Pie Crust Mix and 4 tablespoons water.

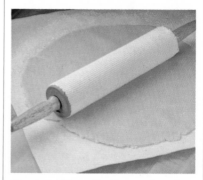

Pastry Tip: Roll out dough in spoke fashion from center to edge, lifting rolling pin at the edge to keep pastry an even thickness.

Decorative Pie Edges

3 Easy-to-Do Pie Edges

  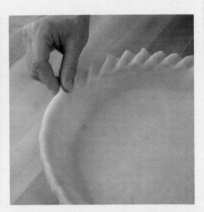

Pinch: Place index finger on inside of pastry edge, right thumb and index finger on outside. Pinch pastry into V-shape. Repeat pinching to sharpen design.

Scallop: Support pastry at outside edge with slightly curved fingers of one hand. With thumb of other hand, press pastry to outside against fingers to form each scallop.

Rope: Trim pastry ½ to 1 inch beyond edge of pie plate; fold under to make plump pastry edge. Press pastry forward diagonally with bent finger while pulling back with your thumb.

Simple Edges with Kitchen Utensils

Fork: Trim pastry overhang ½ inch from edge of pie plate; fold under. Dip fork in flour to prevent sticking, then press firmly on pastry edge.

Knife: Trim pastry overhang 1 inch from edge of pie plate; fold under. Cut pastry edge with knife at ½-inch intervals. Fold alternate squares under.

Spoon: Trim pastry overhang 1 inch from edge of pie plate; fold under. Make a double-ruffle pastry edge by pressing tip of a metal measuring tablespoon into pastry.

Can Opener: Trim pastry overhang ½ inch from edge of pie plate; fold under. Using pointed end of can opener with sharp side down, cut out pastry edge.

Lemon Meringue Pie

Crisco pastry for a single-crust 9-inch pie, page 154

Lemon Filling:
1 cup sugar
6 tablespoons cornstarch
1/8 teaspoon salt
1 1/2 cups cold water
3 egg yolks, slightly beaten
2 tablespoons butter or margarine
1/2 cup lemon juice
1 teaspoon white vinegar
1 teaspoon grated lemon peel

Meringue:
3 egg whites
1/8 teaspoon salt
6 tablespoons sugar
1/2 teaspoon vanilla extract

1. Line a 9-inch pie plate with pastry; bake and cool.
2. For Lemon Filling, combine sugar, cornstarch, and salt in a heavy saucepan. Gradually stir in water, blending until smooth. Cook over medium heat, stirring constantly, until filling comes to boiling. Cook, stirring constantly, for 5 minutes, then remove from heat.
3. Stir a small amount of hot filling into beaten egg yolks, mix thoroughly, then stir into hot filling. Cook, stirring constantly, for 1 minute. Remove from heat and stir in butter, lemon juice, vinegar, and lemon peel. Cool.
4. Preheat oven to 350°.

5. For Meringue, beat egg whites and salt until frothy. Gradually add sugar, beating well after each addition; continue beating until stiff peaks are formed. Blend in vanilla extract.
6. Spoon Lemon Filling into the baked pie shell, then spread Meringue over filling being sure to seal meringue to edge of pie shell.
7. Bake at 350° for 15 to 18 minutes or until golden brown. Cool on a rack. Chill.

One 9-inch pie

Meringue-Topped Pear Pie

Crisco pastry for a single-crust 9-inch pie, page 154
1 can (29 ounces) pear halves in syrup, well drained
3 egg yolks
1/2 cup milk
1/2 cup packed brown sugar
1/2 teaspoon grated orange peel
1 tablespoon orange juice
1/2 teaspoon vanilla extract
3 egg whites
1/3 cup granulated sugar

1. Preheat oven to 350°.
2. Line a 9-inch pie plate with pastry.
3. Arrange pear halves cut-side-down in the unbaked pie shell.
4. Beat egg yolks, milk, brown sugar, orange peel, orange juice, and vanilla extract together until fairly smooth. Pour over pears.
5. Bake at 350° for 40 to 55 minutes or until a knife when inserted near center of filling comes out clean.

6. Beat egg whites until frothy; gradually add granulated sugar, beating until stiff peaks form. Swirl meringue over filling. Return to oven and bake for 15 to 20 minutes or until golden brown. Cool on a rack.

One 9-inch pie

Applesauce Lemon Pie

Crisco pastry for a single-crust 9-inch pie, page 154
1½ cups unsweetened applesauce
¾ cup packed brown sugar
4 eggs, slightly beaten
¼ cup Crisco shortening
3 tablespoons lemon juice
1 teaspoon grated lemon peel
¾ teaspoon salt
¼ teaspoon ground nutmeg
¼ teaspoon ground cinnamon

1. Line a 9-inch pie plate with pastry; set aside.
2. Preheat oven to 450°.
3. Combine applesauce, brown sugar, eggs, Crisco, lemon juice, lemon peel, salt, nutmeg, and cinnamon; mix well.
4. Pour filling into the unbaked pie shell.
5. Bake at 450° for 15 minutes; reduce heat to 300°. Continue baking for 45 to 55 minutes or until a knife inserted in filling halfway between center and edge comes out clean.
6. Cool thoroughly on a rack before cutting.

One 9-inch pie

Tutti-Frutti Ice Cream Pie

Crisco pastry for a single-crust 9-inch pie, page 154
1 quart vanilla ice cream, softened
1 can (20 ounces) crushed pineapple in pineapple juice, divided
1 can (16 ounces) peach halves in heavy syrup
½ cup maraschino cherries, quartered
¼ cup chopped walnuts
½ cup toasted coconut
¼ cup sugar
3 tablespoons cornstarch
¼ cup toasted coconut

1. Line a 9-inch pie plate with pastry; bake and cool.
2. Put ice cream into a large bowl. Drain pineapple; reserve juice. Add ½ cup crushed pineapple to ice cream; reserve remainder. Drain peach halves, reserve syrup. Chop peaches and add to ice cream. Stir in maraschino cherries, walnuts, and ½ cup toasted coconut. Spread mixture evenly in the baked pie shell; cover with plastic wrap and freeze overnight.
3. Meanwhile, combine sugar, cornstarch, reserved pineapple, juice, and peach syrup in a medium saucepan. Bring to boiling over medium heat, stirring constantly. Cook until thick (about 5 minutes), stirring constantly. Refrigerate covered overnight.
4. When ready to serve, spoon pineapple topping over ice cream pie and spread evenly. Decorate with ¼ cup toasted coconut.

8 servings

Apple Raspberry Meringue Pie

Crisco pastry for a single-crust 9-inch pie, page 154
1 can (20 ounces) apple pie filling
½ cup raspberry preserves

Meringue:
2 egg whites
¼ cup sugar

1. Line a 9-inch pie plate with pastry; bake and cool.
2. Preheat oven to 350°.
3. Heat apple pie filling in a heavy saucepan over medium heat, stirring occasionally, until filling comes to boiling. Remove from heat.
4. Spread raspberry preserves over bottom of the baked pie shell. Spoon hot apple filling over preserves.
5. For Meringue, beat egg whites until frothy. Gradually add sugar, beating well after each addition; continue beating until stiff peaks are formed. Spread over filling being sure to seal meringue to edge of pie shell.
6. Bake at 350° for 15 to 18 minutes or until golden brown. Cool on a rack.

One 9-inch pie

How to spread meringue

Place meringue on warm filling in several mounds around edge of pie. Push meringue to edge of crust to seal. Cover rest of filling by gently pushing meringue towards center of pie.

Lime Chiffon Pie

*Crisco pastry for a single-
crust 9-inch pie, page 154*
1 envelope unflavored gelatin
¼ cup cold water
4 egg yolks, slightly beaten
⅔ cup sugar
2 teaspoons grated lime peel
½ cup lime juice
¼ teaspoon salt
*2 or 3 drops green food
coloring*
4 egg whites
½ cup sugar

1. Line a 9-inch pie plate with
pastry; bake and cool.
2. Soften gelatin in cold water.
3. Mix egg yolks, ⅔ cup sugar,
lime peel, lime juice, and salt
in a small saucepan. Cook
over medium heat, stirring
constantly, until mixture is
slightly thickened.
4. Remove from heat and blend
in softened gelatin, stirring
until gelatin is dissolved. Mix
in food coloring, a drop at a
time. Cool; chill until mixture
is partially set.
5. Beat egg whites until frothy.
Add ½ cup sugar gradually,
beating constantly until stiff
peaks are formed. Spread over
partially set gelatin and fold
together. Turn into the baked
pie shell. Chill until firm.

One 9-inch pie

Black Bottom Pie

*Crisco pastry for a single-
crust 9-inch pie, page 154*
1 envelope unflavored gelatin
¼ cup cold water
⅓ cup sugar
1 tablespoon cornstarch
¼ teaspoon salt
2 cups milk
4 egg yolks, slightly beaten
*2 ounces (2 squares) semisweet
chocolate, melted*
1 teaspoon vanilla extract
*1 tablespoon rum or 1
tablespoon milk*
4 egg whites
½ cup sugar

1. Line a 9-inch pie plate with
pastry; bake and cool.
2. Soften gelatin in cold water.
3. Combine ⅓ cup sugar, cornstarch, and salt in a heavy
saucepan. Gradually stir in
milk, blending until smooth.
Cook over medium heat,
stirring constantly, until
filling comes to boiling. Cook,
stirring constantly, for 5
minutes, then remove from
heat.
4. Stir a small amount of hot
filling into beaten egg yolks,
mixing thoroughly, then stir
into hot filling. Cook, stirring
constantly, for 1 minute.
Remove from heat and stir in
gelatin.
5. Blend melted chocolate and
vanilla extract into 1 cup of
the hot filling; pour filling
into the baked pie shell. Chill
until set (about 45 minutes).
6. Stir rum into remaining
filling. Cool.
7. Beat egg whites until frothy.
Gradually add remaining ½
cup sugar, beating well after
each addition; continue beating
until stiff peaks are formed.

Add a fourth of egg whites
to custard to lighten. Fold
remaining egg whites into
filling, gently but thoroughly.
Spoon over chocolate filling in
pie shell. Chill several hours
or overnight until filling is
firm.
8. Decorate with *sweetened
whipped cream* and *chocolate
curls.*

One 9-inch pie

Pecan Pie

*Crisco pastry for a single-
crust 9-inch pie, page 154*
*3 tablespoons Crisco
shortening*
2 teaspoons vanilla extract
½ cup granulated sugar
¼ cup packed brown sugar
3 eggs, well beaten
½ cup chopped pecans
1 cup dark corn syrup
¼ teaspoon salt
½ cup pecan halves

1. Line a 9-inch pie plate with
pastry; set aside.
2. Preheat oven to 450°.
3. Cream Crisco and vanilla
extract. Gradually add sugars,
beating well after each
addition. Add beaten eggs in
thirds, beating well after each
addition. Thoroughly blend in
chopped pecans, corn syrup,
and salt.
4. Pour filling into unbaked
pie shell.
5. Bake at 450° for 10 minutes;
reduce heat to 350°. Arrange
pecan halves over top of
filling. Continue baking for 30
to 35 minutes or until set.
6. Cool thoroughly on a rack
before cutting.

One 9-inch pie

Chocolate Fudge Pie

*Crisco pastry for a single-
crust 9-inch pie, page 154*
¼ cup Crisco shortening
*1 bar (4 ounces) sweet cooking
chocolate*
*1 can (14 ounces) sweetened
condensed milk*
2 eggs, beaten
1 teaspoon vanilla extract
¼ teaspoon salt
½ cup all-purpose flour
1 cup flaked coconut
1 cup chopped pecans

1. Preheat oven to 350°.
2. Line a 9-inch pie plate with
pastry and make a decorative
edge; set aside.
3. Melt Crisco and chocolate
in a heavy saucepan over low
heat. Remove from heat. Stir
in milk, eggs, vanilla extract,
salt, and flour; mix well. Stir
in coconut and pecans. Pour
into the unbaked pie shell.
4. Bake at 350° for 40 minutes
or until toothpick inserted in
center comes out clean. Cool
thoroughly on a rack before
cutting.
5. Serve with unsweetened
whipped cream or scoops of
ice cream, if desired.

One 9-inch pie

Old-Fashioned Cherry Rhubarb Pie

*1 can (16 ounces) pitted tart
red cherries in extra heavy
syrup, drained**
*1 pound fresh rhubarb, cut in
⅛-inch slices*
1¼ cups sugar
¼ cup quick-cooking tapioca
½ teaspoon vanilla extract
¼ teaspoon ground nutmeg
⅛ teaspoon baking soda
*Few drops red food coloring
(optional)*
*Crisco pastry for a double-
crust 9-inch pie, page 154*

1. Mix cherries, rhubarb,
sugar, tapioca, vanilla extract,
nutmeg, baking soda, and red
food coloring in a large bowl;
let stand 20 minutes.
2. Preheat oven to 450°.
3. Divide pastry almost in half.
Roll out larger half to a 13-
inch circle on a lightly floured
surface. Line a 9-inch pie plate
with pastry. Trim edge to ½
inch beyond rim of pie plate.
4. Pour filling into the unbaked
pie shell. Roll out remaining
pastry to an 11-inch circle.
Place top crust over filling
and trim edge to 1 inch
beyond rim of pie plate. Fold
top crust under lower crust
and form a ridge. Flute edge.
Cut slits for steam to escape.
5. Bake at 450° for 15 minutes.
Reduce heat to 350° and bake
for 40 to 45 minutes or until
crust is golden.
6. Cool on a rack. Serve warm
or cooled, topped with scoops
of ice cream, if desired.

One 9-inch pie

* Water-packed pitted tart red
cherries may be used.

160

Peaches 'n' Cream in Chocolate Crust

Chocolate Pastry:
1¹/₃ *cups sifted all-purpose*
   flour
3 tablespoons sugar
2 tablespoons unsweetened
   cocoa
¹/₂ *teaspoon salt*
¹/₂ *cup Crisco shortening*
¹/₄ *cup finely chopped pecans*
¹/₄ *cup cold water*

Peaches 'n' Cream Filling:
1 can (16 ounces) cling peach
   slices in syrup
1 package (3 ounces) lemon-
   flavored gelatin
³/₄ *cup boiling water*
2 tablespoons orange juice
1 pint vanilla ice cream

1. Preheat oven to 400°.
2. For Pastry, sift flour, sugar, cocoa, and salt into a mixing bowl. Cut in Crisco with pastry blender or 2 knives until mixture resembles coarse crumbs. Stir in pecans. Add cold water, 1 tablespoon at a time, mixing until dry ingredients are moistened and dough can be gathered into a ball.
3. Pat dough evenly onto bottom and sides of a 9-inch pie plate; flute edge. Prick bottom and sides of pastry with a fork.
4. Bake at 400° for 10 to 12 minutes or until crust is firm and moist look has disappeared. Cool on a rack.
5. For Filling, drain peach slices, reserving ¹/₂ cup syrup. Dissolve gelatin in boiling water; stir in reserved syrup and orange juice. Chill until slightly thickened. Reserve 6

peach slices for decoration; dice remaining peaches.
6. Whip gelatin until light and fluffy and doubled in volume.
7. Soften ice cream to consistency of whipped cream. Quickly fold ice cream and diced peaches into gelatin. Immediately turn into the baked pie shell. Decorate with reserved peach slices. Chill for several hours or until firm.

One 9-inch pie

Choco Mallow Pie

Crisco pastry for a single-
   crust 9-inch pie, page 154
20 marshmallows, cut in half
¹/₂ *cup milk*
¹/₃ *cup semisweet chocolate*
   pieces
3 ripe bananas
1 container (8 ounces) frozen
   non-dairy whipped topping,
   thawed

1. Line a 9-inch pie plate with pastry; bake and cool.
2. Melt marshmallows with milk in a heavy saucepan over low heat; stir in chocolate pieces until melted. Set aside to cool.
3. Meanwhile, peel bananas, cut into ¹/₄-inch slices, and arrange in the baked pie shell.
4. Fold whipped topping into cooled chocolate-marshmallow mixture. Turn into pie shell over bananas; spread evenly. Chill for 2 hours.

One 9-inch pie

Banana Butterscotch Pie

Crisco pastry for a single-
   crust 9-inch pie, page 154
³/₄ *cup packed brown sugar*
¹/₄ *cup cornstarch*
³/₄ *teaspoon salt*
2 cups milk
2 egg yolks, slightly beaten
2 tablespoons butter or
   margarine
1 teaspoon vanilla extract
3 ripe bananas
Sweetened whipped cream

1. Line a 9-inch pie plate with pastry; bake and cool.
2. Mix brown sugar, cornstarch, and salt in a heavy saucepan. Mix milk and slightly beaten egg yolks. Gradually add milk mixture to dry ingredients, blending until smooth.
3. Place over medium heat and cook, stirring constantly, until mixture comes to boiling. Cook for 1 minute and remove from heat.
4. Stir in butter and vanilla extract. Cover pudding surface with plastic wrap and cool to lukewarm.
5. Spoon half of filling (about 1 cup) into the baked pie shell. Cut 2 peeled bananas into crosswise slices and arrange over filling. Spoon remaining filling over bananas. Chill for 2 hours.
6. Just before serving, cover filling with sweetened whipped cream. Slice remaining banana crosswise and arrange in circle around edge of filling.

One 9-inch pie

Buttermilk Lemon Pie

Crisco pastry for a single-crust 9-inch pie, page 154
3 egg yolks
3/4 teaspoon grated lemon peel
3 tablespoons lemon juice
1/2 cup sugar
2 tablespoons all-purpose flour
1/2 teaspoon salt
3 tablespoons butter or margarine, melted
1 1/2 cups buttermilk
3 egg whites
1/4 cup sugar

1. Preheat oven to 450°.
2. Line a 9-inch pie plate with pastry; set aside.
3. Combine egg yolks, lemon peel, and lemon juice in a bowl. Blend 1/2 cup sugar, flour, and salt. Add to egg yolk mixture and beat until blended. Blend in butter and buttermilk.
4. Beat egg whites until frothy. Gradually add remaining 1/4 cup sugar, beating until soft peaks form. Spread over buttermilk mixture and fold together. Turn into the unbaked pie shell.
5. Bake at 450° for 10 minutes. Reduce heat to 350° and bake for 25 minutes or until a knife comes out clean when inserted in filling halfway between center and edge.
6. Cool thoroughly on a rack before cutting.

One 9-inch pie

Orange Delight Pie

Crisco pastry for a single-crust 9-inch pie, page 154
3 navel oranges
2 tablespoons sugar
Orange juice
1 envelope unflavored gelatin
2 tablespoons cold water
1/4 cup sugar
1 tablespoon lemon juice
3 egg yolks, slightly beaten
3 egg whites, beaten to stiff, not dry, peaks
1 cup whipping cream, whipped
1/2 cup toasted flaked coconut
1/4 cup chopped maraschino cherries, drained

1. Line a 9-inch pie plate with pastry; bake and cool.
2. Grate 1 tablespoon orange peel; set aside. Peel and section oranges; coarsely chop orange sections and put into a sieve over a measuring cup. Sprinkle with 2 tablespoons sugar, stir, and let drain 10 minutes. Add more orange juice to make 1/2 cup juice. Reserve.
3. Soften gelatin in cold water.
4. Combine 1/4 cup sugar, lemon juice, reserved 1/2 cup orange juice, and egg yolks in a heavy saucepan. Cook and stir over low heat until custard coats a metal spoon. Remove from heat; stir in gelatin and reserved orange peel. Cool.
5. Fold beaten egg whites into cooled custard, then fold in whipped cream. Lightly fold in orange pieces, coconut, and cherries.
6. Spoon into the baked pie shell. Refrigerate until firm.
7. Decorate with orange sections, if desired.

One 9-inch pie

Pineapple Cloud Pie

Crisco pastry for a single-crust 9-inch pie, page 154

Filling:
2 envelopes unflavored gelatin
1/2 cup sugar, divided
1/4 teaspoon salt
3 eggs, separated
1/2 cup water
1 can (20 ounces) crushed pineapple in pineapple juice (undrained)
1/2 teaspoon grated lemon peel
1 tablespoon lemon juice
Whipped dessert topping

1. Line a 9-inch pie plate with pastry; bake and cool.
2. For Filling, mix gelatin, 1/4 cup sugar, and salt in the top of a double boiler. Beat egg yolks and water together. Drain pineapple; reserve the juice. Add egg yolk mixture, pineapple juice, and 1 1/3 cups pineapple to gelatin mixture and beat thoroughly; set remaining pineapple aside. Set double-boiler top over boiling water and cook for 5 minutes, stirring constantly.
3. Remove from water; blend in lemon peel and lemon juice. Chill, stirring occasionally, until mixture mounds slightly.
4. Beat egg whites until frothy. Gradually add remaining 1/4 cup sugar, beating until stiff peaks form. Fold into gelatin mixture. Turn filling into the baked pie shell; chill.
5. Decorate pie with whipped topping and remaining pineapple.

One 9-inch pie

Single-Crust Pies

Apricot Cheese Pie

Crisco pastry for a single-crust 9-inch pie, page 154
1 cup dried apricots
1/4 cup slivered blanched almonds
3 eggs
1 teaspoon lemon juice
3/4 cup sugar
1 tablespoon all-purpose flour
1/2 teaspoon salt
1 cup creamed cottage cheese, sieved*
1/2 cup dairy sour cream

1. Preheat oven to 425°.
2. Line a 9-inch pie plate with pastry; set aside.
3. Rinse and drain apricots; cut into small pieces and sprinkle over bottom of the unbaked pie shell. Sprinkle almonds over apricots.
4. Combine eggs and lemon juice in a bowl; beat slightly. Blend sugar, flour, and salt. Gradually add to egg mixture, beating constantly. Add cottage cheese and sour cream; mix until blended. Pour over apricots and almonds in pie shell.
5. Bake at 425° for 45 minutes or until a knife inserted near center of filling comes out clean. If the pie crust edges begin to brown too much during baking, cover them with strips of aluminum foil to prevent overbrowning.
6. Cool thoroughly on a rack, then chill.
7. Decorate each serving with *sliced dried apricots* and *slivered almonds*.

One 9-inch pie

*Force cottage cheese through sieve or colander until no lumps remain.

Sour Cream 'n' Spice Raisin Pie

Crisco pastry for a single-crust 9-inch pie, page 154
1 1/2 cups seedless raisins
1/2 cup granulated sugar
1/4 cup packed brown sugar
1/4 cup cornstarch
1/2 teaspoon ground cinnamon
1/4 teaspoon salt
1/8 teaspoon ground nutmeg
1/8 teaspoon ground cloves
2 cups milk
3 egg yolks, slightly beaten
1 cup dairy sour cream
1 teaspoon lemon juice
2 cups whipped topping

1. Line a 9-inch pie plate with pastry; bake and cool.
2. Combine raisins, sugars, cornstarch, cinnamon, salt, nutmeg, and cloves in a heavy saucepan. Gradually stir in milk, blending until smooth. Cook over medium heat, stirring constantly, until filling comes to boiling. Cook, stirring constantly, for 5 minutes, then remove from heat.
3. Stir a small amount of hot filling into beaten egg yolks, mixing thoroughly, then stir into hot filling. Cook, stirring constantly, for 1 minute.
4. Remove from heat and stir in sour cream and lemon juice. Pour into the baked pie shell.
5. Chill several hours or overnight until filling is firm.
6. Just before serving, cover filling with whipped topping.

One 9-inch pie

Sour Cream Apple Flan

Flan Shell:

1¼ cups sifted all-purpose
    flour
6 tablespoons sugar
¼ teaspoon salt
¼ cup Crisco shortening
¼ cup butter or margarine
2 to 3 tablespoons cold water

Filling:

2¼ pounds tart baking apples
1 cup sugar
1 tablespoon cornstarch
½ teaspoon ground cinnamon
½ cup dairy sour cream
1 egg, beaten
1 teaspoon vanilla extract

1. Preheat oven to 350°.
2. For Flan Shell, combine
flour, sugar, and salt in a
bowl. Cut in Crisco and butter
using a pastry blender or 2
knives until mixture resembles
coarse crumbs. Add cold
water, 1 tablespoon at a time,
mixing until dry ingredients
are moistened and dough can
be gathered into a ball.
3. Roll pastry to a 13-inch
circle on a lightly floured
surface. Place in a 10⅝-inch
flan pan. Prick bottom and
sides with fork. Cover with
aluminum foil, pressing with
hands to cover bottom and
sides of flan shell. Place flan
pan on cookie sheet and bake
at 350° for 10 minutes.
Remove foil and continue
baking for 4 minutes.
4. For Filling, pare, core, and
slice apples. Combine sugar,
cornstarch, and cinnamon,
then lightly toss with apples.
Arrange in the baked shell.

5. Add sour cream to beaten
egg. Stir in vanilla extract.
Carefully pour over apples.
6. Bake at 350° for 50 minutes
or until center is completely
set. Cool on a rack.

One 10⅝-inch tart

Blueberry-Glazed Pie

*Crisco pastry for a single-
    crust 9-inch pie, page 154*
1 cup sugar
3 tablespoons cornstarch
¼ teaspoon salt
¼ teaspoon ground cinnamon
¼ cup cold water
4 cups fresh or dry-pack
    frozen blueberries, rinsed
    and drained
1 tablespoon butter or
    margarine
1 tablespoon lemon juice
1 cup whipped cream

1. Line a 9-inch pie plate with
pastry; bake and cool.
2. Combine sugar, cornstarch,
salt, and cinnamon in a heavy
saucepan. Gradually stir in
water, blending until smooth.
Stir blueberries into saucepan.
Cook over medium heat,
stirring constantly, until mixture comes to boiling (about
10 minutes). Cook, stirring
constantly, for 5 minutes.
Remove from heat and stir in
butter and lemon juice. Cool.
3. Spoon blueberry mixture
into the baked pie shell.
4. Chill several hours or until
firm.
5. To serve, fill a pastry bag
with whipped cream. Pipe a
lattice design on top of pie.

One 9-inch pie

Strawberry-Glazed Pie

*Crisco pastry for a single-
    crust 9-inch pie, page 154*
1 quart fresh strawberries,
    rinsed, hulled, and halved
½ cup sugar
2 tablespoons cornstarch
⅛ teaspoon salt
6 tablespoons cold water
2 packages (3 ounces each)
    cream cheese
2 tablespoons orange juice

1. Line a 9-inch pie plate with
pastry; bake and cool.
2. Set aside 2 cups halved
strawberries; crush remaining
strawberries (1½ cups) with
fork; reserve.
3. Combine sugar, cornstarch,
and salt in a small heavy
saucepan. Gradually add cold
water, blending until smooth;
add reserved crushed strawberries. Cook over medium
heat, stirring constantly, until
mixture comes to boiling.
Cook and stir for 1 minute.
Remove from heat. Cool by
setting pan in a bowl of ice
water.
4. Beat cream cheese until
softened. Gradually add
orange juice, beating until
smooth. Spread over bottom
of the baked pie shell.
5. Arrange reserved halved
strawberries over cheese layer,
then pour cooled strawberry
mixture over halved strawberries. Chill.
6. Top each serving with a
dollop of whipped cream, if
desired.

One 9-inch pie

Tarts and Pastries

Apple Dumplings

Crisco pastry for a double-crust 9-inch pie, page 154
6 baking apples (about 3 inches in diameter), pared and cored
1/3 cup chopped pecans
1/3 cup seedless raisins
1/2 teaspoon ground cinnamon
2 cups packed brown sugar
1 cup water

1. Preheat oven to 425°.
2. Roll out two-thirds of pastry to a 14-inch square on a lightly floured surface, then cut into 4 squares. Roll remaining pastry into a 14x7-inch rectangle, then cut into 2 squares. Place an apple on each square.
3. Mix pecans, raisins, and cinnamon; spoon into centers of apples.
4. Moisten corners of each square, bring 2 opposite corners of pastry up over apple and press together. Repeat with other corners. Press pastry seams together along sides of dumpling.
5. Place dumplings in a 2-quart baking dish. Bring brown sugar and water to boiling and carefully pour around dumplings.
6. Bake at 425° for 40 minutes or until pastry is brown and apples are tender. Spoon syrup over dumplings several times during baking.
7. Serve warm with whipped cream, if desired.

6 servings

Sweet Cherry Tarts

Crisco pastry for a double-crust 9-inch pie, page 154

Filling:
2 packages (3 ounces each) cream cheese
1/4 cup confectioners' sugar
2 tablespoons milk

Glaze:
1 can (17 ounces) dark sweet pitted cherries in syrup
2 tablespoons sugar
1 tablespoon cornstarch
1/4 teaspoon almond extract

1. Preheat oven to 425°.
2. Divide pastry in half. Roll each half to 1/8-inch thickness on a lightly floured surface. Cut six 4-inch circles from each. Place pastry circles over backs of inverted 2 3/4-inch muffin cups or small custard cups. Pinch together in several places so pastry fits cups. Prick with fork. Bake at 425° for 15 minutes or until brown. Cool on a rack, then carefully remove shells from cups.
3. For Filling, beat all ingredients until smooth and creamy. Spoon into the baked shells.
4. For Glaze, drain cherries, reserving syrup. If needed, add water to make 1 cup liquid. Combine sugar and cornstarch in a heavy saucepan. Gradually stir in cherry juice, blending until smooth. Cook and stir over medium heat until glaze comes to boiling. Cook and stir for 5 minutes; remove from heat. Stir in extract and cherries; cool.
5. Spoon cherry glaze into cheese-filled tart shells. Chill.
6. Top with *whipped cream.*

12 tarts

Fried Peach Pies

1 can (16 ounces) cling peach slices, drained
2 cups sifted all-purpose flour
1 teaspoon salt
1/2 cup Crisco shortening
1/2 cup cold water
1 tablespoon red cinnamon candies
2 tablespoons sugar
1 tablespoon cornstarch
1/4 teaspoon ground nutmeg
Crisco shortening for deep frying

1. Set peach slices aside on paper towels to drain.
2. Combine flour and salt in a bowl. Cut in Crisco with pastry blender or 2 knives until mixture resembles coarse crumbs. Add cold water, 1 tablespoon at a time, mixing until dry ingredients are moistened and dough can be gathered into a ball.
3. Divide dough in half. Roll to 1/8-inch thickness on a lightly floured surface. Using the lid from a 3-pound Crisco can as a pattern, cut 6 circles (about 5 1/4 inches) from each half. (Reroll as necessary.)
4. Heat Crisco to 365° in a deep saucepan or deep fryer.
5. Combine peaches, candies, sugar, cornstarch, and nutmeg. Place 1 tablespoon of filling on each dough circle. Moisten edges with water. Fold in half over filling; seal with fork.
6. Fry a few pies at a time in Crisco for 5 minutes or until golden brown, turning once. Remove with a slotted spoon and drain on paper towels.

12 fried pies

Note: Pies may be baked instead of deep-fried. See Note on page 169.

Raspberry-Glazed Petal Tarts

Crisco pastry for a double-crust 9-inch pie, page 154

Filling:
1 package (4-serving-size) vanilla pudding and pie filling mix
2 cups milk
³/₄ teaspoon grated lemon peel
¹/₄ teaspoon almond extract

Glaze:
1 package (10 ounces) frozen red raspberries in syrup, thawed
Orange juice
1 tablespoon sugar
1 tablespoon cornstarch

1. Preheat oven to 425°.
2. Roll pastry to ¹/₈-inch thickness on a lightly floured surface and cut out six 2-inch rounds for each tart. Use 1 round to line bottom of each 2³/₄-inch muffin-pan cup and remaining 5 rounds to line the sides. Moisten edges that overlap with water. Prick pastry with a fork.
3. Bake at 425° for 15 minutes or until golden brown.
4. Cool shells in muffin cups, then carefully remove from cups.
5. For Filling, cook pudding and pie filling mix using 2 cups milk as directed on package. Remove from heat and stir in lemon peel and almond extract. Cool. Cover with plastic wrap and chill until ready to assemble tarts.
6. For Glaze, drain raspberries, reserving syrup. Add orange juice to syrup to make 1 cup liquid.

7. Combine sugar and cornstarch in a heavy saucepan. Gradually stir in liquid, blending until smooth. Cook over medium heat, stirring constantly, until glaze comes to boiling. Cook and stir for 2 minutes. Remove from heat and chill until ready to assemble tarts.
8. Assemble tarts just before serving. To assemble, spoon filling into the baked shells. Spoon reserved raspberries over filling. Spoon glaze over each tart. Serve immediately.

12 tarts

Fried Apple Pies

1¹/₂ cups chopped pared tart cooking apples
¹/₃ cup seedless raisins
¹/₃ cup water
¹/₃ cup packed brown sugar
¹/₄ teaspoon ground cinnamon
¹/₈ teaspoon ground nutmeg
2 cups sifted all-purpose flour
1 teaspoon salt
¹/₂ cup Crisco shortening
¹/₂ cup cold water
Crisco shortening for deep frying

1. Combine apples, raisins, and ¹/₃ cup water in a heavy saucepan. Cook over high heat until mixture comes to boiling, stirring frequently. Reduce heat to low and simmer uncovered for 5 minutes. Stir in brown sugar, cinnamon, and nutmeg. Simmer for 5 minutes, stirring frequently. Remove from heat.
2. Combine flour and salt in a bowl. Cut in Crisco with pastry blender or 2 knives until mixture resembles coarse

crumbs. Add cold water, 1 tablespoon at a time, mixing until dry ingredients are moistened and dough can be gathered into a ball.

3. Divide dough in half. Roll to ⅛-inch thickness on a lightly floured surface. Using the lid from a 3-pound Crisco can as a pattern, cut 6 circles (about 5¼ inches) from each half. (Reroll as necessary.)

4. Heat Crisco to 365° in a deep saucepan or deep fryer.

5. Place about 1 tablespoon of apple filling on each dough circle. Moisten edges with water. Fold in half over filling, pressing with fork to seal.

6. Fry a few pies at a time in hot Crisco for 5 minutes until golden brown, turning once. Remove with a slotted spoon and drain on paper towels. Serve warm or cool.

12 fried pies

Note: If desired, Fried Apple Pies or Fried Peach Pies (page 166) may be baked instead of deep-fried. Place unbaked pies on an ungreased cookie sheet. Prick tops with fork. Bake at 425° for 20 to 25 minutes or until golden brown. If desired, drizzle with confectioners' sugar glaze.

Double Chocolate Tarts

Crisco pastry for a single-crust 9-inch pie, page 154
1 package (6 ounces) semisweet chocolate pieces (1 cup)
1 package (4-serving-size) chocolate instant pudding and pie filling mix
2 cups milk
1 teaspoon vanilla extract

1. Preheat oven to 425°.

2. Roll pastry to ⅛-inch thickness on a lightly floured surface. Using the lid from a 3-pound Crisco can as a pattern, cut 8 circles (about 5¼ inches). Place pastry circles over backs of inverted small custard cups. Pinch together in several places so pastry fits cups. Pierce with fork.

3. Bake at 425° for 15 minutes or until brown. Cool on a rack for 2 to 3 minutes, then carefully remove shells from cups.

4. Melt ½ cup chocolate pieces and divide evenly among the baked tart shells. Spread to coat bottom and sides of each tart shell.

5. Prepare instant pudding and pie filling mix with milk according to directions on package. Stir in remaining chocolate pieces and vanilla extract. Divide evenly among tart shells.

6. Decorate with whipped topping, if desired.

8 tarts

COOKIES

Cookies are the perfect bite-sized snack. They fit into a lunch box very nicely, and are great for gift-giving, too.

Fill up the cookie jar and watch those eager little hands dig in! When you prepare Homemade Crisco Cookie Mix in advance, you'll be able to bake up a new batch of cookies very quickly . . . perhaps almost as fast as the kids eat them!

Southern Pecan Brownies

3 tablespoons Crisco shortening
2 ounces (2 squares) unsweetened chocolate
2 egg yolks, slightly beaten
1 teaspoon vanilla extract
1 cup sugar
1/2 cup all-purpose flour
1/2 cup chopped pecans
2 egg whites
1/2 teaspoon salt

1. Preheat oven to 350°.
2. Melt Crisco and chocolate together in a large saucepan; cool.
3. Stir in egg yolks, then vanilla extract, sugar, flour, and nuts. Mixture will be crumbly.
4. Beat egg whites and salt until stiff, not dry, peaks form. Fold into chocolate mixture.

5. Spread batter in a greased 8-inch square pan.
6. Bake at 350° for 25 to 30 minutes or until a toothpick inserted in center comes out clean.
7. Cool completely before cutting.

About 16 cookies

Toffee Bars

1 cup Crisco shortening
1 cup packed brown sugar
1 egg
1 teaspoon vanilla extract
2 cups all-purpose flour
1/4 teaspoon salt
1 package (12 ounces) semisweet chocolate pieces
1/4 cup chopped walnuts

1. Preheat oven to 350°.
2. Cream Crisco and brown sugar in a bowl. Beat in egg and vanilla extract. Add flour and salt; mix until blended.
3. Put dough into an ungreased 17 1/4x11 1/4x1-inch pan; smooth out dough.
4. Bake at 350° for 12 minutes or until edges begin to brown.
5. Remove from oven and sprinkle chocolate pieces over hot baked layer. Cover with aluminum foil and let stand for a few minutes. Remove foil and spread chocolate evenly over top. Sprinkle with nuts.
6. When cool, cut into bars or squares.

5 to 6 dozen cookies

Almond Crunchies

1/2 cup Crisco shortening
2 teaspoons grated lemon peel
1/2 cup sugar
1 cup all-purpose flour
1/2 teaspoon salt

Almond Topping:
1/4 cup Crisco shortening
1 cup unblanched almonds, finely chopped
1/2 cup sugar
1/2 cup whipping cream
1 teaspoon vanilla extract

1. Preheat oven to 375°.
2. Cream 1/2 cup Crisco with lemon peel and 1/2 cup sugar. Combine flour and salt; add in halves, mixing until blended after each addition.
3. Turn dough into an 11x7x 1 1/2-inch pan and press into an even layer.
4. Bake at 375° for 12 minutes.
5. Meanwhile, for Almond Topping, melt Crisco in a heavy saucepan. Add almonds and sugar. Stir in cream and heat to boiling; cool slightly. Stir in vanilla extract. Pour almond mixture over partially baked layer.
6. Continue baking for 20 minutes or until light golden.
7. Cool completely. Cut into bars or squares.

About 30 cookies

Top Tray: Almond Crunchies.

Bottom Tray: Toffee Bars (left) and Southern Pecan Brownies (right).

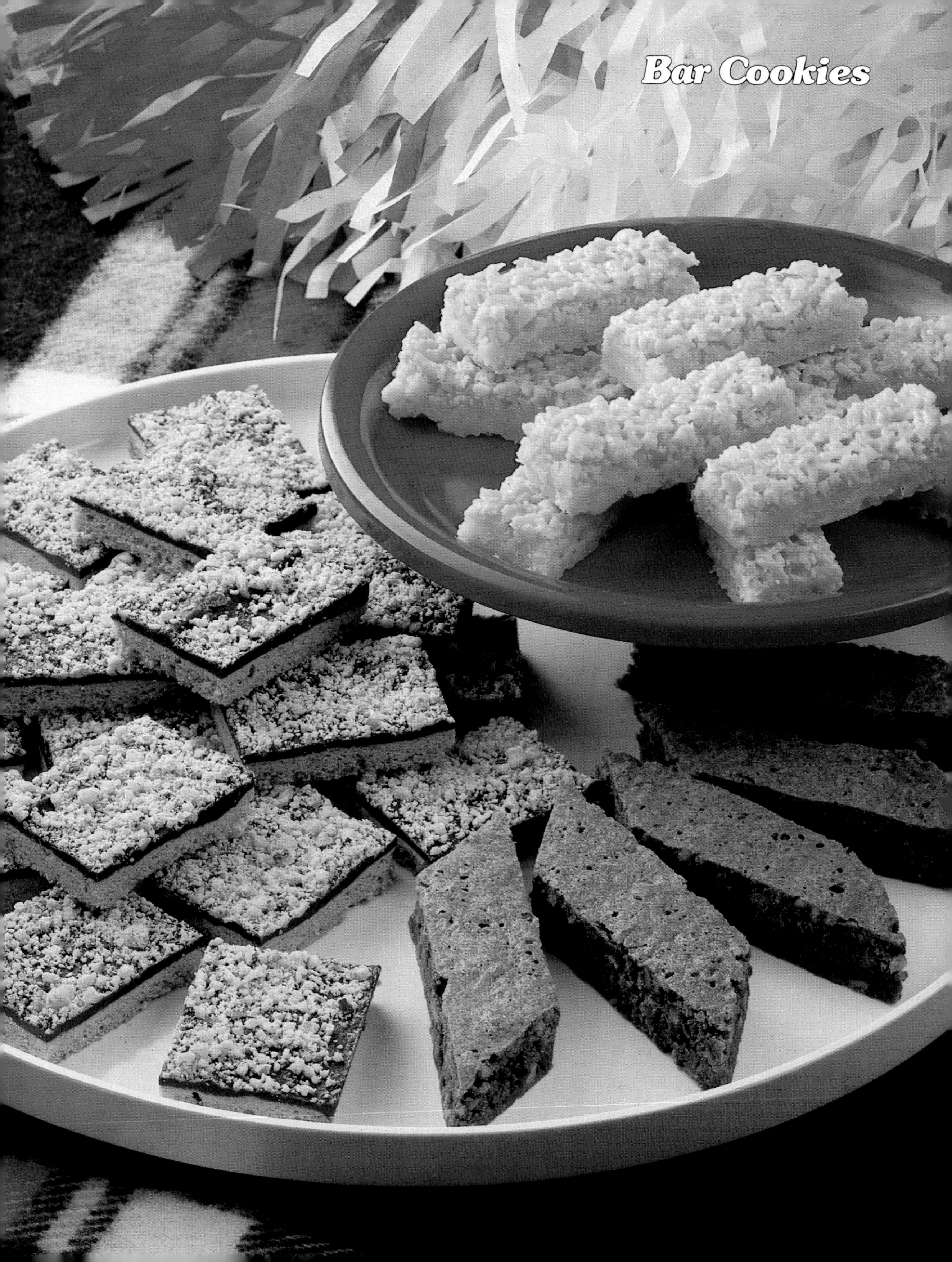
Bar Cookies

Bar Cookies

Chocolate Chip Bars

¹/₂ cup Crisco shortening
¹/₄ cup sugar
¹/₄ cup packed brown sugar
1 egg yolk
1 cup all-purpose flour
¹/₄ teaspoon baking powder
¹/₄ teaspoon salt
1 package (6 ounces)
  semisweet chocolate pieces
  (1 cup)
¹/₂ cup chopped pecans

Meringue:
1 egg white
¹/₄ cup packed brown sugar

1. Preheat oven to 325°.
2. Cream Crisco and sugars in a mixer bowl. Beat in egg yolk.
3. Combine flour, baking powder, and salt. Add to creamed mixture and beat until blended.
4. Spread in an ungreased 8x8x2-inch glass baking dish.
5. Bake at 325° for 20 minutes. Remove from oven. Sprinkle chocolate pieces and nuts over top.
6. For Meringue, beat egg white to stiff, not dry, peaks. Add brown sugar gradually while beating. Spread meringue carefully over mixture in baking dish.
7. Bake at 325° for 10 minutes or until meringue is golden brown. Cool before cutting into bars.

2 dozen cookies

Pecan Surprise Bars

³/₄ cup Crisco shortening
¹/₂ teaspoon almond extract
¹/₂ teaspoon vanilla extract
²/₃ cup sugar
1 egg
1³/₄ cups all-purpose flour
1 teaspoon salt
1 cup apricot or raspberry
  preserves

Pecan Topping:
3 egg whites
¹/₄ teaspoon salt
¹/₂ cup sugar
²/₃ cup finely chopped pecans
  or walnuts

1. Preheat oven to 350°.
2. Cream Crisco and extracts in a mixer bowl. Add sugar gradually while beating. Beat in egg. Blend in flour and salt.

3. Spread dough evenly in an ungreased 11x7x1¹/₂-inch pan.
4. Bake at 350° for 20 minutes.
5. Remove from oven. Spread preserves over baked layer.
6. Bake at 350° for 5 minutes. Remove from oven and cool on a rack while preparing topping.
7. For Pecan Topping, beat egg whites and salt until stiff, not dry, peaks form. Add sugar gradually while beating. Fold in pecans. Spread topping carefully and evenly over preserves.
8. Bake at 350° for 15 to 20 minutes or until topping is golden brown. Cool before cutting into bars or squares.

32 cookies

Apricot Pecan Bars

1/2 cup Crisco shortening
1 1/4 cups all-purpose flour
1/4 cup confectioners' sugar
1 egg
1/2 cup packed light brown
 sugar
1/4 teaspoon vanilla extract
1/2 cup finely snipped apricots,
 cooked*
1/2 cup pecans, chopped

Lemon Glaze:
3/4 cup confectioners' sugar
2 tablespoons lemon juice

1. Preheat oven to 350°.
2. Cut Crisco into flour and confectioners' sugar until particles resemble coarse crumbs. Press mixture evenly and firmly into a 9x9x2-inch pan.
3. Bake at 350° for 15 minutes.
4. Meanwhile, beat egg, brown sugar, and vanilla extract until thick; stir in a mixture of apricots and pecans.
5. Drop by teaspoonfuls over entire partially baked layer and spread to cover.
6. Continue baking for 15 minutes or until lightly browned.
7. For Lemon Glaze, blend confectioners' sugar with lemon juice.
8. Remove pan from oven and immediately drizzle Lemon Glaze over top. When cool, cut into bars.

About 4 dozen cookies

Note: If packaged dried apricots are extremely soft, it may not be necessary to cook the apricots.

* Put snipped apricots into a heavy saucepan with a small amount of water (3 to 4 tablespoons). Cover tightly and cook over low heat for 10 minutes or until apricots are soft and liquid is absorbed. Cool.

Glazed Lemon Bars

Bottom Layer:
1 cup sifted all-purpose flour
1/4 cup confectioners' sugar
1/4 teaspoon salt
1/2 cup Crisco shortening

Filling:
1 cup sugar
2 tablespoons all-purpose flour
1/2 teaspoon baking powder
1/8 teaspoon salt
2 eggs, slightly beaten
2 tablespoons lemon juice
1 teaspoon grated lemon peel

Glaze:
1/2 cup confectioners' sugar
1 tablespoon lemon juice
1/2 teaspoon grated lemon peel
1 tablespoon Crisco
 shortening

1. Preheat oven to 325°.
2. For Bottom Layer, combine flour, confectioners' sugar, and salt in a bowl. Cut in Crisco with pastry blender or 2 knives until mixture is well blended. Turn dough into a 9-inch square pan and press into an even layer.
3. Bake at 325° for 12 to 15 minutes or until lightly browned.
4. Meanwhile, for Filling, combine sugar, flour, baking powder, and salt in a large bowl. Add eggs, lemon juice, and peel; mix thoroughly.
5. Remove baked layer from oven and pour filling over bottom layer.
6. Return to oven and bake for 25 minutes.
7. For Glaze, combine all ingredients. Remove pan from oven and spread Glaze over lemon filling. Cool thoroughly before cutting into bars.

2 dozen cookies

Chocolate Cream Cheese Tiers

Chocolate Layer:
1/3 cup Crisco shortening
2 ounces (2 squares)
 unsweetened chocolate
2 eggs
1 cup sugar
1 teaspoon vanilla extract
1/2 cup sifted all-purpose flour
1/2 teaspoon salt
1/2 cup chopped salted pecans
 (or chopped unsalted pecans)

Chocolate Cream Cheese Frosting:
1 package (3 ounces) cream
 cheese, softened
1 ounce (1 square) semisweet
 chocolate, melted
1 1/2 cups confectioners' sugar
1 tablespoon milk

1. Preheat oven to 350°.
2. For Chocolate Layer, melt Crisco and chocolate together; set aside to cool.
3. Beat eggs, sugar, and vanilla extract until thick. Add cooled chocolate mixture and beat until blended. Stir in flour and salt, then pecans. Turn into a greased 11x7x1 1/2-inch pan and spread evenly.
4. Bake at 350° for 25 minutes.
5. Cool in pan on a rack.
6. For Chocolate Cream Cheese Frosting, combine all ingredients in a small mixer bowl and beat until smooth and of spreading consistency. Spread on chocolate layer.
7. Chill and cut into bars.

About 30 bars

Drop Cookies

Lacy Crisps

1/3 cup blanched almonds, finely chopped
1/4 cup sugar
2 teaspoons all-purpose flour
1/4 teaspoon salt
3 tablespoons Crisco shortening
1 tablespoon milk

1. Preheat oven to 350°.
2. Mix almonds, sugar, flour, and salt in a bowl. Blend in Crisco and milk.
3. Drop batter by measuring teaspoonfuls about 4 inches apart onto greased and lightly floured cookie sheets.
4. Bake 4 cookies at a time at 350° for 6 to 7 minutes or until golden brown.
5. Let set about 1 minute on cookie sheets; remove carefully with a spatula to racks. Cool completely. Store in an airtight container.

About 2 dozen 3-inch cookies

Snow-Capped Chocolate Drops

1 1/2 cups sifted all-purpose flour
1/2 teaspoon baking soda
1/2 teaspoon salt
1 egg
2/3 cup packed brown sugar
1/2 cup Crisco shortening
1/3 cup maraschino cherry liquid
2 envelopes (1 ounce each) premelted unsweetened chocolate
1/3 cup chopped walnuts
1/4 cup chopped maraschino cherries
3/4 cup marshmallow creme

1. Preheat oven to 350°.
2. Combine flour, baking soda, and salt in a large mixer bowl. Add egg, brown sugar, Crisco, cherry liquid, and chocolate; blend well at low speed. Stir in walnuts and cherries.
3. Drop by rounded teaspoons onto ungreased cookie sheets.
4. Bake at 350° for 10 to 12 minutes. Cool on racks.
5. When cool, frost each cookie with 1 teaspoon marshmallow creme.

3 dozen cookies

Nutty Chocolate Drops

4 ounces (4 squares) unsweetened chocolate
1 cup Crisco shortening
2 cups sugar
2 teaspoons vanilla extract
3 eggs
2 3/4 cups all-purpose flour
1 teaspoon salt
1/2 teaspoon baking powder
1/2 teaspoon baking soda
1 cup buttermilk
1 1/2 cups chopped walnuts

Rich Chocolate Frosting:
1/2 cup Crisco shortening
4 ounces (4 squares) unsweetened chocolate
2 2/3 cups confectioners' sugar
1 egg
6 tablespoons water
2 teaspoons vanilla extract
1/8 teaspoon salt

1. Preheat oven to 350°.
2. Melt chocolate; set aside to cool.
3. Cream Crisco, sugar, and vanilla extract in a bowl. Add eggs, one at a time, beating thoroughly after each addition. Blend in cooled chocolate.
4. Combine flour, salt, baking powder, and baking soda; add to creamed mixture alternately with buttermilk, mixing until blended after each addition. Stir in walnuts.
5. Drop by teaspoonfuls onto ungreased cookie sheets.
6. Bake at 350° for 12 to 15 minutes. Cool on racks.
7. For Rich Chocolate Frosting, melt Crisco and chocolate together. Pour into a bowl. Beat in, in order, confectioners' sugar, egg, water, vanilla extract, and salt. Set bowl in a larger bowl of ice and water. Beat with electric mixer about 5 minutes or until frosting is of spreading consistency.
8. Spread frosting on cooled cookies.

About 7 dozen cookies

Crisco cans with their reusable lids are especially handy for storage as well as cookie-gift-giving containers. They can be decorated creatively with fancy paper, ribbon, lacy doilies, rickrack, napkins, and greeting cards.

Drop Cookies

Irresistibles

1/4 cup Crisco shortening
1/3 cup packed light brown
  sugar
2 tablespoons honey
2 tablespoons light corn syrup
1 tablespoon heavy cream
3/4 cup sifted cake flour
1/2 teaspoon salt
1 cup slivered blanched
  almonds
3 ounces mixed candied fruit,
  finely chopped (about 1/2 cup)
1/2 cup semisweet chocolate
  pieces

1. Preheat oven to 350°.
2. Cream Crisco and brown
sugar in a bowl until fluffy.
Add honey, corn syrup, and
cream gradually, beating well
after each addition.
3. Combine cake flour and
salt; add to creamed mixture
and mix until blended. Stir in
almonds, candied fruit, and
chocolate pieces.
4. Drop by level tablespoonfuls
3 inches apart onto greased
and lightly floured cookie
sheets; spread into 2-inch
rounds.
5. Bake a few cookies at a
time at 350° for 7 minutes
until cookies are delicately
browned around edges.
6. Cool for 2 to 3 minutes on
cookie sheets. Carefully
remove cookies to racks and
cool completely.

About 3 dozen cookies

Top Can: Chocolate Raisin Clusters
Botton Can: Irresistibles

Chocolate Raisin Clusters

1 1/2 cups raisins
1/2 cup Crisco shortening
1 cup packed brown sugar
1 egg
2 ounces (2 squares)
  unsweetened chocolate,
  melted and cooled
1 teaspoon vanilla extract
1 1/4 cups all-purpose flour
1/2 teaspoon baking powder
1/2 teaspoon salt
1/3 cup milk
1/2 cup chopped walnuts

1. Preheat oven to 350°.
2. Rinse and drain raisins;
set aside.

3. Cream Crisco and brown
sugar in a bowl. Add egg and
beat thoroughly. Blend in
melted chocolate and vanilla
extract.
4. Combine flour, baking powder, and salt; add to creamed
mixture alternately with milk.
Stir in raisins and walnuts.
5. Drop by level tablespoons
about 2 inches apart onto
lightly greased cookie sheets.
6. Bake at 350° for about 15
minutes.
7. Cool cookies on racks.
8. Frost cooled cookies with
chocolate frosting, if desired.

5 dozen cookies

Drop Cookies

Chocolate Crunch Cookies

1 cup Crisco shortening
1 cup packed dark brown sugar
1/2 cup granulated sugar
1 teaspoon vanilla extract
2 eggs
2 1/4 cups all-purpose flour
1 teaspoon baking soda
1 teaspoon salt
1 cup chopped pecans
1 package (12 ounces) semisweet chocolate pieces

1. Preheat oven to 375°.
2. Cream Crisco, sugars, and vanilla extract in a large mixer bowl. Add eggs, one at a time, beating well after each addition.
3. Combine flour, baking soda, and salt; add to creamed mixture and beat until blended. Stir in pecans and chocolate pieces.
4. Drop by tablespoonfuls onto ungreased cookie sheets.
5. Bake at 375° for 10 to 12 minutes or until set.

About 4 dozen cookies

Apple Spice Cookies

1/2 cup Crisco shortening
1 cup packed brown sugar
1 egg
2 cups sifted all-purpose flour
1 teaspoon baking soda
1 teaspoon salt
1 teaspoon ground cinnamon
1/4 teaspoon ground allspice
1/4 teaspoon ground cloves
1/4 cup milk
2 Golden Delicious apples

Vanilla Glaze:
1 tablespoon butter or margarine, melted
1 cup sifted confectioners' sugar
1 teaspoon vanilla extract
4 to 5 teaspoons milk

1. Preheat oven to 400°.
2. Cream Crisco and brown sugar in a bowl. Beat in egg.
3. Combine flour, baking soda, salt, and spices; add to creamed mixture alternately with milk, mixing well after each addition.
4. Core and finely chop apples (about 2 cups). Stir chopped apple into batter.
5. Drop by rounded teaspoonfuls onto ungreased cookie sheets.
6. Bake at 400° for 10 to 12 minutes. Cool on racks.
7. For Vanilla Glaze, combine butter and confectioners' sugar. Stir in vanilla extract. Add milk, mixing until smooth and of desired consistency. Spread Vanilla Glaze over cooled cookies.

About 5 dozen cookies

Drop Cookies

Hermits

³/₄ cup Crisco shortening
1¹/₂ cups packed brown sugar
3 eggs
2¹/₂ cups all-purpose flour
1 teaspoon ground cinnamon
¹/₄ teaspoon ground nutmeg
¹/₈ teaspoon ground cloves
1 teaspoon salt
³/₄ teaspoon baking soda
1 cup dark seedless raisins
³/₄ cup chopped walnuts

1. Preheat oven to 400°.
2. Cream Crisco and brown sugar in a large mixer bowl. Add eggs, one at a time, beating thoroughly after each addition.
3. Combine flour, spices, salt and baking soda; add gradually to creamed mixture, mixing until blended. Stir in raisins and walnuts.
4. Drop by teaspoonfuls 2 inches apart onto ungreased cookie sheets.
5. Bake at 400° for 7 to 8 minutes or until set.

About 8 dozen cookies

Ranger Cookies

1 cup Crisco shortening
1 cup sugar
1 cup packed brown sugar
1¹/₂ teaspoons vanilla extract
2 eggs
2 cups sifted all-purpose flour
1 teaspoon baking powder
1 teaspoon baking soda
¹/₂ teaspoon salt
2 cups uncooked oats
1 cup flaked coconut
³/₄ cup crisp rice cereal

1. Preheat oven to 375°.
2. Cream Crisco, sugars, and vanilla extract in a large

mixer bowl. Add eggs, one at a time, beating well after each addition.
3. Combine flour, baking powder, baking soda, and salt; add gradually to creamed mixture, mixing until blended. Stir in oats, coconut, and rice cereal.
4. Drop batter by teaspoonfuls about 2 inches apart onto ungreased cookie sheets.
5. Bake at 375° for 10 minutes.

About 6 dozen cookies

Blueberry Drop Cookies

1 cup fresh, canned, or dry-pack frozen blueberries
³/₄ cup Crisco shortening
1 cup sugar
1¹/₂ teaspoons grated lemon peel
2 eggs
2 cups sifted all-purpose flour
2 teaspoons baking powder
¹/₄ teaspoon salt
¹/₂ cup milk

1. Preheat oven to 375°.
2. Rinse blueberries and spread on paper towels to dry thoroughly.
3. Cream Crisco, sugar, and lemon peel. Add eggs, one at a time, beating well after each addition.
4. Combine flour, baking powder, and salt. Add flour mixture alternately with milk to creamed mixture, beating until smooth after each addition. Lightly fold in blueberries.
5. Drop by teaspoonfuls on greased cookie sheets.
6. Bake at 375° for 10 to 12 minutes.

About 5 dozen cookies

Chewy Oatmeal Cookies

1 cup Crisco shortening
1 cup sugar
1 cup packed brown sugar
2 eggs
2 cups all-purpose flour
1 teaspoon baking powder
1 teaspoon baking soda
1 teaspoon salt
1¹/₂ cups uncooked oats
¹/₂ cup flaked coconut
¹/₂ cup chopped nuts

1. Preheat oven to 350°.
2. Cream Crisco and sugars in a mixer bowl. Add eggs, one at a time, beating well after each addition.
3. Combine flour, baking powder, baking soda, and salt. Add to creamed mixture; mix just until smooth. Stir in oats, coconut, and nuts.
4. Drop by teaspoonfuls onto ungreased cookie sheets.
5. Bake at 350° for 8 to 10 minutes or until lightly browned.

About 5 dozen cookies

Crisco Cookie Mix Recipes...

Homemade Crisco Cookie Mix

4 cups sifted all-purpose flour
2 cups sugar
2 teaspoons baking powder
1½ teaspoons salt
1⅓ cups Crisco shortening

1. Combine flour, sugar, baking powder, and salt in a large bowl. Cut in Crisco with a pastry blender or 2 knives until mixture resembles coarse meal.
2. Store in covered container up to 6 weeks at room temperature. For longer storage, place in freezer.
3. To measure, spoon mix into measuring cup and level with a spatula.

About 7⅓ cups mix

Chocolate Chip Cookies

2½ cups Homemade Crisco Cookie Mix (above)
½ cup packed brown sugar
1 egg
3 tablespoons milk
1 teaspoon vanilla extract
1 package (6 ounces) semisweet chocolate pieces
½ cup chopped walnuts

1. Preheat oven to 375°.
2. Combine Crisco mix and brown sugar in a bowl. Mix egg, milk, and vanilla extract with a fork. Add to bowl and stir until well blended. Stir in chocolate pieces and nuts.
3. Drop by level tablespoons onto ungreased cookie sheets.
4. Bake at 375° for 10 to 12 minutes or until lightly browned. Cool on racks.

About 3 dozen cookies

Raisin Cookies

Follow recipe for Chocolate Chip Cookies except use *1 cup raisins* in place of chocolate pieces.

Date Cookies

Follow recipe for Chocolate Chip Cookies except use *1 cup finely chopped dates* in place of chocolate pieces.

Coconut Cookies

Follow recipe for Chocolate Chip Cookies except use *1 cup flaked coconut* in place of chocolate pieces.

Butterscotch Cookies

Follow recipe for Chocolate Chip Cookies except use *1 cup butterscotch chips* in place of chocolate pieces.

Frosted Banana Cookies

*1¹/₂ cups Homemade Crisco
   Cookie Mix (opposite page)*
¹/₂ teaspoon ground cinnamon
¹/₄ teaspoon ground cloves
1 cup bran flakes
¹/₂ cup mashed banana
1 egg, slightly beaten
*¹/₂ cup coarsely chopped
   pecans*

Frosting:
*3 tablespoons Crisco
   shortening*
4 teaspoons water
1¹/₂ teaspoons vanilla extract
1¹/₃ cups confectioners' sugar
Toasted flaked coconut

1. Preheat oven to 375°.
2. Combine Crisco mix and spices in a bowl.
3. Combine bran flakes, banana, and egg; add to Crisco mix in bowl and mix well. Stir in pecans.
4. Drop by slightly rounded teaspoonfuls onto greased cookie sheets.
5. Bake at 375° for 10 to 12 minutes.
6. Cool cookies on racks.
7. For Frosting, mix ingredients until smooth.
8. Frost cooled cookies and dip in toasted coconut.

About 2 dozen cookies

Candied Fruit Cookies

Follow recipe for Chocolate Chip Cookies (opposite page) except use *1 cup chopped candied fruit* in place of chocolate pieces.

Gingersnaps

*2¹/₂ cups Homemade Crisco
   Cookie Mix (opposite page)*
1 teaspoon ground ginger
¹/₂ teaspoon ground cinnamon
¹/₄ teaspoon ground nutmeg
¹/₂ teaspoon baking soda
1 egg, slightly beaten
¹/₄ cup molasses
Sugar for rolling

1. Combine Crisco mix, spices, and baking soda in a bowl. Add egg and molasses; mix well.
2. For ease in handling, chill dough for 3 hours.
3. Preheat oven to 350°.
4. Shape dough into 1-inch balls and roll in sugar. If dough becomes sticky, rechill. Arrange balls about 3 inches apart on lightly greased cookie sheets.
5. Bake at 350° for 12 to 15 minutes.

About 3 dozen cookies

Peanut Cookie Faces

*3 cups Homemade Crisco
   Cookie Mix (opposite page)*
¹/₂ cup sifted all-purpose flour
¹/₂ cup chopped salted peanuts
1 egg
¹/₄ cup milk
1 teaspoon vanilla extract

Peanut Butter Frosting:
*¹/₃ cup Jif Creamy Peanut
   Butter*
1¹/₂ cups confectioners' sugar
¹/₄ cup milk
Raisins

1. Preheat oven to 375°.
2. Combine Crisco mix and flour in a bowl. Stir in peanuts.
3. Mix egg, milk, and vanilla extract. Add to dry ingredients and stir with a wooden spoon until dry ingredients are moistened and dough can be shaped into a ball.
4. Divide dough into 9 equal portions. Shape each into a ball, place on a greased cookie sheet, and flatten into a 4-inch round.
5. Bake at 375° for 15 minutes or until golden. Cool on racks.
6. For Peanut Butter Frosting, blend peanut butter, confectioners' sugar, and milk in a small bowl. Frost each cookie with a scant 2 tablespoons frosting. Decorate with raisins to make a smiling face.

9 large cookies

Peanut Butter Cookies

³/₄ cup Jif Peanut Butter
¹/₃ cup packed brown sugar
1 egg
2 tablespoons milk
*2 cups Homemade Crisco
   Cookie Mix (opposite page)*
¹/₂ cup chopped salted peanuts

1. Preheat oven to 375°.
2. Cream peanut butter and brown sugar in a bowl. Beat in egg and milk. Stir in Crisco mix and chopped peanuts until mixed.
3. Shape dough into 1-inch balls and place on ungreased cookie sheets. Flatten with a floured fork, making a criss-cross pattern on the tops. Dip fork in flour as needed to prevent sticking.
4. Bake at 375° for 10 to 12 minutes.

About 4 dozen cookies

Molded Cookies

Chocolate Crackles

1 package Duncan Hines Deluxe II Devil's Food Cake Mix
2 eggs, slightly beaten
1 tablespoon water
1/3 cup Crisco shortening
Confectioners' sugar

1. Preheat oven to 375°.
2. Put dry cake mix, eggs, water, and Crisco into a bowl. Mix with a spoon until well blended.
3. Drop batter by 1/2 teaspoons into a bowl of confectioners' sugar. Coat well and roll into balls. Put onto greased cookie sheets.
4. Bake at 375° for 10 to 12 minutes.

About 4 1/2 dozen cookies

Orange Crescents

1 cup Crisco shortening
1/2 cup confectioners' sugar
1 teaspoon orange extract
1 teaspoon grated orange peel
2 1/2 cups all-purpose flour
1/2 teaspoon salt
1 cup finely chopped pecans

Orange Glaze:
3/4 cup confectioners' sugar
1 1/2 tablespoons orange juice

1. Cream Crisco and confectioners' sugar in a bowl. Stir in orange extract, orange peel, flour, salt, and pecans.
2. Wrap dough and chill for 3 hours or overnight.
3. Preheat oven to 350°.

4. Shape level tablespoons of dough into crescents. Place on ungreased cookie sheets.
5. Bake at 350° for 20 minutes or until lightly browned.
6. Cool cookies on racks.
7. For Orange Glaze, stir ingredients together until smooth.
8. Spread glaze over cooled cookies.

About 3 1/2 dozen cookies

Molasses Crinkles

3/4 cup Crisco shortening
1 cup packed brown sugar
1 egg
1/4 cup molasses
2 1/4 cups all-purpose flour
2 teaspoons baking soda
1 teaspoon ground cinnamon
1 teaspoon ground ginger
1/2 teaspoon ground cloves
1/4 teaspoon salt
Granulated sugar

1. Preheat oven to 350°.
2. Cream Crisco and brown sugar in a bowl. Add egg and molasses; beat thoroughly.
3. Combine flour, baking soda, spices, and salt. Add to creamed mixture and mix until blended.
4. Shape teaspoonfuls of dough into balls. Dip tops in granulated sugar.
5. Arrange balls on ungreased cookie sheets.
6. Bake at 350° for 9 to 11 minutes.
7. Cool cookies on racks.

About 4 1/2 dozen cookies

Filled Star Cookies

2 cups Crisco shortening
1 cup sugar
1 1/2 teaspoons vanilla extract
3 egg yolks
1/3 cup orange juice
4 cups all-purpose flour
1/2 teaspoon salt
Preserves or jam for filling
Confectioners' sugar

1. Cream Crisco, sugar, and vanilla extract. Beat in egg yolks and orange juice. Combine flour and salt; mix in 2 cups at a time until dough is soft; add more flour if needed.
2. Wrap in waxed paper or plastic wrap. Set in refrigerator overnight.
3. Preheat oven to 350°.
4. Roll out chilled dough to about 1/4-inch thickness on a floured surface.
5. Use a star cutter to cut out star shapes; these are the top cookies. Put stars on ungreased cookie sheets. With thimble or tiny round cutter, cut out 5/8-inch centers from stars; reserve scraps of dough.
6. Bake at 350° for 10 to 12 minutes.
7. Gather scraps of dough into a ball and chill if necessary. Roll out dough to 1/4-inch thickness.
8. Cut out stars and put onto ungreased cookie sheets.
9. Bake at 350° for 10 to 12 minutes.
10. When cool and ready to serve, spread preserves on plain stars, then top with remaining stars. Sift confectioners' sugar over tops.

2 or 3 dozen filled cookies
(A 3 3/4-inch cookie cutter makes about 2 dozen; a 2 3/4-inch cookie cutter makes about 3 dozen)

Refrigerator Cookies

Lemon Cutouts

2¼ cups all-purpose flour
1 cup confectioners' sugar
¾ teaspoon salt
1 cup Crisco shortening
2 tablespoons milk
1 teaspoon lemon extract
1 teaspoon grated lemon peel

Lemon Frosting:

3 tablespoons Crisco
   shortening
¼ teaspoon salt
3 cups confectioners' sugar
3 tablespoons lemon juice
Yellow food coloring (optional)

1. Combine flour, confectioners' sugar, and salt in a large bowl. Cut in Crisco with a pastry blender or 2 knives until mixture resembles coarse crumbs. Stir in milk, lemon extract, and lemon peel.
2. Divide dough in half; form into 2 flat patties. Wrap in plastic wrap and chill for 1 hour.
3. Preheat oven to 350°.
4. Roll out dough to ⅛-inch thickness on a lightly floured surface. Cut with a floured 2¼-inch round or scalloped cutter. Place on ungreased cookie sheets.
5. Bake at 350° for 8 to 10 minutes or until edges just begin to brown.
6. Cool cookies on racks.
7. For Lemon Frosting, beat Crisco and salt in a small mixer bowl. Add confectioners' sugar alternately with lemon juice, beating until smooth. Tint with yellow food coloring, if desired. Frost cooled cookies.

About 7 dozen cookies

Coconut Surprises

1 cup Crisco shortening
1 teaspoon vanilla extract
1 cup sugar
1 egg
2¼ cups flaked coconut,
   divided
1¾ cups all-purpose flour
½ teaspoon baking soda
½ teaspoon salt

1. Cream Crisco with vanilla extract; add sugar gradually, beating until fluffy. Add egg and beat well.
2. Thoroughly blend in 1¾ cups of the coconut.
3. Combine flour, baking soda, and salt; add in fourths to creamed mixture, mixing well after each addition.
4. Knead lightly with fingertips 5 to 10 times until mixture holds together.
5. Shape into six 1-inch rolls; coat with remaining ½ cup coconut; wrap and chill thoroughly (at least 3 hours).
6. Preheat oven to 325°.
7. Cut each roll into ⅓-inch slices; place ¾ inch apart on lightly greased cookie sheets.
8. Bake at 325° for about 15 minutes.

About 8 dozen cookies

Refrigerator Cookies

Dreamy Treats

1/2 cup Crisco shortening
3/4 cup sugar
4 egg yolks, well beaten
1/2 teaspoon salt
1 cup all-purpose flour
Sugar for tops

1. Cream Crisco and sugar in a bowl. Add egg yolks gradually while beating. Blend in salt.
2. Add flour in halves, mixing until blended after each addition. Chill thoroughly (about 2 hours).
3. Preheat oven to 350°.
4. Using rounded teaspoon of dough for each cookie, drop dough aout 2 inches apart onto ungreased cookie sheets; flatten each with a glass dipped in sugar.
5. Bake at 350° for about 8 minutes.
6. Cool cookies on racks.

About 3 1/2 dozen cookies

Lemon Overnight Cookies

3 1/4 cups all-purpose flour
1 cup sugar
3/4 teaspoon salt
1 cup Crisco shortening
1/2 cup whipping cream
1 tablespoon grated lemon peel
1 tablespoon lemon juice
1 teaspoon vanilla extract

1. Combine flour, sugar, and salt. Cut in Crisco with pastry blender or 2 knives until mixture resembles coarse crumbs.
2. Blend cream, lemon peel, lemon juice, and vanilla extract; add gradually to flour mixture, mixing with a fork until well blended.

3. Chill dough until easy to handle.
4. Shape dough into two 1 1/2-inch rolls. Wrap and chill overnight.
5. Preheat oven to 350°.
6. Cut each roll into 1/4-inch slices; place on ungreased cookie sheets.
7. Bake at 350° for 10 to 12 minutes.

5 to 6 dozen cookies

Raisin Oat Treats

1 1/2 cups all-purpose flour
1 teaspoon baking soda
1/2 teaspoon cream of tartar
1/2 teaspoon salt
1/2 cup uncooked oats
3/4 cup Crisco shortening
1 teaspoon vanilla extract
1 cup packed dark brown sugar
1 egg
3/4 cup raisins

1. Combine flour, baking soda, cream of tartar, and salt; mix in oats and set aside.
2. Cream Crisco with vanilla extract; add brown sugar gradually, beating until fluffy. Add egg and beat thoroughly.
3. Add the dry ingredients in fourths, mixing until well blended after each addition. Stir in raisins.
4. Shape into 6x1 1/2-inch rolls. Wrap each roll and chill several hours or overnight.
5. Preheat oven to 375°.
6. Cut each roll into 1-inch slices. Cut each slice into quarters. Place each quarter point-side-up on ungreased cookie sheets.
7. Bake at 375° for 7 to 8 minutes.

About 6 dozen cookies

Brown Sugar Cookies

1 cup Crisco shortening
1 cup sugar
1 cup packed brown sugar
2 eggs
1 teaspoon vanilla extract
3 cups all-purpose flour
1 teaspoon baking soda
1 teaspoon salt
1 cup finely chopped pecans

1. Cream Crisco and sugars in a large mixer bowl. Blend in eggs and vanilla extract. Combine flour, baking soda, and salt; add gradually to creamed mixture, blending well. Stir in nuts.
2. Divide dough into 4 portions; put each portion onto a piece of waxed paper and shape into a roll, 8 inches long. Wrap in waxed paper.
3. Chill until cold and firm.
4. Preheat oven to 350°.
5. Cut each roll into 1/4-inch slices. Cover cookie sheets with aluminum foil. Place cookies on the foil-covered cookie sheets.
6. Bake at 350° for 10 minutes or until lightly browned.
7. Lift cookies on aluminum foil to a rack to cool. When cooled, remove cookies from foil.

About 10 dozen cookies

Deep-Fried Cookies

Orange Knot Cookies

Crisco shortening for deep
  frying
1/3 cup sugar
3/4 teaspoon ground cinnamon
3 egg yolks
1 teaspoon grated orange peel
2 tablespoons sugar
1/2 teaspoon vanilla extract
1 teaspoon orange extract,
  divided
1 cup all-purpose flour
1/4 teaspoon salt
1/4 cup dairy sour cream
1 package (6 ounces)
  semisweet chocolate pieces
  (1 cup)

1. Melt Crisco to a depth of 3 inches in a 3-quart saucepan. Heat to 365° while preparing dough. Combine 1/3 cup sugar and cinnamon. Set aside.
2. Beat egg yolks until thick. Add orange peel. Gradually beat in 2 tablespoons sugar, beating until light and fluffy. Blend in vanilla extract and 1/2 teaspoon orange extract.
3. Sift flour and salt together. Stir in sour cream until mixture is crumbly. Add egg yolk mixture, stirring until dry ingredients are moistened. Turn out onto a lightly floured surface. Knead gently 4 or 5 times.
4. Roll dough to a 15-inch square. Cut into 20 narrow strips, using a pastry wheel or sharp knife. Cut strips crosswise into thirds. Tie each strip into a knot.

5. Fry 10 knots at a time in hot Crisco about 1 1/2 minutes or until golden brown, turning once. Drain on paper towels. Sprinkle with cinnamon sugar.
6. Put chocolate pieces into the top of a double boiler. Set over hot water until chocolate is melted, then stir in 1/2 teaspoon orange extract; remove from hot water. Generously dip both ends of cookies into chocolate. Set on waxed paper until chocolate is firm.

About 60 cookies

Deep-Fried Cookie Drops

1 1/2 cups all-purpose flour
1/2 cup sugar
1 teaspoon baking powder
1/4 teaspoon salt
1/2 cup milk
1 egg, beaten
1/2 teaspoon vanilla extract
Crisco shortening for deep
  frying
Confectioners' sugar

1. Combine dry ingredients, milk, egg, and vanilla extract in a large mixer bowl. Beat at medium speed until smooth (about 2 minutes).
2. Heat Crisco to 365° in a deep saucepan or deep fryer.
3. Drop cookie batter by teaspoonfuls into hot Crisco a few at a time. Fry for 2 1/2 to 3 minutes, turning if necessary to brown evenly. Drain on paper towels. Roll in confectioners' sugar. Serve immediately.

About 6 dozen cookies

Almond-Filled Cookies

4 cups sifted all-purpose flour
1/4 cup sugar
2 teaspoons salt
1 cup Crisco shortening
1 cup cold water
1 can (12 1/2 ounces) almond
  filling
Crisco shortening for deep
  frying

1. Combine flour, sugar, and salt in a large bowl. Cut in Crisco with pastry blender or 2 knives until mixture resembles coarse crumbs. Add cold water, 2 tablespoons at a time, mixing until dry ingredients are moistened and dough can be gathered into a ball.
2. Divide dough into 4 equal portions and wrap each in plastic wrap.
3. Roll out 1 portion of dough at a time into a 12x10-inch rectangle on a lightly floured surface. Cut into 2-inch squares.
4. Place 1 level teaspoon almond filling in center of half of the squares. Moisten edges with water. Place a plain square on top of each, pressing edges with fork to seal. Prick tops with fork.
5. Repeat using remaining portions of dough and filling.
6. Heat Crisco to 365° in a deep saucepan or deep fryer. Fry a few squares at a time in hot Crisco for 3 minutes or until golden brown, turning once. Remove with a slotted spoon and drain on paper towels.

5 dozen filled cookies

Deep-Fried Cookies

Jumbo Snacks

2 tablespoons Crisco
  shortening, melted
1/2 cup whipping cream
1 teaspoon salt
1 teaspoon vanilla extract
1/4 cup sugar
4 eggs
3 1/4 cups all-purpose flour
1/4 cup cornstarch
Crisco shortening for deep
  frying
1/3 cup sugar
1 to 2 teaspoons ground
  cinnamon

1. Combine Crisco, cream, salt,
vanilla extract, 1/4 cup sugar,
and eggs in a bowl and beat
thoroughly.
2. Combine flour and cornstarch; add, about 1/2 cup at a
time, to egg mixture, mixing
until well blended after each
addition. Chill thoroughly.
3. Heat Crisco to 365° in a
large deep saucepan or deep
fryer.
4. Divide dough into 32 equal
portions and cover until ready
to use.
5. Roll rounds paper thin.
6. Fry, one round at a time, in
hot Crisco for 1 to 2 minutes
or until golden brown; turn
once.
7. Drain over Crisco a few
seconds, then remove to paper
towels. Cool.
8. Combine 1/3 cup sugar and
the cinnamon. Sprinkle both
sides of snacks with mixture.

32 (6-inch) snacks

Apple Rosettes

3/4 cup all-purpose flour
1 tablespoon grated lemon
  peel
1 teaspoon sugar
1 teaspoon ground nutmeg
3/4 teaspoon salt
1/3 cup applesauce
1 cup milk
2 egg yolks
1 tablespoon Crisco
  shortening, melted
Crisco shortening for deep
  frying
Confectioners' sugar

1. Combine flour, lemon peel,
sugar, nutmeg, and salt.
2. Blend applesauce, milk, egg
yolks, and melted Crisco; beat
into dry ingredients using a
wire whisk or wooden spoon
until smooth. Chill thoroughly
or overnight.

3. Heat Crisco to 365° in a
deep saucepan or deep fryer.
4. Prepare desired shape of
rosette iron by dipping in hot
Crisco until thoroughly
heated. Tap gently to remove
excess Crisco. Lower hot iron
into batter, not more than
three-fourths the depth of the
iron (if batter goes over top,
cookie will be difficult to
remove). Lower coated iron
into hot Crisco and fry until
delicately browned (about 30
seconds). Remove from Crisco
and slip cookie from iron.
5. Drain, inverted, on paper
towels. Repeat process until
all batter is used.
6. Dip cookies while warm in
confectioners' sugar.

3 to 4 dozen rosettes

Recipe Index

Recipe Index

Recipe Index